Environmental Law and Policy

STEPHEN R. CHAPMAN

Clemson University

PRENTICE HALL
Upper Saddle River, New Jersey   Columbus, Ohio

Library of Congress Cataloging-in-Publication Data

Chapman, Stephen R.
    Environmental law and policy / by Stephen R. Chapman
       p.   cm.
    Includes bibliographical references and index.
    ISBN 0–13–848706–5
    1. Environmental law—United States.   2. Environmental policy—
United States.   I. Title.
KF3775.C46   1998
344.73'046—DC21   97–30111
                                                  CIP

Editor: Ed Francis
Production Editor: Mary M. Irvin
Design Coordinator: Karrie M. Converse
Cover Designer: Russ Maselli
Production Manager: Pamela D. Bennett
Marketing Manager: Danny Hoyt

This book was set in Times Roman by BookMasters, Inc., and was printed and bound by R. R. Donnelley & Sons Company. The cover was printed by Phoenix Color Corp.

 © 1998 by Prentice-Hall, Inc.
Simon & Schuster/A Viacom Company
Upper Saddle River, New Jersey 07458

Printed in the United States of America

10 9 8 7 6 5 4 3 2 1

ISBN: 0-13-848706-5

Prentice-Hall International (UK) Limited, *London*
Prentice-Hall of Australia Pty. Limited, *Sydney*
Prentice-Hall of Canada, Inc., *Toronto*
Prentice-Hall Hispanoamericana, S. A., *Mexico*
Prentice-Hall of India Private Limited, *New Delhi*
Prentice-Hall of Japan, Inc., *Tokyo*
Simon & Schuster Asia Pte. Ltd., *Singapore*
Editora Prentice-Hall do Brasil, Ltda., *Rio de Janeiro*

To my wife, Barbara, whose love, constant support, and assistance made this book possible.

Preface

Environmental regulations, or "regulations," refers to the laws, rules, and regulations that address the full spectrum of environmental issues and problems affecting human health and the protection, conservation, and preservation of natural resources in the United States.

A comprehensive study of environmental law and policy involves a range of complex concepts, some of which are relatively independent, but most of which interact with elements of other issues. This opens a variety of potential starting points and areas of emphasis in the study of environmental law and policy that accommodate different interests, personal and professional needs, and time limits.

Environmental law and policies is an appropriate starting point for a comprehensive, in-depth academic program in the traditional area of environmental science. It is an equally appropriate capstone subject and, because it integrates problems and solutions, provides an ideal framework for a single-survey course.

STRUCTURE OF THE TEXT

The text considers the definition of *environment* to include preservation and protection of natural resources, and regulations affecting all elements of the environment. Some readers may choose to emphasis specific subject areas more than others. Within fairly wide limits, the text accommodates this approach. The text is organized into five general subject areas:

1. general concepts starting with
   i. a survey or overview of today's environmental concerns
   ii. an introduction to the legislative process expanded to consider the diverse sources of environmental regulations
   iii. an introduction to issues of risk assessment and management, introducing conflicting perceptions of the concept of risk as it relates to the environment and conflicts over management strategies

2. the regulation of natural resources, with a major focus on the resource land as an example of the growth of regulations and legislative statements of environmental policy, and the impact of environmental regulations on private property ownership rights

3. the major pollution control efforts expressed in air and water quality control legislation and the policies imposed by the legislation in addition to seeking environmental restoration

4. the continuing and varied problems associated with disposal of the waste generated by households and by industry in the form of toxic substances and materials, plus waste generated by efforts to improve the environment

5. the critical aspects of environmental implications of food safety as they relate to the use and regulation of pesticides, along with several personal issues

The goal of the text is to establish a logical bridge between environmental problems and regulations so that the reader can effectively analyze each in terms of a simple model involving formulating answers to four questions for the problems as well as their regulatory solutions. Introducing this simple model or approach is effectively the first step in using the text: WHERE ARE WE? HOW DID WE GET HERE? WHERE SHOULD WE GO? HOW SHOULD WE GET THERE?

PART ONE: GENERAL CONCEPTS

To stress the breadth of environmental issues considered throughout the text, it starts with an overview of the major environmental concerns expressed by the public and by scientists today. The interrelation among issues or problems is established, noting that many "problems" are the product of other problems, and that regulations should ultimately address the basic problems, but shorter term solutions are frequently encountered. The impact of lifestyle and the fact that humans cause pollution emerge as inescapable conclusions. Next, the complex and controversial subject of risk assessment is explored, with a focus on two points: the impact of science technology on the process and the point that for many "natural resources" (such as wilderness) technical approaches do not provide adequate assessment or evaluate appropriate factors. The place of the environmental impact statement is introduced, and arguments stressing the separation of assessment from risk management are introduced. The final chapter in Part One introduces the various sources of law. Understanding the sources of law provides an essential basis for understanding the law and regulatory process. This includes two sources not frequently examined in general texts: lobbying, and the voice of the individual and administrative law. This section looks at practical significance, not a scholarly, law school approach.

PART TWO: NATURAL RESOURCE REGULATION

The regulation of natural resources, or conservation, starts with the most common resource—land. The text traces the history of the regulation of this fundamental resource from acquisition of land from Native Americans under the Discovery Doctrine through the massive distributions of land by the federal government, followed by increasing restrictions of land distribution and unrestricted use, leading to the establishment of the National Forest and National Park System. This has now come full circle to current policies of retention of federal ownership. In addition, the basics of private land (real estate) ownership are introduced with the limits on the exercise of ownership rights stemming from environmental laws and policies. Following this introduction, the continuing evolution of natural resource regulation is explored with emphasis directed to major legislation and policies: the adoption of multiple use sustained yield as a national management policy; the impact of the Federal Land Policy Management act and resulting empowerment of the Bureau of Land Management and termination of homesteading; and the National Environmental Policy Act and requirements of environmental impact statements, for example. Congress also addressed specific resource issues: wilderness, wild rivers, and even hiking trails are part of the discussion. The discussion includes examination of the social forces that encouraged the continued evolution of protective resource regulation.

PART THREE: POLLUTION CONTROL

Air and water pollution represent a major area of environmental concern throughout the nation. The test examines issues of air and water quality in a thorough analysis of the Clean Air Act (including its amendments), the Clean Water Act, and the Safe Drinking Water Act. For both subject areas, emphasis first is placed on careful analysis of the stated congressional findings of facts that explain the basis of congressional actions, goals, and statements of national policy expressed by Congress. From these foundations, the acts are analyzed to determine whether they satisfy the stated goals and respond to the problems (facts) identified by Congress. This includes examining specific definitions used in the acts, as well as rules promulgated by authority of the acts and specific sources or types of pollutants addressed by Congress in the legislation. Basic policies, such as Congress requiring states to comply with federal standards, and citizens' private rights of action to enforce provisions of the act are noted, as are limitations such as mandated consideration of economic factors in setting certain standards. Interfaces among the several acts are identified and developed. Areas of environmental improvement are discussed in terms of the impact of the various acts.

PART FOUR: WASTE AND WASTE MANAGEMENT

The most obvious environmental problem facing Americans today is the sea of waste we generate and in which we are drowning. The text carefully separates two major areas of waste: abandoned dump sites and current disposal issues and problems. It examines the problems and relates them to the water quality issues introduced in the previous sections and unifies the several sets of concepts related to definitions of toxic and hazardous substances. Major emphasis is placed on the purposes and effectiveness of two acts: the SuperFund (CERCLA) and RCRA. The scope of CERCLA is simply presented in the definitions of the title, focusing on *comprehensive, environmental,* and *liability.* The intent of

RCRA to minimize land disposal is stressed, along with the distinctions of municipal solid waste versus hazardous waste and the disposal requirements associated with each. In addition, the association between the Emergency Preparedness and Community Right to Know Act and OSHA specifications is developed, with emphasis on hazards associated not only with storage, but also with the daily transport of hazardous materials and the all-too-frequently reported mishaps from transportation, including defective pipelines. The basic principles of nuclear energy regulation and the disposal of nuclear waste are also included to complete this diverse unit.

PART FIVE: PESTICIDE SAFETY, FOOD SAFETY, AND PERSONAL ISSUES

Discussion in this section starts by establishing that both pesticide safety and food safety are appropriately a part of any comprehensive study of environmental regulation. The discussion of food safety is limited for obvious reasons to issues related to pesticide residues. The basic approach is an analysis of the two most relevant acts: The Federal Fungicide, Insecticide, and Rodenticide Act; and the Federal Food, Drug, and Cosmetic Act. Emphasis is placed on the activities regulated and problems addressed by each act, the agencies responsible for enforcement of the acts (FIFRA by the USDA and FFDCA by the EPA), and the rules promulgated under the acts. These materials provide the ideal format to review issues related to risk assessment and illustrate the impact of a single action: the publication of *Silent Spring* or the passage of the Delaney amendment to FFDCA. The 1996 amendments to both acts are discussed in terms of the continued evolution of environmental regulation.

ACKNOWLEDGMENTS

"Thanks" seems like so little to say to the following who have contributed so significantly to the completion of *Environmental Law and Policy*:

In addition to my wife, our daughters, Cindy and Cheryl, and their families for their constant encouragement.

Students at Clemson, who for the last five years have challenged and encouraged me with their friendship, interest, and intellect.

Faculty associates at Clemson who have shared ideas, listened patiently, and offered precise criticisms: Dr. O. J. Dickerson, Dr. Horace Skipper, and Mr. John Gentry, Esquire.

Dean Steven Bahls and the library staff at Capital Law School, and Dean Ed Eck and the library staff at the University of Montana Law School.

The great team at Prentice Hall whose personal interest, encouragement, and professional expertise were always available: Jane Manning Hyatt, Ed Francis, Mary Irvin (the Production Editor responsible for converting a manuscript to a book), and Melissa Gruzs, (the copyeditor whose patience and assistance defy description).

And to the reviewers who offered their professional reviews and helpful critiques of the original manuscript: Terence Centner, University of Georgia; James D.

Halderman; Kelley MacIsaac, Palmar College; and Scott Wolcott, Rochester Institute of Technology.

To each of you, my most sincere thanks. To the many I have failed to name, my apology, and my thanks. In spite of all assistance, errors and omissions remain, and I alone stand responsible for them.

S. R. C.

■ Table of Contents

3   RISK ASSESSMENT AND MANAGEMENT   54

7 CLEAN WATER AND WATER QUALITY CONSIDERATIONS   142

■ PART FOUR Waste Management   165

8 WASTE AND WASTE DISPOSAL   167

9   SPECIFIC POLLUTION CONTROL LEGISLATION   195

PART ONE

General Principles

1

Overview of Environmental Issues and Concerns

The environment can be defined as the aggregate of surrounding things, conditions, or influences especially as effecting the existence or development of someone or something, or the sum of all external forces affecting the growth and development of an organism. These definitions must include natural resources as part of the environment. Analysis of these definitions in today's world reveals a complex, potentially all-encompassing subject. Virtually everyone agrees that, regardless of the definition, the quality of our environment is declining.

For discussion and analytical purposes, deterioration of the environment can be divided into two interdependent components: 1) the overuse or depletion of "natural resources" such as land and water, the loss of biodiversity (endangered species), and the loss of solitude; 2) pollution (which more directly threatens human health and well-being) in all of its direct and insidious forms: threats to air and water quality and to safe drinking water, and growing, serious concerns over waste production and disposal, nuclear safety and the disposal of nuclear waste, and food safety.

Some issues are immense in scope and can be viewed as megaconcerns—global warming, loss of the tropical rain forests, atmospheric radon, and atmospheric ozone depletion, for example. These issues may involve elements related to both health and natural resource depletion. Other issues, such as workplace safety and certain aspects of food safety, are very specific, and some might question their inclusion in a discussion of environmental issues. Certain aspects of workplace safety may logically be excluded from environmental issues, whereas others could be discussed—for example, exposure to toxic fumes, radioactive materials, or even loud noises. Some food safety issues may include environmental elements, such as pesticide residues in food. Food spoilage generally would not be an environmental issue, although it certainly would be a significant health issue.

ORGANIZATIONAL APPROACHES TO ENVIRONMENTAL ISSUES AND LAWS

Subject Matter Organization

In addition to the sheer magnitude and complexity of environmental issues today, many discussions are distorted by strong emotions and opinions, and frequently involve serious, but not readily measured, economic considerations. Such issues include the value of solitude, protecting the wilderness, and conserving virgin stands of timber. Frequently, the problems and proposed solutions are technically extremely complex. In addition, regulatory considerations have grown to involve fundamental issues of constitutional law and associated policy questions.

No single system exists for addressing these concerns, which must ultimately be treated as part of many problems. Nonetheless, a consistent approach to any problem should simplify its analysis and facilitate the comparison of alternative courses of action. Such an analytical approach should be equally applicable to the evaluation of a problem, to proposed solutions, and to regulatory proposals.

A Simple Four-Step Approach

One approach that can be applied to problems, solutions, or regulations involves four simple steps, or the formulation of responses to four questions. This four-step approach provides a common framework to discuss and interpret a full spectrum of environmental problems.

With respect to the type of problem, the technical level of resolving the problem, or the extent of regulations, the first step is to determine the current status: "Where are we now?" Individuals may differ in their responses, but this step is a critical starting point. The second question asks, "How did we get here?" Room for disagreement exists, but the focus is on a specific facet of the issue. The third question requires formulating goals or solutions: "Where should we go?" The final question identifies potential action: "How should we get there?" If the first three steps lead to the conclusion that some action is needed, then this final question demands the formulation of a plan of action. This plan could be a call for technical steps to reduce air pollution from coal-burning generators; it could be a call for stricter regulations or enforcement of existing regulations; or it could be a recognition that at a given point in time, action is not feasible or essential.

TODAY'S ENVIRONMENT: A SITUATION ANALYSIS

Virtually every day, every American and many citizens of other nations are affected by American laws, rules, and regulations that have been implemented to protect the environment, guard human health, and conserve natural resources. These laws, rules, and regulations can be introduced and discussed from a purely regulatory perspective. However, a brief discussion of the nature and type of issues existing today—a survey of the question "Where are we?"—provides a practical foundation to explore and better understand the major emphasis of this text: the structure, intent, and formulation of environmental laws and the regulation of individuals and industry in the United States.

Few would deny that we face serious environmental deterioration throughout the world today, or that human activity lies at the heart of many of the problems. Many facts support this generalization. Unfortunately, this rather bleak position has merit; nearly every day, some element of the national media reports some environmental issue or problem, and too frequently the media report "man-made" environmental disasters.

Environmental Concerns Related to Human Health

Analysis of the current state of our environment can be approached from several perspectives: regulations, causes of environmental degradation, types of solutions, aspects of the environment affected, or a general consideration of the nature of the environmental degradation. A general survey provides the best starting point to examine other areas and, ultimately, to establish interrelations among the diverse elements of this complex topic. Table 1.1 lists 35 environmental concerns that have been expressed by the general public, by scientists, and by various special interest groups.

Table 1.1 reveals a variety of important concepts related to environmental issues, which can be classified as related to health or to conservation and protection of natural resources or ecology. Of course, even this broad classification is arbitrary in many situations. The two major categories are not mutually exclusive, and neither the major groupings nor the order of listing in a group represent any documented or suggested relative importance.

Major Health Concerns

Waste Disposal

The first item, waste disposal and the location of waste disposal sites, represents a complex topic of major controversy. This issue involves not only the question of dumps (or landfills, as they are now designated) and the fact that space for such use is at a premium, but also directly involves issues related to alternative methods of waste disposal: incineration and recycling, plus energy recovery. Moreover, landfills represent very real threats to the contamination of both groundwater and surface water supplies (item 14). Clearly, this issue cannot be separated from item 10, solid waste and litter, nor can it be separated from concerns related to water quality (items 2 and 9, for example). When incineration is considered as an alternative, item 3, industrial air pollution, cannot be ignored.

Of course, water quality involves two sets of concerns, aquatic habitat issues (natural resource protection) and issues focused on water quality. The second area, although involved in other concerns, is specifically noted in item 19, which includes the specific pollutant, lead, a serious pollutant of both water and air.

General Environmental Concerns Related to Health

1. Waste disposal and the location of waste disposal sites.
2. Industrial pollution of water as a by-product of manufacturing
3. Accidental release of industrial pollutants
4. Workplace exposure to toxic chemicals
5. Oil spills
6. Ozone destruction
7. Nuclear plant accidents
8. Exposure to radioactivity (other than from nuclear plants)
9. Defective underground storage tanks
10. Solid waste and litter
11. Pesticide risks and food safety
12. Agriculturally related (nonpoint source) pollution of water
13. Pollution from urban runoff (nonpoint source pollution)
14. Water pollution from sewage
15. Air pollution from vehicles
16. The greenhouse effect and ozone depletion
17. Exposure to radon
18. Exposure to asbestos
19. Safe drinking water
20. Disposal of medical wastes
21. Biotechnology

General Environmental Concerns Related to Natural Resources or Ecology

22. Loss of wetlands
23. Contaminated coastal waters
24. Pesticide risks to wildlife
25. Loss of biodiversity
26. Habitat destruction
27. Loss of endangered species
28. Acid rain

More Specific Environmental Concerns Related to Natural Resources or Ecology

29. Soil erosion
30. Effective multiple use and sustained yields of natural resources
31. Sustainable agricultural productivity
32. Forest management and protection
33. Rangeland management and protection
34. Management and protection of groundwater and surface water supplies
35. Wilderness preservation

TABLE 1.1 Areas of environmental concern based on environmental degradation as expressed by the general public, scientists, special-interest groups, and various regulatory agencies and as reflected in political attention to the various topics. Items are not in order of priority. They represent an arbitrary composite from the popular media, technical publications, and over twenty, widely used, current undergraduate environmental

Medical Waste Disposal

Medical wastes (item 20) represent a special case of problems associated with disposal of solid wastes. The potential health hazards are obvious, with public exposure to dressings, bedding, and infectious materials, plus glassware, contaminated syringes, and other materials requiring special care. In the future, this specific waste problem may become more critical as home care of terminally ill individuals results in the inclusion of medical waste in less dangerous household solid waste that is considered as part of the municipal solid waste stream. In the case of medical waste, the concern is both with exposure to the raw material and with possible pollution of water supplies.

Water Pollution

Generally, *nonpoint source pollution* (items 12 and 13) refers to water pollution from diffuse sources. Agricultural nonpoint source pollution includes leaching of fertilizers, particularly nitrogen, pesticide residues in runoff water, and pollutants from animal waste carried to water sources. Urban nonpoint source pollutants include materials such as toxic petroleum residues carried in runoff water from streets and parking lots. In either situation, the environmental issue is water pollution. Of course, water pollution leads to habitat destruction and ultimately may affect biodiversity.

Materials leaked from defective underground storage tanks contribute to environmental degradation. Greatest concern has focused on petroleum products and potential contamination of water sources from defective tanks. In addition, the ground itself can become contaminated with leaked materials, which may reduce or destroy its productive and economic value.

Air Pollution

Air pollution (items 3 and 15) represents a continuing threat to health, although significant progress has been achieved in reducing levels of certain types of pollutants. This general cause of environmental degradation comprises two subunits: industrial pollutants and pollutants related to transportation, mainly automobiles, but including trucks, buses, and even aircraft. Both subunits contribute particulate matter that is at the very least a serious irritant. Sulfur oxides, primary components of acid rain, represent serious pollutants produced by burning coal with a high sulfur content, which is common in electrical generation facilities and in the iron smelting industry.

The most common automobile-generated pollutant is smog. Smog includes particulate matter, carbon monoxide, and oxides of nitrogen. The elimination of leaded fuels has reduced the lead problem significantly, yet lead from nonfuel sources remains a serious pollutant. Other industrial pollutants of major concern include many organic compounds used in the manufacture of synthetic materials (plastics and man-made fibers) and pesticide residues.

Certain organic compounds have the potential to adversely affect the protective layer of atmospheric ozone (items 6 and 16). These pollutants include compounds such as certain coolants used in air conditioning units (freon, or chlorofluorohydrocarbons) and fumigants such as methyl bromide. Damage to the ozone layer contributes to the potential greenhouse effect, the trapping of radiant heat in the earth's atmosphere and subsequent warming of the earth resulting in global climatic changes, including the potential melting of polar ice caps. The actual danger from these substances is disputed, but they are recognized as a serious threat by the government and are the subject of active basic research projects.

Scientists recognize asbestos (item 18) (particularly as it exists in old buildings as insulation) an air pollutant, and radon (item 17), a naturally occurring radioactive gas that may accumulate in buildings, as potential carcinogens. An additional issue, disposal of unwanted or worn materials, arises with asbestos.

Food Safety

Pesticide risks and food safety (item 11) present a complex set of problems:

1. Residues from pesticides applied during crop production may reach the final food product and affect the consumer.

2. Too little is known regarding the differences in sensitivity to residues in infants versus older children and adults. Also, the diets of infants frequently contain proportionately far more food that may have pesticide residues (fruits and vegetables).

3. Pesticides that may occur in seemingly minute amounts may accumulate in the food chain and harm other life-forms (in this case, the issue extends to general ecological concerns).

4. Workers who are constantly exposed to pesticides or pesticide residues may face health risks (such as item 4, workplace exposure to toxic chemicals).

The Workplace

Some of the issues listed in Table 1.1 may seem more related to job safety and thus not appropriate as environmental concerns. Item 7 might also be placed in this category, although a nuclear plant accident clearly represents potential harm to more than plant workers. Because many people spend more waking hours in the workplace than in any other location, inclusion of workplace issues in this discussion is justified.

Radiation

Exposure to radiation other than as a result of a nuclear plant accident (item 8) presents a complex series of subconcerns. Radiation has become a major resource in both medical research and in clinical applications. Exposure for clinical purposes (from routine dental x-rays to cancer therapy) must be included in totaling human exposure to radiation. Medical sources of radioactive materials represent the major source of low-level nuclear waste, a product that has become a serious waste management issue. The waste represents a significant environmental hazard that requires special handling to minimize possible pollution from improper waste disposal.

In addition to medical applications, a variety of industries use radioactive materials either in manufacturing processes or as a part of the completed product. Radioactive materials are also used to sterilize some products and to reduce foodborne pathogens in poultry and some vegetables. The products do not become radioactive. Government uses of nuclear materials in the defense industry is a significant contributor to the radioactive waste problem, as is the nuclear power industry. The nature of nuclear materials justifies their separate consideration and regulation even though they fit into the broad category of waste materials with the potential to pollute water and air.

Biotechnology

Like radiation, biotechnology (item 21) comprises at least two subsets of environmental concerns. The first focuses on potential harm from the application of biotechnological techniques during manufacture of a product, and the second concerns the environmental implications of the use or release of the products of biotechnology. (The number of products is growing constantly. Included are human hormones, such as insulin, produced by genetically engineered bacteria, and new varieties of soybeans and cotton that are resistant to otherwise toxic weed killers. Also, bacteria have been developed that can neutralize oil, thus reducing pollution, but these have not yet been widely used. Much of the progress in biological control of agricultural pests is the product of biotechnology.) The issues can be classed as process or product issues. Chapter 3 considers these implications in some detail.

Transporting Hazardous Materials

Oil spills (item 5) have been recognized as major environmental problems. The "Exxon Valdez" disaster in Alaska remains a tragic example of the damage such activities can cause to human health and to the environment. Oil spills relate to a serious, more general environmental problem that has not received extensive public scrutiny: safe transportation of materials that can harm the environment. Transportation concerns must include problems associated with transporting essential manufacturing or consumer products and waste materials. In the final analysis, consideration must be given to finding effective alternatives for the toxic materials and acceptable technologies to minimize waste products and to render such products environmentally safe.

Environmental Concerns Related to Natural Resources or Ecology

Natural resources and ecological issues continue to attract significant attention; historically such issues represent the earliest subject of environmental regulation by the federal government. Government concern about natural resources is not new, nor is government regulation of the environment. In the United States, early land management practices reflect the government's concern with the environment. Clearly, land must be regarded as a major natural resource and a significant component of the environment.

Soil Erosion

Since at least the Dust Bowl era of the mid-1930s, soil erosion (item 29) has been recognized as a major environmental problem related directly to the loss of a critical natural resource as well as a problem having great economic consequences. Soil erosion, caused by wind and water, remains a leading conservation problem throughout the United States. Although most frequently viewed as agricultural problems, erosion and related sediment problems also directly affect urban settings. These problems include loss of topsoil critical for sustained agricultural output, damage from silt accumulations in rivers, lakes, and reservoirs, and resulting losses of habitat and decreased recreational opportunities.

Protection of All Life-forms

Items 25, 26, and 27 reflect a growing national concern about the need to protect all forms of life. To some, the need is a matter of practical considerations: Many life-forms may be of currently unrecognized, but ultimately significant, human value. These proponents place emphasis on the potential medicinal value of many plants. Some also suggest their potential value as alternative sources of food or for industrial purposes, such as sources of industrial oil. Others, most notably the animal rights activists, regard the issue from an ethical position and assert that all organisms have a right to survive.

Destruction of Habitat and Loss of Biodiversity

Habitat destruction (item 26) results from changing land use. Most frequently claims of damage are associated with timbering and mining activities in areas of native forests, with excessive grazing or intensified farming practices, or as a result of building and urbanization. Part of the timbering and mining claims include concerns that the development of roads into otherwise secluded sites will disrupt animal life. Habitat destruction includes destruction of food sources and reproductive (e.g., nesting) sites, and disruption of the normal life cycles or reproductive cycles of organisms.

The concept of biodiversity (item 25) involves both a community and a population concept related to the need for minimum levels of inherited differences for a community or population to survive. In the case of community, the diversity includes different species as well as differences among individual members of the same species. Populations are subdivisions of a community, and diversity is expressed as inherited differences among intermating individuals. Loss of the Brazilian rain forests has attracted great concern in relation to loss of biodiversity. Because of the complex interrelationships among organisms and their environment, a loss of the rain forest could also result in significant changes in air quality (carbon dioxide concentration) and potential global warming or increased greenhouse effects.

The ultimate loss of biodiversity is the biological extinction of a species. Species designated as endangered species (item 27) require special protection, including protection of habitat critical to their survival. Arguments supporting the protection of designated endangered species follow either the general concerns of the animal rights advocate or the philosophy that until the potential value of an organism is known, its survival should be guarded. Although more attention appears focused on animal species, the concept includes both plants and animals.

Pesticides

Pesticides represent a threat to human health and have already been discussed in that light. They also may harm various forms of wildlife (item 24), and are known to accumulate in the food chain, so that low levels of concentration in one organism may lead to higher, damaging levels in organisms that feed on the lower forms, a phenomenon known as *bioaccumulation*.

Acid Rain

Acid rain (item 28) is a product of air pollution previously discussed as item 3, industrial pollution of air as a by-product of manufacturing. Acid rain results from simple chemical reactions between water and sulfur oxides that are produced predominantly by burning coal high in sulfur. Electrical generating plants are chief, but not exclusive, consumers of such coal and as a result, are major sources of acid rain. The effects of the production of sulfur compounds are felt great distances from the consumption of the coal, because winds can carry the pollutants great distances before they are deposited. Acid rain and related acid deposits destroy native vegetation and have been blamed for sterilizing lakes in Scandinavia as well as for damaging buildings and other structures.

Wetlands

In recent years, the federal government has recognized the ecological significance of wetlands and the rapid rate of loss of the nation's wetlands (item 22). Wetlands play several important roles: natural filters for water, flood control, and a variety of unique ecological niches and habitats for migratory waterfowl as well as fish and shellfish. Wetlands continue to be a subject of regulatory controversy and legal issues related to constitutional protection of private property; see chapter 2.

Item 23, contaminated coastal waters, again shows the relationship among the items. This issue relates to water pollution, and coastal waters have received special attention because they represent unique habitats for waterfowl, fish, and shellfish.

Issues Related to Natural Resource Management

The final six items could be treated under the preceding heading; however, each addresses a unique topic, and all involve patterns of policy development. In addition, each has received significant legislative attention and reflects major policy posture or philosophies. However, significant problems remain unresolved for each item, and additional evolution of policy should be expected.

Land Management

Item 30, effective multiple use and sustained yields of natural resources, expresses the federal land-management policy as it has evolved over the history of the nation. Management policy has moved from special interests to shared use of natural resources. This policy recognizes conflicts of interest between groups seeking to use various resources, from timber and livestock interest to wildlife conservation and wilderness preservation, and it is evolving to "ecosystem management" that considers entire, complex systems as a unit.

Item 31, sustainable agriculture, cannot be separated in concept from the philosophy of multiple use and sustained yield. The majority of intensely cultivated agricultural land is privately owned, and the Constitution strictly limits government management. Nonetheless, regulatory efforts to protect the agricultural resources include water distribution from federal water projects and funding through the diverse agricultural support programs. As a result, a variety of federal programs have an impact on the agricultural environment: The growing policy is the support of sustainability rather than maximum yields. This philosophy has found favor with many environmental interests.

Items 32, 33, and 34 (management and protection of forests, rangeland, and groundwater and surface water supplies) represent special-interest concerns related to the issues just addressed under items 30 and 31. Conflicting interest continues regarding timber activities in the national forests, including economic factors (the need for jobs related to the timber industry) and the loss of critical habitat and virgin stands of various tree species. The major issue with rangeland focuses on overgrazing and the problems of erosion resulting from overgrazing plus the loss of wildlife and the negative impact on recreational use.

Agriculture represents one of the major export industries in the United States, and the strength of the nation's productive capacity is a source of national pride. The issue of sustainable agriculture (item 32) reflects a serious concern that current production practices deplete the natural resources on which our agricultural production system depends.

Many might blame government price-support policy over the past fifty to sixty years for fostering environmentally destructive practices. Regardless of the blame, the issue emerges that, to ensure sustainable production, agricultural practices that protect resources must be identified and producers encouraged, if not required, to adopt such practices: to minimize erosion, to protect soil fertility, to minimize pollution from pesticides as well as nonpoint source pollutants, fertilizers, and animal wastes, and to utilize available water more effectively while protecting supplies.

Wilderness Preservation

In the minds of many, wilderness preservation (item 35) represents the ultimate in special-use classification. The federal government has recognized areas to be protected as wilderness areas and imposed management strategies designed to minimize the impact of human activities on such areas. Current controversies include protecting existing areas, expanding areas designated as wilderness areas, and limiting activities in areas adjacent to wilderness areas to protect the designated wilderness. Pressure to allow development in these areas comes from both mining and timber interests. Arguments that frequently have strong economic overtones center on the basic issue of intrinsic value of wilderness and the justification of denying the development of essential natural resources, including oil and natural gas.

Groups of the Issues for Simplification

The organization of the issues in Table 1.1 represents only one possible grouping of issues. Some critical issues may appear to be ignored or be minor components of broader concerns. The intent of Table 1.1 is to provide an introductory scope of the diversity and complexity of environmental issues subject to regulation and management. The issues discussed, and others that may be inferred, can be organized into fewer, larger units that allow a simpler review of possible causes and solutions and lead more directly to the consideration of environmental rules, regulations, and laws.

For convenience, the issues included in Table 1.1 can be discussed in groups that parallel regulations and allow the inclusion of other issues. The categories in this broader grouping are not mutually exclusive. The grouping has been suggested by the three sub-groups of concerns identified in the discussion of Table 1.1

1.   One obvious major group is ecology or natural resource conservation. This group includes issues ranging from soil conservation and land use to biodiversity (which includes habitat destruction, rain forest preservation, and endangered species), concerns over forest and range management, damage from acid rain, and protection of water supplies and re-sources. Note the immediate overlaps: Rain forest preservation also is a concern related to global warming and air quality (carbon dioxide accumulation), and waste disposal has be-come a major water quality consideration.

2.   A second major grouping is health-related issues. These can be divided into three subgroups: air quality and air pollution, water quality and water pollution of both surface water and groundwater resources, and issues related to waste accumulation and disposal.

Waste accumulation and disposal cannot be separated from concerns related to both air and water quality. Incineration has been considered as an alternative to waste disposal in landfills, which leads to problems with air pollution from incinerators and to issues re-lated to the disposal of the incinerator ash that may contain concentrated forms of some pol-lutants. Landfills, a common method of waste disposal, are significant potential sources of water pollution in the form of raw materials or products of waste decomposition leached from the landfill sites into surface water or groundwater supplies. Certain aspects of waste disposal are best considered independently; these include radioactive (nuclear) waste, cer-tain very toxic materials, and perhaps medical wastes.

In addition to potential danger to water quality from leachate from landfills, water quality has deteriorated as a result of the discharge of pollutants from manufacturing plants, as either by-products or waste materials, into rivers, lakes, bays, and oceans. These pollutants, which include chemicals and raw organic (plant and animal) materials, are commonly called *point source pollutants*. Nonpoint source—urban and agricultural—pollutants continue to pose serious threats to water quality. The safety of drinking water has received special attention, but as a generalization, it logically falls under the area of health and water quality.

Air pollution has two major sources or causes: manufacturing and automotive. This topic also shares potential impact related to rain forest destruction and global warming con-cerns that frequently are discussed as independent issues.

3.   A third area of regulation addresses broad policy issues and is not directed to any specific problem area or obvious cause. This area may provide the fundamental, common thread among all environmental concerns. It includes the formulation of general policy con-siderations as articulated in legislation such as the National Environmental Policy Act, the Federal Land Policy Management Act, and the Multiple Use/Sustained Yield Act (see the discussion of land management policy in chapter 4 and the National Environmental Policy Act and Endangered Species Act in chapter 5 as examples of statements of general policy).

CAUSES OF ENVIRONMENTAL DEGRADATION

The most significant environmental degradation can be attributed to three causes (which are not mutually exclusive): population growth, technology, and lifestyle. However, these causes do not take into account naturally occurring pollution such as sulfur emissions from volcanic eruptions and even naturally occurring soil erosion.

The Human Impact

The impact of people on the environment takes two forms. First, humans consume natural resources: As the population increases, demands for resources increase. Second, many human activities directly damage the environment.

Increased demand for food is an obvious and familiar example of the burden a growing population places on the environment. Space to produce food is limited. As the population grows, demand for greater production per acre and for more intense farming practices (e.g., double cropping, increased irrigation, and increased use of fertilizers and pesticides) grows too. These requirements burden the productive capacity of the land, increase demands on water resources for irrigation, encourage the extensive use of agricultural chemicals, and can lead to habitat destruction as marginal lands are cultivated. Said another way, valuable, irreplaceable farm land is too frequently converted to nonagricultural uses, as is clearly reflected in the suburban sprawl of America.

The concern over population growth exceeding increases in food productivity is not new. In the eighteenth century, Thomas Malthus, an English economist and clergyman, predicted the potential of imminent mass starvation as a result of the geometric increase in the human population and linear increase in food production; see Figure 1.1. However, Malthus could not have foreseen the extent to which "science" would increase crop yields or the vast areas of land that would be brought under cultivation. As a result, his dire predictions of mass starvation have not come true. Recently, others have made similar predictions based not only on availability of food, but on crowding, resource depletion, and general environmental degradation. Although the warnings must be considered seriously, most "worst-case situations" have not materialized. Nevertheless, hunger remains a critical worldwide concern with enormous environmental implications.

Several other measures illustrate the impact of increasing population growth. Figures 1.2 through 1.6 dramatically illustrate the impact of increased population in one area, the drainage of the Chesapeake Bay. Figure 1.2 identifies this extensive region, which includes parts of at least five states—New York, Pennsylvania, Virginia, West Virginia, and Maryland. Figure 1.3 shows the population growth since the seventeenth century including predictions into the twenty-first century: the critical parts are the rapid growth starting about 1930. Figures 1.4, 1.5, and 1.6 illustrate patterns of environmental degradation that are directly associated with the periods of most rapid population growth.

Figure 1.4 characterizes air pollution from all sources and contrasts 1952 and 1986. The increase is undeniable, and the extensive concentration along the northwest region of the area (the Greater District of Columbia area) plainly parallels the massive population growth in that area. Figure 1.5 reveals a similar pattern for solid waste accumulation, as does Figure 1.6 for energy consumption. Increased energy consumption also contributes to increased air pollution. The patterns found in this area are not unique; similar patterns exist for growing metropolitan areas throughout the United States. The message is clear: People cause pollution!

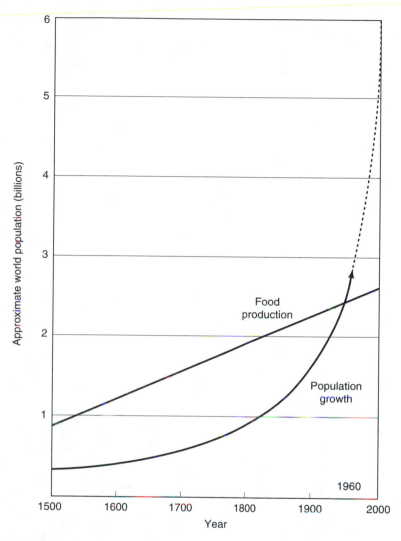

FIGURE 1.1 Pattern of world population growth from 1500 with prediction to 2050. Malthus predicted that food production could not keep pace with the increasing rate of population growth.

The Impact of Technology

Every facet of life in America benefits from various aspects of advanced technology: It has reduced the demand for physical labor, increased the yields and quality of many crops through the development of highly effective pesticides and fertilizers, made available convenience products from precooked and packaged meals to paper diapers, brought entertainment and current events to the homes of millions, and contributed to the mobility of the average citizen through the availability of automobiles. However, these benefits carry three

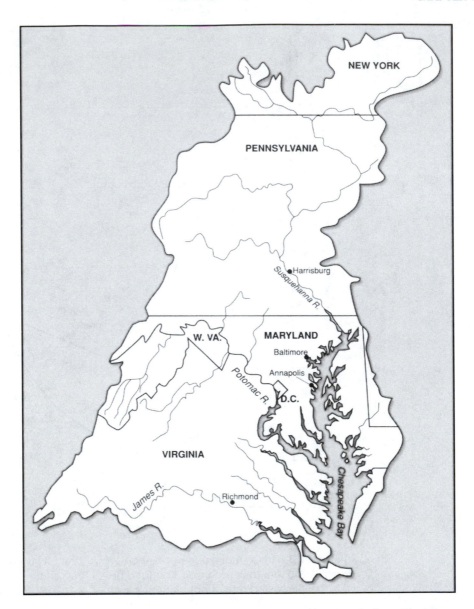

FIGURE 1.2 The Chesapeake Bay drainage, which extends from Virginia into New York. Granted with permission from *Turning the Tide: Saving the Chesapeake Bay*. Horton, Tom, and William M. Eichbaum, Copyright © Island Press, 1991. Published by Island Press, Washington, DC and Covelo, CA.

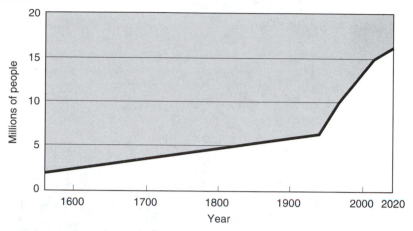

Population after 1980 is projected

FIGURE 1.3 Population in the Chesapeake Bay Watershed. Granted with permission from *Turning the Tide: Saving the Chesapeake Bay.* Horton, Tom, and William M. Eichbaum, Copyright © 1991. Published by Island Press, Washington, DC and Covelo, CA.

unavoidable environmental costs: (1) manufacturing the product, (2) using the product, and (3) disposing of the used product or residues associated with its use.

Pesticides represent a typical example of the impact of technology. Major growth in the development and use of pesticides, especially insecticides, occurred during and immediately after World War II. According to the Environmental Protection Agency, pesticides include approximately 47,000 products. Agricultural uses account for about 75 percent of the billion pounds of pesticides sold annually in the United States. Weed killers (herbicides) constitute the majority of the pesticides used. Technology yields new, more effective and environmentally less threatening pesticides. The EPA reports that since 1970, over 120 new chemicals have been registered as pesticides and that 10 to 15 new pesticides are registered annually. (Pesticide registration and regulation are discussed in detail in chapter 10.)

The use of pesticides on fruits and vegetables is a matter of greatest concern to many. Common formulations of insecticides have included chlorinated hydrocarbons and organic mercury and phosphorous compounds. The raw materials used in formulating these products are dangerous to human health.

Excessive use or misuse of pesticides can contaminate lakes and streams and can result in residues on food products. Residues of some pesticides are known to accumulate in the food chain, thereby increasing the potential harm to humans and wildlife. Many residues are thought to be carcinogenic. In addition to the issues of user and consumer safety, a final issue concerns the environmentally safe disposal of pesticide containers. Perhaps as much as the improper use of the product, careless disposal of containers represents a serious environmental threat, particularly when the containers find their way into municipal landfill sites or other land disposal areas, and from there, potentially into water supplies.

Americans are mobile people. The family car, which for many families now is two, three, or more cars in daily use, presents a complex set of environmental problems. Normal

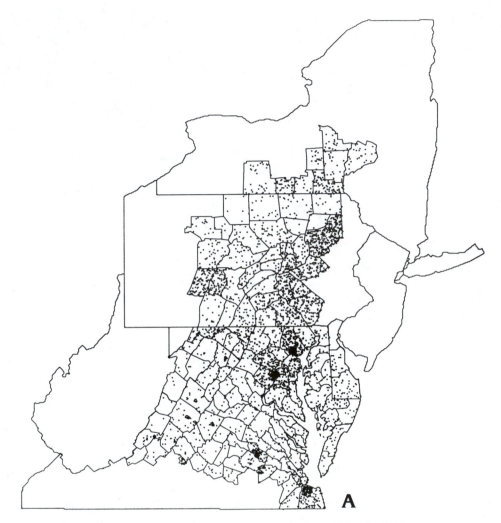

FIGURE 1.4 Air pollution in the Chesapeake Bay Watershed. Map A
shows 1952 conditions, and map B on p. 19 shows 1986 conditions.
Granted with permission from *Turning the Tide: Saving the Chesapeake
Bay.* Horton, Tom, and William M. Eichbaum, Copyright © Island Press,
1991. Published by Island Press, Washington, DC and Covelo, CA.

operation of a gasoline engine produces air pollutants. The elimination of lead as a gasoline additive has improved a serious problem, but the fact remains—cars pollute, and more than people of any other nation, Americans drive. To add to the problem, production of gasoline, starting with oil exploration and continuing through refining and storage of the finished products, represents an environmentally threatening activity.

Moreover, the automobile manufacturing industry requires large supplies of steel, and steel production remains a significant source of pollution. Cars consume products other than gasoline, and these also become environmental hazards. Lead batteries and used tires are two of the obvious products, and junk cars still litter the landscape.

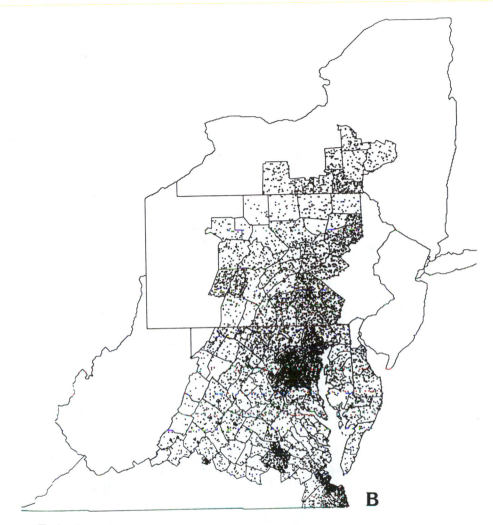

B

Technology since World War II has given us a variety of artificial fibers and materials. Their manufacture involves the use of toxic chemicals and the related need to dispose of toxic wastes and residues, and the end products are a serious source of accumulation of slowly degradable materials entering municipal solid waste landfills. The materials generally classified as polymers are used in packaging materials, as insulation, clothing, carpets, and building materials from pipe to maintenance-free siding materials for homes and businesses. Table 1.2 lists the most common plastic and artificial fibers produced in the United States.

Health care uses increasing amounts and diverse sources of radioactive materials, and the benefits are dramatic for many. Nevertheless, this use leads to problems of safety and with disposal of expended radioactive sources. The same issue exists with other commercial uses, including nuclear power for generating electricity. As a source of electrical generation, nuclear power no longer holds the bright promise it appeared to have in the late 1960s and early 1970s, but plants nationwide continue to produce waste that must be stored or neutralized.

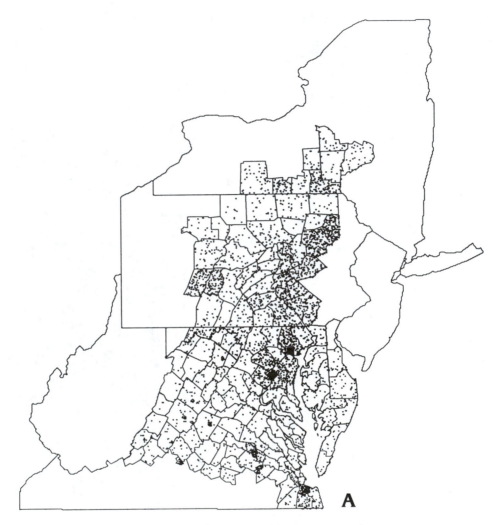

FIGURE 1.5 Waste production in the Chesapeake Bay Watershed. Map A shows 1952 conditions, and map B on p. 21 shows 1986 conditions. Granted with permission from *Turning the Tide: Saving the Chesapeake Bay*. Horton, Tom, and William M. Eichbaum, Copyright © Island Press, 1991. Published by Island Press, Washington, DC and Covelo, CA.

The Impact of Lifestyle

Without minimizing very serious socioeconomic problems, the United States can be characterized generally as an affluent society. This fact appears to explain in part many of the very real, serious environmental problems confronting the nation today.

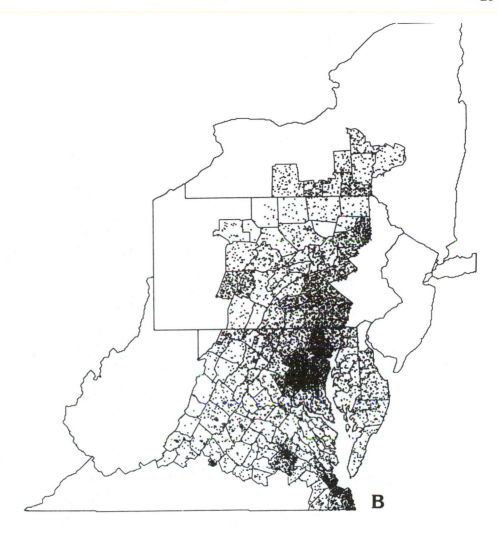

B

Our affluence has led us to become a mobile society, and air pollution (smog) from motor vehicles is a significant problem. We also demand convenience in other forms of transportation, and this convenience has a small but real environmental cost.

As a nation, we have become a convenience demanding, throwaway society. Affluence, technology (particularly the amazing array of plastic items available), and relatively inexpensive imports contribute to this mind-set. In addition, the pace of society seems to demand convenience. Consider the items used daily and the items most frequently purchased.

The fast-food industry serves thousands of meals daily. Although several chains have taken significant, if not dramatic, steps to reduce the use of synthetic materials for carryout customers, local highways are littered with plastic utensils, boxes, wrappers, and throwaway cups and containers, and landfills receive even more. The shelves of large grocery chains and smaller local stores are filled with "convenience foods." These include precooked, single-serving meals, and a vast array of fresh and processed products that are individually

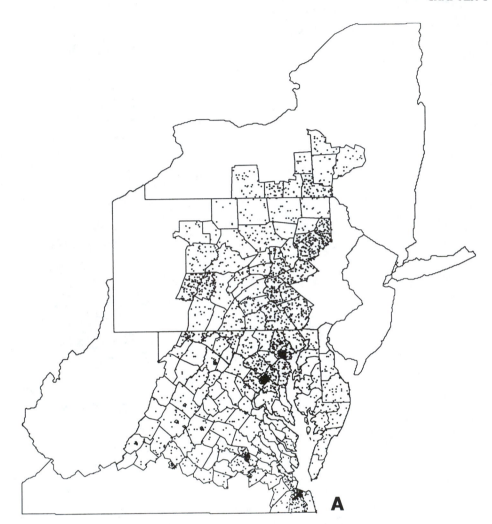

FIGURE 1.6 Energy consumption in the Chesapeake Bay Watershed.
Map A shows 1952 conditions, and map B on p. 23 shows 1986 conditions. Granted with permission from *Turning the Tide: Saving the Chesapeake Bay.* Horton, Tom, and William M. Eichbaum, Copyright © Island
Press, 1991. Published by Island Press, Washington, DC and Covelo, CA.

packaged. Once used, the packages become waste. The trend continues with personal products,
from throwaway razors to disposable washcloths. Paper diapers have been the subject of controversy, but use of the alternative, cloth diapers, is not without significant environmental cost:
water use, heating water, and detergent residues entering water supplies from sewage systems.

Consider, in addition, the vast array of throwaway small appliances found in virtually
every home today. These range from flashlights to kitchen appliances and small radios. The
number of disposables seems to be increasing endlessly.

The environmental issues of convenience are twofold: the energy, raw materials, and
pollution associated with manufacture, plus the increasingly serious problem of disposal.

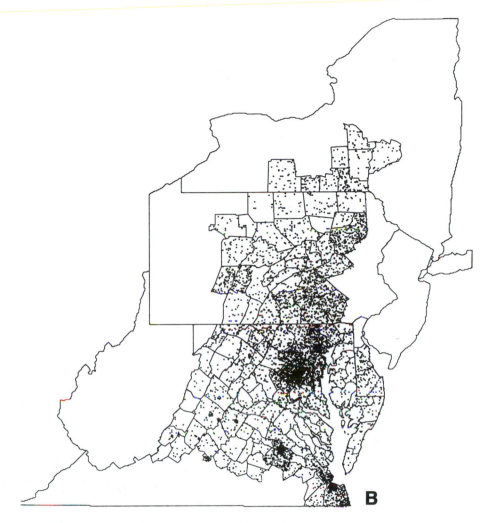

B

The magnitude of the problem is expressed by a simple figure with unbelievable implications: Taking into account reductions from composting and recycling, every day each American produces approximately 3.5 pounds, or more, of municipal solid waste (what we have traditionally called garbage). The level of waste production is increasing, although recycling efforts are helping. Figure 1.7 describes the composition of the waste. The total amount generated will continue to increase, led by paper products. Note that neither mining nor agricultural waste generally enters the reported waste stream, although agriculture (animal waste and fertilizer) is recognized as a serious nonpoint source of water pollution.

SOLUTIONS

Solutions to problems of environmental degradation are as varied and complex as the problems, and they involve additional considerations. At least four general aspects of a problem enter into the formulation of solutions. These factors are clearly not mutually exclusive.

Polymer Produced	Billions of Tons Produced
Plastic	
1. polyethlene	21.75
2. poly (vinyl chloride)	9.97
3. polypropylene	8.40
4. polystyrene	5.04
5. phenol and other tar resins	2.90
6. urea resins	1.54
7. unsaturated polyesters	1.19
Synthetic Fibers	
8. polyester	3.56
9. nylon	2.55
10. olefin	1.98
11. acrylic	0.44

TABLE 1.2. Production of synthetic polymers in the United States in 1992. Products represent new technology and also significant components of materials disposed of in landfills. Reprinted in part with permission from *Chemical Engineering News*, 71 (15):16 "Biodegradation and Bioremediation," by Martin Alexander. Copyright 1994, American Chemical Society.

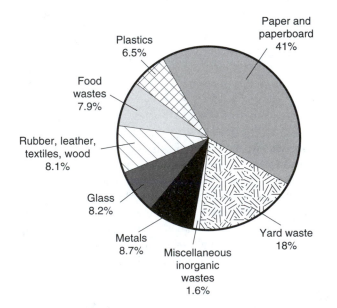

FIGURE 1.7 Composition of municipal solid waste estimated for the year 2000 by EPA. US EPA DATA.

1. The first factor is the magnitude of the problem. Environmental degradation always has some ultimate local component, but in some instances either the basic concern (the cause or the effect of the degradation) or simply the "local" component surpasses the capacity of local resolution; examples are efforts to protect the Brazilian rain forests and to address the emerging issues of global warming, although individual efforts in either case cannot be ignored. Clearly issues that cross political boundaries, either national or even state boundaries, may require consideration different from those that involve a single political entity.

2. The second factor to consider focuses on whether the solution is corrective (remedial) or preventive. In many situations, this decision can result in assigning blame for a problem instead of determining who or what is to be regulated and in what manner. Commonly efforts address both the corrective and preventive aspects of a problem. Solid waste disposal regulations illustrate this in several ways. From a regulatory position, certain major laws (that is, those with very widespread application—and, in this case, with a high level of federal funding) focus on cleaning up old waste sites (CERCLA: the Comprehensive Environmental Response Compensating and Liability Act, discussed in chapter 8), or both laws and rules related to laws regulating currently active landfill sites and encouraging recycling. The same pattern is seen in regulations seeking to protect the nation's surface waters. Both technology and laws focus on prevention of pollution by water treatment at the source of the potential pollutant and by treatment of sewage water to reduce pollutants before the water reenters a body of water.

3. Costs, or economic factors, cannot be ignored and must be balanced with benefits (or with potential harm) a given condition might cause, which leads to a consideration of the complex topic of risk assessment. Risk assessment is difficult; even when economic harm can be estimated, it becomes far more complex when issues affecting human health are involved, even if the health costs themselves can be estimated. Ideally, risk could be assessed without economic considerations, but practically, this is rarely feasible. In some situations, determining cost can be virtually impossible, such as calculating the cost of lost wilderness. (The complex issue of risk assessment is addressed in chapter 3.)

4. The final factor also addresses the proposed type of solution needed or being considered: Either technology must remedy or prevent environmental degradation or rules and standards must control activities within acceptable, agreed-upon limits. Commonly, both aspects are at work in any given situation. For example, laws and rules establish limits of the discharge of certain air pollutants. Technology has established what is feasible and what might be practical. In the opposite situation, standards are established, and the world of technology is called upon to formulate methods to satisfy the standards. In spite of criticism and shortcomings, overall, technology has demonstrated a remarkable capacity to protect and restore the environment. Reductions in air pollutants illustrate this capacity dramatically.

Because many environmental problems cross national and international political boundaries, because of conflicting economic interests in the environment, because of the magnitude of the problems to be addressed, and despite well-documented attempts to protect or enhance the environment without laws, rules, and regulations, continued progress in protecting our environment will depend on the formulation and enforcement of appropriate laws at all levels of government—federal, state, and local. The remainder of this text focuses on forces that shape laws, rules, and regulations, addresses how laws are formulated, considers the major federal laws that regulate the environment, and draws comparisons with the effects of state laws. Consideration is given to laws regulating natural resources or ecology as well as to health-related issues; risk assessment as an essential element of formulating laws, rules, and regulations is given separate attention.

QUESTIONS AND CONCEPTS FOR DISCUSSION AND RESEARCH

1. What are the major environmental issues facing society today? Are they more health or resource related? Is the "health" versus "resource" distinction important, or is it a matter of convenience that can be arbitrary?

2. Does the four-step approach to environmental analysis presented in this chapter apply more to problems and issues, to rules and regulations, or to technology and solutions? Is it more appropriate to health-related or resource-related considerations?

3. What are the major causes of environmental degradation today? What are the possible solutions?

REFERENCES AND SELECTED READING

Alexander, Martin. 1994. *Biodegradation and Bioremediation.* San Diego, CA: Academic Press.

Focusing on the Garbage Crisis. An Interview with Sylvia Lowrance. 1989. *EPA Journal* 15(2), 10–14.

Horton, Tom, and William M. Eichbaum. 1991. *Turning the Tide: Saving the Chesapeake Bay.* Washington, DC and Covelo, CA: Island Press.

Kubasek, Nancy K., and Gray S. Silverman. 1994. *Environmental Law.* Englewood Cliffs, NJ: Prentice Hall.

Lewis, Jack. 1989. What's in the Solid Waste Stream? *EPA Journal* 15(2), 15–17.

Nebel, Bernard J., and Richard T. Wright. 1993. *Environmental Science: The Way the World Works.* 4th ed. Englewood Cliffs, NJ: Prentice Hall.

U.S. Environmental Protection Agency. 1996. *Environmental Backgrounder: Pesticides.* Washington, DC.

———. January 1989. *Recycling Works! State and Local Solutions to Solid Waste Management.* EPA/530-SW-89-014. Washington, DC.

2

Sources of Environmental Policy, Laws, Rules, and Regulations

Increasingly in recent years, environmental issues have become a recognized specialty field of law and policy. The topic is extremely broad, complex, and diverse and is subject to strong, emotional, and conflicting opinions. Nonetheless, policy and law development follow the same basic governmental/political pattern followed by any other area subject to government regulation. Understanding how policies are formulated and how laws, rules, and regulations are made and implemented in general provides an essential foundation for understanding major environmental policies, laws, and rules. This understanding can also provide significant insight into the nature of the problems as seen by policy makers and lawmakers.

OVERVIEW

The following discussion will focus first on the formulation of federal environmental law. This focus is logical because the United States Constitution empowers Congress, within prescribed limits, to enact legislation with which individual states must comply. In the field of environmental regulation, federal laws set the minimum standards of compliance, and states may enact stricter laws, such as the stricter automobile smog control laws passed by California. In many states, environmental standards established by federal law comprise all

27

state environmental regulations for major areas of controversy and regulation, such as air and water pollution.

Constitutional Empowerment for Legislative Action

Although the Constitution empowers Congress to enact certain types of laws with which all states must comply, the Constitution also specifically limits the legislative authority of Congress. The American form of government, as expressed by the United States Constitution, is built on the philosophy of limited government with emphasis on individual and states' rights.

For a law to be constitutional (enforceable if challenged in court), Congress must either show direct or implied constitutional authority to enact the type of legislation the law represents. Surprisingly, the Constitution does not specifically empower Congress to enact legislation to protect the environment, but it does call for legislation to protect the property of the United States. Much environmental legislation is justified by implied constitutional empowerment to take certain legislative actions under the broad regulatory authority of the Commerce Clause. Other portions of the Constitution also affect the interpretation of environmental regulation, but the Commerce Clause has been interpreted to provide the basic constitutional empowerment.

Public Input

Assuming legitimate constitutional congressional empowerment to act, the starting point for regulation appears to be congressional action: Congress enacts a law. Although certainly a highly visible element of the process, it is not the first step. Generally, Congress reacts to "public pressure," and as a result of such public pressure exerted through lobbying efforts, legislation is proposed. Thus, the voice of the public must be considered as the starting point for regulatory legislation, although commonly the individual feels that a single voice is rarely heard.

The Role of the Courts

Courts play a major role in the ultimate expression of environmental policy and law. At the extreme, the highest courts may decide whether a law is constitutional and therefore can be enforced. Appellate courts at both the federal and state levels interpret laws and ultimately establish what the law allows or prohibits. Lower, trial courts must follow these decisions; thus appellate courts become valid sources of law. Some would insist that courts are the ultimate source of law. Most commonly the role of the court is viewed through trials as deciding when laws have been violated and assessing penalties. This is the traditional judicial role of law enforcement.

Administrative Rules

Administrative rules—the rules and regulations of numerous governmental departments and agencies such as the Environmental Protection Agency (EPA) and the U.S. Department of Agriculture (USDA)—are major sources of environmental law and policy. Through legislation, Congress empowers the agencies to formulate and enforce rules and regulations to implement legislation. This is the complex and important field of administrative law. The federal Administrative Procedure Act limits the extent of agency rule making and requires public notice of proposed rules and the opportunity for public input to proposed rules.

Executive Actions

Other factors directly add to the pool of environmental regulations. At the federal level, for example, the president can exercise significant authority over the operation of executive agencies, such as the EPA, the USDA, or the United States Department of the Interior (which includes the Bureau of Land Management), by requiring them to follow specific executive policies, which are not generally subject to public input or court review.

State Government

State governments exercise the same authorities as the federal government, but for certain subjects, if any conflict arises, the federal law or rule will prevail. States exercise several sources of law that the Constitution has reserved exclusively to the states, and thus, these types of law are not available to the federal government.

Unique State Powers

States can exercise "police power," which is law that protects the public security, health, safety, and morality. The United States Constitution grants exercise of this power to the states. Many health laws and rules trace their origin to this authority. In addition, states can call on the precedent of "common law" as a basis of action. (American common law traces to England. It is unwritten law that, over time, has generally been accepted as good, proper, or appropriate.) Common law is not a source of federal law, although this fundamental doctrine may be changing.

THE VOICE OF THE PEOPLE

Individual Input

Frequently, individual citizens feel far removed from decision making and believe their opinion or voice is not heard by the government. However, the Founding Fathers intended that the voice of the individual must be heard: The Preamble of the Constitution of the United States, which clearly represents the voice of the people, begins "WE the people of the United States. . . . " The American form of democratic government calls for the voice of the individual to be heard. Obviously, as the nation has grown and issues have become more numerous and complex, individual input has become increasingly difficult, but not impossible.

With but a few exceptions, Americans are governed at all levels by some form of representative government. Elected representatives and officials formulate, enact, and enforce laws and rules. These representatives are elected by the vote of the people. If the people do not approve of the actions of elected officials, they can refuse to reelect them, or, in extreme situations, the voters can remove an elected official from office during his or her term. In some instances, the public, by referendum, has the right to vote directly on issues. The power of the ballot cannot be overlooked.

In recent years, public pressure has forced political candidates to include environmental issues in their campaign positions. The major political parties have been variously identified as pro- or anti-environment, based in large part on the party's position regarding executive policy and stricter rules and enforcement, and frequently based on promises of continued fiscal support for agencies that formulate and enforce environmental rules and policies.

Candidates for local government, from city council to the state legislature, must assume a position regarding one or more local environmental issues, such as selecting locations for landfills, support for recycling, or zoning for land use. The system may be far from perfect, but opportunities for direct input on environmental issues do exist—although measuring the effectiveness of such input may be difficult.

Group Input or Lobbying

The opportunity for individual input is fundamental to the American form of government; however, in the real world of politics, group input is more effective and efficient in terms of identifiable legislative responses. Group input may be highly organized and formal, or relatively informal and ad hoc in nature. Regardless, all such input qualifies as lobbying. In this sense, lobbying involves two related types of activities: (1) support of (or opposition to) a particular cause, such as the location of a nuclear waste disposal facility, and (2) support of the election of specific political candidates. Lobbying provides essential services to both the government and to the private citizen. In addition to providing the majority of campaign support, it keeps the public informed of issues and of the positions assumed by elected representatives.

Table 2.1 summarizes a number of types of lobbying organizations and the general positions they have taken on a variety of issues.

Lobbying in support of a cause involves a variety of activities. The ultimate purpose is to convince elected representatives to vote in favor of a given position or course of action. Lobbying efforts range from providing officials with factual material in support of the position to exerting pure political pressure in terms of financial support for campaigns and asserting that certain actions will be "unpopular" with the voters.

Lobbying for political candidates usually takes the form of supporting specific candidates for election or reelection because of the positions they have taken or promise to take if elected. Activities involve direct participation in campaign affairs to financial support of candidates so they can appear in the public eye and explain their positions.

Federal law restricts lobbying by limiting the amount of direct financial support any individual or organization can give to a particular candidate for a federal office, Congress, or the presidency; however, contributions to national political organizations, which in turn reallocate funds to candidates or virtually in direct support of candidates, tend to circumvent this limit. Despite regulations on campaign funding, the issue has been subject to extensive criticism during recent national campaigns, and changes in the law should be expected.

States differ in terms of limiting lobbying activities and contributions to candidates for state and local offices. Like the federal government, most states require lobbyists to reg-

Lobbying Group	Interests or Positions Supported
Nature Conservancy	Emphasis on real estate protection for all aspects of conservation, including wildlife habitat
Sierra Club	Grown to become a national voice for most environmental concerns, with widely respected publications on conservation
National Audubon Society	Widely recognized conservation organization, with emphasis on campgrounds and wildlife
National Resource Defense Council	Has supported litigation in a wide variety of "pro-environment" causes
Greenpeace USA	Very active organization that has encouraged nonviolent civil disobedience in support of environmental causes
Earth Day Resources	Acts to perpetuate and continue Earth Day
Earth Day 2000	Stresses and supports disclosure of truth in environmental claims and issues
National Rifle Association	Generally supports wildlife and related conservation activities
United Auto Workers (Union)	Has supported limits on environmental regulation in the interest of manufacturing and jobs
AFL/CIO (COPE—Committee on Political Education)	Support of political candidates frequently favoring employment over the environment
EXXON Corporation	Like many energy companies, favors less restriction on resource exploration

TABLE 2.1 Lobbying groups and the varied interests they have represented.

ister and to report contributions made to candidates, and candidates are subject to a high level of accountability for contributions received.

Lobbyists represent virtually all sides of an amazing number of issues. Considering only "environmental issues," lobbyists span the full range of interest of essentially all natural resource conservation and health and pollution control legislation. Obviously, politicians and political parties are involved, but to date no major party can reasonably claim to be the only pro-environment party.

Certain organizations are widely recognized for their general philosophy and the stances they take on major issues. For example, the Sierra Club stands for the protection of wildlife and its habitat.

Some organizations seem to be unlikely environmental lobbyists. For example, certain labor organizations have taken surprising stands on environmental issues: When faced with the issue of jobs versus the environment on behalf of their membership, they have favored jobs or employment at the expense of environmental considerations. This situation parallels the position of manufacturers who otherwise frequently find themselves on the opposite side of an issue from labor's interests.

BASIC CONSTITUTIONAL EMPOWERMENT

The United States Constitution

Few people realize the direct impact the Constitution exerts on the daily life of the individual. This impact includes virtually all aspects of environmental law and regulation. The Constitution establishes a limited form of federal government: Unless authorized and empowered by the Constitution, Congress cannot enact laws. The original document, including the first ten amendments, the Bill of Rights, and court interpretations have confirmed this basic, essential limitation of federal power. Obviously, the provisions of the Constitution, either specifically or by implication, have been interpreted to grant broad, but certainly not unlimited, authority to the Congress. Understanding constitutional authorization and limitations, which requires a basic review of the structure and content of the Constitution, provides an essential foundation to understanding existing environmental laws and regulations.

The Constitution is a relatively short document consisting of the Preamble and seven articles. The Preamble is perhaps the best known and most frequently quoted portion of the Constitution.

> We the People of the United States, in Order to form a more perfect Union, establish Justice, insure domestic Tranquility, provide for the common defense, promote the general Welfare, and secure the Blessings of Liberty to ourselves and our Posterity, do ordain and establish this Constitution for the United States of America.

This statement of fundamental principles has provided the foundation on which this nation has grown but, in fact, it is not considered to be empowerment for any type of governmental action.

The empowerment of government comes from the seven articles and amendments to the Constitution. The first three articles establish the basic structure of the federal government, including the clear-cut separation of powers and the system of checks and balances among the three branches of the federal government.

Article 1 establishes the Congress and sets the basic limit of its authority. This article requires certain actions and allows Congress latitude in others. The Constitution does not authorize or empower Congress to promulgate laws to regulate the environment, which leads to the obvious issue of the assumed source of such authority. For many laws, the courts have said this authority is given by the Commerce Clause of Article I. This clause empowers Congress to regulate trade among the states and with foreign nations. The environmental authorization is found in the "policy" that environmental quality may affect interstate trade; therefore, Congress, in the interest of regulating interstate trade, can regulate the environment. This general provision has provided the justification for federal pollution control. Federal land management policy, including timber, mining, and certain aspects of wildlife management, stem from the constitutional authority for Congress to "manage" the property of the United States. The federal government has deferred to state hunting and fishing rules and regulations on federal (public) lands.

Article II establishes the executive branch of the government—the presidency. The president influences environmental issues, as well as other subjects, in at least three ways. The authority of the president has evolved to include a significant role in environmental regulation that is not clearly authorized by the Constitution. The president can issue executive orders directing agencies to act in specific ways. For example, President Theodore Roosevelt directed the preservation of what is now Yellowstone National Park and thereby started what has become the National Park Service. More recently, executive policy declared that there should be no net loss of wetlands in the United States. This statement of policy directly affects the actions of several agencies, including the EPA, the U.S. Army Corps of Engineers, and the USDA.

With congressional approval, the president can create agencies and, of course, can exercise the enormous political power of the office to influence congressional action. Finally, through the power of the veto, the president can stop the implementation of actions approved by Congress. However, Congress can override a presidential veto by passing the vetoed material by a two-thirds majority vote.

Article III establishes the federal court system. The Constitution requires the establishment of the United States Supreme Court, and authorizes Congress to establish other courts as it deems them to be needed. The amazing power the courts exercise in interpreting the law is not clearly granted by the Constitution, but it certainly is real, and is of immense importance in the field of environmental law and regulation.

The remaining four articles are all important, but of less direct significance to environmental issues. The second paragraph of Article IV empowers Congress to manage the property of the United States. The concept of ownership has emerged with respect to other aspects of the environment, such as the authority of the federal government to "sell" air pollution credits. Some have argued that the government, by selling such credits (see the discussion of the Clean Air Act in chapter 6) has exercised ownership authority over at least air quality. Article 4 requires all states to respect the laws of other states and recognizes that the rights of all citizens are protected in every state.

Article V details the steps to ratify the Constitution, and Article VI acknowledges (Revolutionary) war debts. Article VII addresses amending the Constitution.

Amendments to the Constitution

The Constitution has been amended only twenty-seven times, and ten of these, the Bill of Rights, are considered by many virtually as part of the original document itself. Several of the amendments have unique potential to affect the nature and enforcement of environmental laws, rules, and regulations.

The Fifth Amendment guarantees "due process of law," which protects individual interests from all forms of government action, including acting, or potentially failing to act, on an environmental issue. This same amendment prohibits the taking of private property without "due process" and without "just compensation": " . . . nor be deprived of life, liberty, or property without due process of law; nor shall private property be taken for public use without just compensation." In recent years, the issues of due process and just compensation have emerged frequently as the government, in attempts to protect the environment, has limited the use of private property. Such limitations are most commonly associated with restrictions on the use and development of wetlands and on the protection of habitat for species listed under the provisions of the Endangered Species Act.

The Tenth Amendment guarantees states' rights and limits federal authority: "The powers not delegated to the United States by the Constitution, nor prohibited by it to the States, are reserved to the States respectively, or to the people." This amendment reserves both police power and common law doctrines exclusively to the states. Both of these sources of law play significant roles in environmental regulation at the state level more than at the federal level.

The Fourteenth Amendment also has direct implications to environmental regulation. Recall that the Bill of Rights limits the role of the federal government. The Fourteenth Amendment limits the actions of state government with respect to the individual. This amendment includes the guarantees to all persons of "due process" and of "equal protection of the law," which parallels limits of the federal government imposed by the Fifth Amendment.

In summary, the Constitution must be viewed as the basic source of law in the United States. A key concept focuses on the fact that Congress cannot enact any law without specific or implied constitutional empowerment that authorizes action. The Constitution says little, if anything, about authorizing environmental laws, but it authorizes Congress to manage the property of the United States, and the Commerce Clause has been found to justify environmental legislation. The Constitution prohibits Congress from basing laws on common law doctrine or on police power to protect the public health and welfare. Both of these sources of law are reserved to the states, and states have used them to further regulate or protect the environment.

State Constitutions

Individual states also have constitutions that both empower and limit the actions of state government. This includes authority of state governments to regulate the environment. States differ in the posture they have assumed regarding constitutional authorization to regulate the environment. Consider a few selected examples.

The Montana Constitution (art. 2, sec. 3) grants the state legislature perhaps the clearest and greatest authority to enact environmental regulations. That constitution guarantees a clean and healthful environment to the people of the state. This provision is unique among the states. Clearly, this very specific provision empowers the Montana legislature to enact all forms of laws.

Although less specific, the South Carolina Constitution (art. 12, sec. 1) directs the state legislature to create agencies necessary to protect the natural resources of the state. Although this empowerment is not as dramatic as that of Montana, it implies the state is to care for natural resources and the environment. Some states, such as Colorado, have no specific constitutional authorization or mandate to protect the environment. Authorization may be implied, or actions may be justified on the exercise of common law authority or on the exercise of the state's police powers and authority.

Additional State Powers

The U.S. Constitution gives to the states both common law authority and police power. Both of these have potential as sources of environmental regulatory authority.

The concept of common law traces generally to England; the underlying philosophy of the Constitution has its origins in this basic philosophy. From an environmental regulatory perspective, common law may provide the basis for state governments to establish water rights among different users, to protect water sources from pollution, and to manage wildlife for the benefit of the public. In addition, the concepts of nuisance and trespass find their roots in common law, and both may be used to regulate activities to protect the environment, or to protect the individual from environmental degradation. Air and water pollutants have been found to be forms of trespass at the state level, and noise and odors have been regulated by states under nuisance concepts. Frequently, these concepts provide the basis for the individual citizen to seek relief from environmental degradation.

Police power gives states broad legislative authority; it is far more than crime prevention and may address environmental issues. Like common law, it is a power retained for the states by the Constitution. Frequently, however, states defer to local (city and county) government for the exercise of much of police power.

Police power includes laws related to public health, welfare, and morality. Such laws include zoning and related activities that may affect land use and clearly must be considered to have significant impact on environmental regulation. In the future, such authority may become extremely important in resolving issues regarding the locations of landfills and related facilities.

STATUTORY LAW

Basic Concept

Most general references to law are to statutory law, the laws enacted by federal or state legislative bodies (Congress or the state assemblies) and ultimately published in the books of law (the codes or statutes) of the government. Remember, no legislative body can pass laws without authority that comes from the Constitution or, in the case of individual states, that comes from its constitution, common law roots, or is authorized under the precepts of police power. The vast majority of environmental regulations stem from federal statutory laws.

A detailed discussion of the legislative process is far beyond the scope of this material. Nonetheless, a brief review will help explain the concepts of statutory law. Because federal and state processes are similar, only the federal process will be reviewed.

Statutory law starts formally as a bill proposed by an elected representative and represents the "solution" to an issue or problem brought to the attention of the representative by lobbying efforts. Frequently, several representatives sponsor the same bill. Rarely does the elected official actually write the bill. This may be done by staff assistants, or at times the lobbying organization may provide a draft of legislation its members propose. Most frequently, a bill is passed through a series of subcommittees before action by the full committee sends it to the floor.

Frequently significant lobbying pressure is exerted at this stage to modify the original proposal. Ultimately, if the bill is approved by the committee, it comes to the floor of the House (or Senate) for vote. If passed, it then is forwarded to the other body, the Senate or House, where it again is passed through committees and ultimately emerges to the floor for a vote. If passed, differences between the versions of the two houses are resolved by conference committees, and when a final version is approved, the bill is sent to the president for his approval. At this point, the president can approve the bill, in which case it becomes law, or he can veto it. In the latter situation, Congress can override the presidential veto if each house casts a two-thirds majority vote in favor of the bill in spite of the veto; then the bill becomes law. However, if the presidential veto is not overridden, the bill dies.

Bills that are approved by the president or passed over his veto become public laws; for each session of Congress, the public laws are published in volumes designated as *U.S. Statutes at Large.* The individual laws are also published as the *United States Code* (the *Code,* abbreviated and cited as USC). The *Code* comprises all the statutory laws of the United States; the *Statutes at Large* are the actions of a single session of Congress. Reference to statutory laws generally implies reference to the *Code.* All federal environmental law traces to statutory laws; therefore, understanding the basic structure of the *Code* provides the logical starting place for understanding environmental laws and regulations.

The *United States Code*

The *Code* comprises several volumes and is republished periodically, generally every eight years. In the interim, annual supplements are published to include the cumulative new laws and amendments to existing laws. Thus, in looking for a statutory law, after reviewing the main volume, each annual supplement must be examined to find additions or amendments to the law. For example, the current *Code* was published in 1994; the volumes include all laws passed up to 1994. To find new laws, or amendments since this publication, the subsequent supplements must be checked. Each supplement includes all changes since the last printing of the *Code.* The *Statutes at Large* never integrate laws; they contain only the annual congressional acts.

Basic Structure

The statutory laws of the United States are organized into subject matter groups called titles. All of the statutory law is combined into fifty specific titles. Some titles fill more than one volume of the *Code;* because other titles are relatively brief, more than one is included in a volume.

The key point to remember is that reference to statutory law starts with a title number, not with a volume number. The subject matter of the fifty titles of statutory law is given in Table 2.2. This table is reproduced on the inside cover of every volume of the *Code,* so reference to the very broad subject matter of any title is simple. Of course, the *Code* is fully indexed, and the index is a logical starting point to find specific laws.

The Fifty Titles

Examine Table 2.2. Note first that among the fifty titles, Title 6 has been repealed and replaced by Title 31. In addition, Title 34 has been eliminated by enactment of Title 10. Thus, all of the current laws are included in forty-eight titles. Review the general topics of the titles: Each apparently reflects types of law authorized by the Constitution, although no title specifies environmental protection. Statutory law affecting environmental regulation is found in several titles, including Title 16, Conservation; Title 33, Navigation and Navigable Waters; and Title 42, The Public Health and Welfare. The individual titles clearly represent

Title	Title
[1]1. General Provisions.	26. Internal Revenue Code.
2. The Congress.	27. Intoxicating Liquors.
[1]3. The President.	[1]28. Judiciary and Judicial Procedure; and Appendix.
[1]4. Flag and Seal, Seat of Government, and the States.	29. Labor.
[1]5. Government Organization and Employees; and Appendix.	30. Mineral Lands and Mining.
	[1]31. Money and Finance.
[2]6. [Surety Bonds.]	[1]32. National Guard.
7. Agriculture.	33. Navigation and Navigable Waters.
8. Aliens and Nationality.	[3]34. [Navy].
[1]9. Arbitration.	[1]35. Patents.
[1]10. Armed Forces; and Appendix.	36. Patriotic Societies and Observances.
[1]11. Bankruptcy; and Appendix.	[1]37. Pay and Allowances of the Uniformed Services.
12. Banks and Banking.	[1]38. Veterans' Benefits.
[1]13. Census.	[1]39. Postal Service.
[1]14. Coast Guard.	40. Public Buildings, Property, and Works.
15. Commerce and Trade.	41. Public Contracts.
16. Conservation.	42. The Public Health and Welfare.
[1]17. Copyrights.	43. Public Lands.
[1]18. Crimes and Criminal Procedure; and Appendix.	[1]44. Public Printing and Documents.
19. Customs Duties.	45. Railroads.
20. Education.	[1]46. Shipping; and Appendix.
21. Food and Drugs.	47. Telegraphs, Telephones, and Radiotelegraphs.
22. Foreign Relations and Intercourse.	48. Territories and Insular Possessions.
[1]23. Highways.	[1]49. Transportation; and Appendix.
24. Hospitals and Asylums.	50. War and National Defense; and Appendix.
25. Indians.	

[1]This title has been enacted as law. However, any Appendix to this title has not been enacted as law.
[2]This title was enacted as law and has been repealed by the enactment of Title 31.
[3]This title has been eliminated by the enactment of Title 10.

TABLE 2.2 The fifty titles comprising the *United States Code*.

extremely large and frequently diverse subject matter areas. Each title is subdivided at several levels to isolate a specific field or topic of a law.

Subdivisions of Titles

Titles are subdivided for convenience into chapters. Table 2.3 provides an example of this arrangement for Title 16, Conservation. This title contains 114 chapters, numbered from 1 through 74 with numerous alphanumeric designations of related chapters. Depending on the complexity of the subject matter, chapters may be further divided into subchapters and parts. Although these subdivisions are helpful in understanding the law and its organization and in finding parts of the law, in formally citing the law, reference is made only to the title and to the section. Each title is divided into specific, consecutively numbered sections. Thus, in Title 16, the Endangered Species Act is found in Chapter 35, but this act starts at section 1531 and continues through section 1600. Forest and Rangeland Renewable Resources Planning, also in Title 16 (Chapter 36), starts at section 1601. The specific wording of the Endangered Species Act that defines the prohibited acts of "taking" an endangered species is found in Title 16, sections 1532 and 1538. This law is cited as 16 USC 1532, 1538. In some instances, sections are divided into numbered paragraphs or units. The portion just referred to in section 1532 is in fact 16 USC 1532(14) and in section 1538 it is 16 USC 1538(a)(1)(B). Because environmental law is extensive and complex and involves very specific points, understanding this arrangement is essential to understanding many laws and the problems they address.

Throughout this text, and in legal writing generally, when a law is mentioned or quoted, the citation is given immediately following its mention. The citation takes the form of the title number followed by USC, which is immediately followed by the section number, and sometimes by subsection designations (letters and numbers). In reading, a citation can be ignored, much as a reference in other text materials, unless it is of critical importance to the reader.

Nongovernmental Editions of the *Code*

The federal government publishes the *United States Code*. In addition, several commercial publications are produced. These contain the same statutory material, word for word. They are of primary interest to attorneys and law students because they include additional references concerning the law. Most frequently the references are to cases involving judicial interpretation of the meaning of a particular section of the law (note that this reflects how the courts have in fact "made the law"), or to scholarly publications concerning a section of the law. Such commercial publications include the *United States Codes Annotated* (USCA) and the *U.S. Code Service*.

ADMINISTRATIVE LAW

Basic Concepts

Commonly, through statutory law, Congress sets the general guidelines—statements of policy or goals, intentions—for various types of regulation, but does not establish specific details. This is dramatically true for many aspects of environmental laws. Congress delegates setting details to regulatory agencies that it has established. In the area of environmental regulation, the EPA is the prime example, although other agencies are also involved, such as the USDA and the U.S. Department of the Interior (USDI).

The Federal Administrative Procedure Act allows Congress to empower agencies to make rules and to enforce rules and regulations that have the force and effect of law. Through this process, Congress addresses major issues, such as air pollution, waste management, and similar technical, long-term problems, in a single major legislative act. The legislation identifies the "problem" and empowers an agency to develop solutions to the problem or issue and authorizes the agency to formulate and enforce rules needed to resolve the issue. Frequently, the rules include the multitudes of standards that must be satisfied to comply with an act. These standards include, for example, specific limits on hundreds of chemicals discharged into the air by all types of manufacturing plants as well as the design criteria for new landfill facilities.

TABLE 2.3 Chapters comprising Title 16, Conservation, of the *United States Code,* including first section of each chapter.

TABLE 2.3   Title 16, Conservation, continued

This process allows the agency to work on long-term issues more nearly free of political pressures. It also allows the agency to use its essential technical expertise to address the issues. Generally, in its legislative actions, Congress seems to avoid dealing with the same issue repeatedly. Assigning long-term issues, such as many environmental issues, to an agency supports this basic legislative posture. In addition, although Congress has access to all types of technical expertise, supporting the development of special expertise in agencies and calling on those agencies to address specific problems have been efficient in the eyes of Congress.

Key Parts

Administrative law and procedure can be complex, but the basics, in terms of environmental regulation, are relatively simple. Administrative agencies such as the EPA have two critical roles in the formulation of rules and regulations: a *quasi-legislative* function and a *quasi-judicial* function. The quasi-legislative function is the actual role of making rules. Because these rules effectively amount to laws, the agency is acting in a legislative capacity. However, because only Congress can truly act in a legislative capacity, the agency acts in a quasi (nearly) legislative capacity. Similarly, the agencies can enforce rules they make. To this extent, the agencies act as courts, deciding when rules have been violated. Only courts truly adjudicate conflicts, so this judicial activity of the agency is identified as a quasi-judicial activity.

The rule-making authority of agencies is strictly limited. First, agencies cannot make rules unless Congress has directly, or by clear implication, authorized such action in a law. Second, agencies are required to take two steps before making any rule: (1) give public notice of the proposed rule and reasons for making the rule, and (2) provide opportunity for the public to comment on proposed rules. By law, federal agencies must give notice of proposed rules in the *Federal Register* (FR), the official federal document in which such notices and other actions are announced. It is published daily for all federal working days. The announcement must explain the nature of the proposed rule, give its assumed legislative authority (by what statute the agency justifies making the rule), and state to whom comments regarding the proposed rule must be addressed. The Administrative Procedure Act requires no public hearings, although for controversial issues, the agency may choose to schedule such hearings. In some instances, Congress may require public hearings prior to rule making. Also, the agency must acknowledge the input or comments, but it is not required to agree with or follow the will of the majority of comments in making rules.

Lobbying groups play a key role in the formulation of rules, just as they can affect statutes. In the case of administrative actions, lobbyists not only seek to influence the nature of rules in the interests of their constituencies, the lobbying organizations also do a real service by monitoring the daily publication of the FR and by informing constituencies when matters of their interest are under congressional or agency consideration.

Final rules are initially published in the FR. Following this publication, all rules are published in the *Codes of Federal Regulations* (CFR). The CFR is organized in a manner similar to the *U.S. Code,* although the titles of the CFR are not numbered the same as the titles of the statutes that authorize a particular rule. The CFR consists of numerous paperback volumes that are updated quarterly. Understanding the CFR and its contents is very important in environmental regulation because it contains most of the rules and regulations, lists of toxic water pollutants, allowable pesticide residues for all types of food and feed, and detailed standards for testing both engines and fuels for compliance with the provisions of the Clean Air Act.

To be certain that the most recent rules have been located, the FR should be consulted. The CFR is clearly indexed, but reference is based on specific enabling statutes. The index includes a cross-reference table that facilitates finding rules that have been promulgated by an agency under the authority of specific sections of the law. For example, the Endangered Species Act directs the EPA to develop a list of endangered and threatened species and to update this list periodically. Taking (hunting, killing, or otherwise harming individuals on this list) is illegal; thus, the list states what is illegal. Congressional empowerment of the EPA to prepare this list is given by 16 USC 15631(5). Consulting the cross-index of the CFR leads to the Endangered Species Lists found in 50 CFR 17.11, which is the list of endangered (protected) species. In this citation, *50* identifies the title under which the rule or standard is found.

Titles are divided into parts, and the parts are divided into sections. Thus, the citation 50 CFR 17.11 identifies Section 11 of Part 17 of Title 50 of the CFR. Remember, the USC is also divided into chapters and parts, but citations do not include reference to these subdivisions.

Generally, when Congress empowers an agency to make rules, it also empowers that agency to enforce those rules. Enforcement follows two types of hearing procedures, either informal or formal adjudication. In these hearings, the agency actually acts as a court, and in initial stages, an agency administrator may serve as the hearing officer or judge. Formal hearings are far more court-like in nature. The distinction can be of major significance if the issue moves from the agency to a court because the record on which a court may hear the issue can be limited to that established in the initial hearing. A formal agency hearing establishes a more extensive record. Although agencies can enforce rules, the process of administrative law does not deny an individual the ultimate opportunity for a court hearing or trial to challenge the decision of the agency.

State Administrative Laws

The individual state agencies also formulate a wide variety of rules and regulations, many of which affect the environment, including provisions to comply with multitudes of federal regulations and state matters, such as hunting and fishing regulations. The state procedures are quite similar to the Federal Administrative Procedure Act, with several marked exceptions. Most require notice and comment, but notice, of course, is given in an appropriate state publication. Many states have requirements for public hearings on the request of certain numbers of individuals who will be directly affected by a proposed rule, and some states invoke legislative oversight of agency rule making: A legislative body may be empowered to veto a rule promulgated by an agency. Clearly, this potential returns the rule making much closer to the legislature and direct political pressures. Given the importance of administrative rule making to environmental regulation, it is critical to understand how rules are formulated to have the greatest opportunity to influence those rules.

Unmonitored Rule Making

Agencies may take many actions that are not subject to procedures and limitations of administrative law and are not specifically authorized by statute or other legislative mandate. These actions generally fall under one of two topics: internal operating procedures, which can involve agreements among agencies, and standards involved in issuing permits and licenses. In this way, an agency has the same type of authority that the president exerts in issuing executive orders or policy statements.

THE COURTS AS A SOURCE OF LAW

Although the Constitution establishes a clear division of the branches of the federal government and a system of checks and balances among the branches of government, the courts have emerged as significant actual sources of law, a legislative function. Some have maintained that the courts are the ultimate source of law, because they interpret the finite meaning of the law. Courts have played significant roles in shaping environmental law.

Basic Concepts of the Court System

The American judicial system comprises several interrelated parts that play very different roles. First, the Constitution created a federal court system requiring only the Supreme Court. It authorized Congress to create additional courts, which Congress has done. States have separate, parallel court systems, and these systems are not entirely independent.

Understanding several basic concepts related to courts and the court systems will clarify the role courts play in formulating laws. The concepts involve several fundamental legal principles and the basic structure of the court systems in the United States.

Jurisdiction

Jurisdiction is the authority of a court to hear a case, reach a decision, and enforce that decision. Jurisdiction comprises two elements: personal jurisdiction, the authority of the court over the individual accused of some "wrong," and subject matter jurisdiction. Some courts, such as local traffic courts or state family law courts, have very limited subject matter jurisdiction. (See also the definition of jurisdiction on p. 49.)

Court Systems

Understanding the structure and functions of the various court systems in the United States will help clarify the importance of the concept of jurisdiction as it relates to all areas of law, including environmental law. First, the United States has two major court systems: the federal court system and a separate, independent court system in each state. In some instances courts have exclusive jurisdiction, and in others, jurisdiction can be shared.

The Federal District Courts

With the exception of a few very specific situations designated in the Constitution, trials in the federal system are held in the federal district courts. These are the first element of the federal court system. Congress established these courts in every state, and some states are partitioned into divisions. The subject matter jurisdiction is federal laws, including Constitutional issues, and disputes between citizens of different states, situations of diversity of citizenship, in which cases a federal district court may hear and decide cases involving issues related to violations of state laws.

In most states, the federal district court is held in several locations, which are specified by federal statute. Examples of the statutory organization of the federal district courts for several states are given in Table 2.4.

Trials arising over alleged violations of federal environmental laws would be heard in the federal district court, probably in the state in which the violation occurred. The trial is a matter of determining facts (the task of the jury) and applying the law to those facts (the task of the court or the judge) from which a verdict is reached and penalties, if any, assessed. The trial is generally the end point for determining facts.

Circuit Courts of Appeal

Jury decisions can be appealed, but appeals must be on matters of law, not simply based on disagreement with how a jury viewed facts. In the federal system, initial appeals are heard in the federal circuit courts, the second of the three elements of the federal court system. The circuit courts are organized in an umbrella-like fashion. The circuit court system is divided into thirteen circuits, eleven representing groups of states and numbered one through eleven, plus the Federal Circuit and the District of Columbia. The latter two circuits play unique roles that are beyond the scope of this discussion, except to note that Congress can specify that controversies arising from certain legislation must be tried in the federal circuit.

The composition of the eleven numbered circuits is summarized in Table 2.5. Note that each circuit encompasses several states. For example, the Second Circuit is composed of Connecticut, New York, and Vermont, and the Eleventh Circuit Alabama, Florida, and Georgia. Remember, federal district courts are located in each state. Appeals from a federal district court decision must be made to the circuit court serving the state in which the trial was held. Thus, a trial involving violations of provisions of the Clean Air Act by a utility company in Kentucky would be appealed to the Sixth Circuit, which encompasses Kentucky, Michigan, Ohio, and Tennessee. Similarly, an appeal from a case in California would be heard in the Ninth Circuit.

The Supreme Court

The circuits are not the final arbitrator. The United States Supreme Court is the final element of the federal judicial system. The Supreme Court hears appeals from all circuit courts, and for certain Constitutional issues may hear appeals from state courts. The Supreme Court selects the cases it will hear. Thus very few cases reach the Supreme Court.

State Courts

Every state has a system of courts that is generally parallel to the federal system, although the names of the courts may vary and apparently conflict with the federal system. Excluding a wide range of special courts, the systems start with a trial court variously called the superior court (California), the district court (Montana), or the circuit court (South Carolina). These courts have jurisdiction over all issues, both civil and criminal, for state law. In addition, they can hear and decide issues involving federal law. Most states also have one or more levels of appellate courts, and a supreme court. Recall that in the federal court system, the initial appellate courts serve circuits, or groups of states. The comparable courts in states (the initial appellate courts) generally do not serve subdivisions of the state, but hear cases from throughout the state, although the court may meet at various locations in a state. Also, unlike the federal system, most states guarantee access to the states' highest court for appeals. State Supreme Courts do not "select" the cases they will hear.

Judicial Precedent

Understanding the structure of the federal court system provides the basis for understanding the concept of judicial precedent, which explains how courts effectively make laws. The trial courts, the federal district courts, are effectively independent of each other. Obviously,

§105. Missouri

Missouri is divided into two judicial districts to be known as the Eastern and Western Districts of Missouri.

Eastern District

(a) The Eastern District comprises three divisions.

(1) The Eastern Division comprises the counties of Crawford, Dent, Franklin, Gasconade, Iron, Jefferson, Lincoln, Maries, Phelps, Saint Charles, Saint Francois, Saint Genevieve, Saint Louis, Warren, and Washington, and the city of Saint Louis.

Court for the Eastern Division shall be held at Saint Louis.

(2) The Northern Division comprises the counties of Adair, Audrain, Chariton, Clark, Knox, Lewis, Linn, Macon, Marion, Monroe, Montgomery, Pike, Ralls, Randolph, Schuyler, Scotland, and Shelby.

Court for the Northern Division shall be held at Hannibal.

(3) The Southeastern Division comprises the counties of Bollinger, Butler, Cape Girardeau, Carter, Dunklin, Madison, Mississippi, New Madrid, Pemiscot, Perry, Reynolds, Ripley, Scott, Shannon, Stoddard, and Wayne.

Court for the Southeastern Division shall be held at Cape Girardeau.

Western District

(b) The Western District comprises five divisions

(1) The Western Division comprises the counties of Bates, Carroll, Cass, Clay, Henry, Jackson, Johnson, Lafayette, Ray, Saint Clair, and Saline.

Court for the Western Division shall be held at Kansas City.

(2) The Southwestern Division comprises the counties of Barton, Barry, Jasper, Lawrence, McDonald, Newton, Stone, and Vernon.

Court for the Southwestern Division shall be held at Joplin.

(3) The Saint Joseph Division comprises the counties of Andrew, Atchison, Buchanan, Caldwell, Clinton, Daviess, De Kalb, Gentry, Grundy, Harrison, Holt, Livingston, Mercer, Nodaway, Platte, Putnam, Sullivan, and Worth.

Court for the Saint Joseph Division shall be held at Saint Joseph.

(4) The Central Division comprises the counties of Benton, Boone, Callaway, Camden, Cole, Cooper, Hickory, Howard, Miller, Moniteau, Morgan, Osage, and Pettis.

Court for the Central Division shall be held at Jefferson City.

(5) The Southern Division comprises the counties of Cedar, Christian, Dade, Dallas, Douglas, Greene, Howell, Laclede, Oregon, Ozark, Polk, Pulaski, Taney, Texas, Webster, and Wright.

Court for the Southern Division shall be held at Springfield.

§ 102. Michigan

Michigan is divided into two judicial districts to be known as the Eastern and Western Districts of Michigan.

Eastern District

(a) The Eastern District comprises two divisions.

(1) The Southern Division comprises the counties of Genesee, Jackson, Lapeer, Lenawee, Livingston, Macomb, Monroe, Oakland, Saint Clair, Sanilac, Shiawassee, Washtenaw, and Wayne.

Court for the Southern Division shall be held at Ann Arbor, Detroit, Flint, and Port Huron.

(2) The Northern Division comprises the counties of Alcona, Alpena, Arenac, Bay, Cheboygan, Clare, Crawford, Gladwin, Gratiot, Huron, Iosco, Isabella, Midland, Montmorency, Ogemaw, Oscoda, Otsego, Presque Isle, Roscommon, Saginaw, and Tuscola.

Court for the Northern Division shall be held at Bay City.

Western Division

(b) The Western District comprises two divisions.

(1) The Southern Division comprises the counties of Allegan, Antrim, Barry, Benzie, Berrien, Branch, Calhoun, Cass, Charlevoix, Clinton, Eaton, Emmet, Grand Traverse, Hillsdale, Ingham, Ionia, Kalamazoo, Kalkaska, Kent, Lake, Leelanau, Manistee, Mason, Mecosta, Missaukee, Montcalm, Muskegon, Newaygo, Oceana, Osceola, Ottawa, Saint Joseph, Van Buren, and Wexford.

Court for the Southern Division shall be held at Grand Rapids, Kalamazoo, Lansing, and Traverse City.

(2) The Northern Division comprises the counties of Alger, Baraga, Chippewa, Delta, Dickinson, Gogebic, Houghton, Iron, Keweenaw, Luce, Mackinac, Marquette, Menominee, Ontonagon, and Schoolcraft.

Court for the Northern Division shall be held at Marquette and Sault Sainte Marie.

§ 106. Montana

Montana, exclusive of Yellowstone National Park, constitutes one judicial district.

Court shall be held at Billings, Butte, Glasgow, Great Falls, Havre, Helena, Kalispell, Lewistown, Livingston, Miles City, and Missoula.

TABLE 2.4 Statutory required organization of federal district courts in three states. 28 USC 102, 105, and 106.

Circuits	Composition
District of Columbia	.District of Columbia.
First	.Maine, Massachusetts, New Hampshire, Puerto Rico, Rhode Island.
Second	.Connecticut, New York, Vermont.
Third	.Delaware, New Jersey, Pennsylvania, Virgin Islands.
Fourth	.Maryland, North Carolina, South Carolina, Virginia, West Virginia.
Fifth	.District of the Canal Zone, Louisiana, Mississippi, Texas.
Sixth	.Kentucky, Michigan, Ohio, Tennessee.
Seventh	.Illinois, Indiana, Wisconsin.
Eighth	.Arkansas, Iowa, Minnesota, Missouri, Nebraska, North Dakota, South Dakota.
Ninth	.Alaska, Arizona, California, Idaho, Montana, Nevada, Oregon, Washington, Guam, Hawaii.
Tenth	.Colorado, Kansas, New Mexico, Oklahoma, Utah, Wyoming.
Eleventh	.Alabama, Florida, Georgia.
Federal	.All Federal judicial districts.

TABLE 2.5   Statutory required composition of each of the thirteen Circuits comprising the U.S. Circuit Courts. 28 USC 41.

all courts seek to be consistent in applying the law, but differences can arise. When a case is appealed, the circuit court interprets the law, and that interpretation then becomes binding on all district courts within the circuit. Thus, the district courts within a circuit are inferior to the circuit court in which they are located. It is not surprising, then, that when the United States Supreme Court decides a case, that is, interprets a law, that interpretation is binding on all circuit courts, hence on all district courts. In this manner, court decisions actually become the law.

When an appellate court, circuit court, or the Supreme Court decides a case, the intention is that the interpretation of the law in that case will be permanent; this is the doctrine of *Stare decisis*. This legal doctrine effectively says that once an issue is properly decided, the decision should remain unchanged. This is a type of common law, in that the decisions are assumed to be appropriate and to represent the law, without legislation.

Consider a simplified example: The Fifth Amendment to the Constitution prohibits taking of private property without just compensation. Increasingly, landowners claim that limits on the use of their lands imposed by compliance with certain environmental laws amount to an unconstitutional taking of their land. A provision of the Endangered Species Act prohibits destruction of critical habitat for species listed as endangered. Courts have varied in defining a "taking" of property. The Supreme Court ultimately addressed this issue; at present, for a government action to be considered a "taking" of private property, that action must have totally destroyed the value of the property to the individual. Merely reducing the value is not, according to this decision, an unconstitutional taking. Given this standard, any court hearing a case in which an unconstitutional taking of property is claimed must determine whether the owner has lost all value of the property. However, had the appellate decision been accepted at a circuit court, then the standard of "total loss of value" would apply only to district courts in states within the circuit in which the decision was made.

Note that many appeals do not concern the specific law on which the case is tried. Frequently appeals are based on legal, procedural matters, such as the admissibility of evidence or other considerations. These decisions also make law in terms of procedures, but not in terms of the specific statute being tested.

The same basic pattern exists for state courts. However, the initial appeal decision may be binding on all trial courts, statewide, unless the state supreme court overrides or reverses the lower appellate court.

Publication of Court Decisions

Most decisions rendered by appellate courts are published; these publications are the heart of much legal research and the basis for many appeals. They are referred to as case or court law and may be the ultimate form of written law. They interpret the *Code* or CFR or, at the state level, even common law doctrines. Decisions of the various courts are published in different journals, generally called "reporters." For some courts, the decisions are published in several different reporters. Regardless, the publications are verbatim records of the decision of the court, including, frequently, lengthy explanations by the judges of how and why a decision was reached.

Publication of federal appellate decisions is fairly simple. The federal government publishes decisions made by the United States Supreme Court in a reporter entitled *United States Reports* (abbreviated U.S.). The volumes are numbered consecutively, and cases are reported in volumes by the names of the parties involved. Reference is by the names of the parties, plaintiff and defendant, followed by the citation to a volume and pages. For example, a major case interpreting the intent of Congress regarding enforcing the provisions of the Endangered Species Act is commonly referred to as the "Snail Darter case," because the snail darter was the endangered species at the heart of the controversy. The case actually involved the federal government, the Tennessee Valley Authority, and an individual named Hill. The citation to the Supreme Court decision is *TVA v. Hill,* 437 U.S. 153 (1976). This citation says the case TVA versus Hill is found in volume 437 of the *United States Reports,* starting at page 437, and the Supreme Court decided the case in 1976.

Like the *U.S. Code,* Supreme Court decisions are also published in at least two commercial volumes, *Supreme Court Reports* (abbreviated S.Ct.) and *Lawyer's Edition* (abbreviated L.Ed.), with special notations to assist legal research. The Snail Darter case would be found under the same name as in U.S., but cited in these publications as follows: 98 S.Ct. 2518 and 57 L.Ed. 117. Each of these listings contains the full decision of the Supreme Court.

Decisions made by all the circuit courts of appeals are published in a reporter entitled simply the *Federal Reporter,* abbreviated F. Publication started with volume 1 in January 1890 and included both the circuit and district court decisions. After 999 volumes were filled, a second series of the *Federal Reporter* was initiated, abbreviated F2d, which led to 999 additional volumes. July 1993 witnessed the initiation of the third series of the *Federal Reporter,* F3d. Starting in October 1932, decisions of the federal district courts were published in a reporter designated as the *Federal Supplement,* abbreviated F.Supp.; to date, there is only one series of this reporter. Citations for both of these reporters follow the same pattern as for that of the Supreme Court, except for the abbreviation of the appropriate reporter.

Individual states also publish decisions of state appellate courts in state reporters, although some states have stopped this practice. The same decisions are also published in seven regional reporters, summarized in Table 2.6. These reporters also duplicate publication of decisions of the federal district courts.

The key point to remember concerning courts as a source of law is that the interpretation of the law comes from appeals of trial court decisions, and jurisdiction of the appellate court determines the scope of authority of the decision. Based on the doctrine of *Stare decisis,* decisions of appellate courts tend to remain for relatively long periods, but they do change. For example, constant pressure suggests that some change from appellate courts might be expected concerning the very strict definition of governmental actions that constitute an unconstitutional taking.

Stare decisis provides stability to the law. Congress can enact laws to circumvent court decisions, so long as those new laws are not found to be unconstitutional. In addition, ultimately many appellate court decisions are modified, if not reversed. Case law is stable and slow to change, but it is not immutable.

Certain aspects of environmental law are in a state of flux, whereas others seem to be fairly well established. Logically, the laws addressing older issues appear to be more stable than those addressing more recently exposed problems. Thus, many of the laws relating more to natural resource conservation, starting with laws regulating federally owned land, are quite firm, whereas laws, rules, and regulations related to pollution issues, solid waste disposal, and similar topics seem to be evolving more rapidly. Understanding the sources of law should help understand and shape this evolution.

LITIGATION

Litigation is the process through which disputes between parties are resolved in an adversarial setting in which one party "wins" and the other party "loses." Most commonly, litigation is equated with some type of court and trial. Environmental litigation represents nothing unique to the basic litigation process, and a detailed discussion of it is beyond the scope of this material. Nonetheless, an overview of the process will foster understanding two critical concepts: (1) how environmental laws are enforced by the government, and (2) the rights private citizens have to seek enforcement of such laws and to seek payment of damages for injuries suffered as a result of violations of environmental laws, rules, and regulations.

Basic Terms and Concepts

The following terms and concepts apply in general to all trials:

1. "Action"—A lawsuit.
2. "Parties"—The individuals directly involved in the action. The party initiating the action and claiming damages or other relief is the plaintiff, and the party against whom the claim is made is the defendant. Corporations and governmental agencies at all levels can be parties to lawsuits.
3. "Relief"—In civil cases, decision by the court to satisfy a claim made by a plaintiff. This may be money or equitable relief, which is commonly an order to do or to refrain from doing some specific act.

Atlantic Reporter	Pacific Reporter, *continued*
Connecticut	Hawaii
Delaware	Idaho
District of Columbia	Kansas
Maine	Montana
Maryland	Nevada
New Hampshire	New Mexico
New Jersey	Oklahoma
Pennsylvania	Oregon
Rhode Island	Utah
Vermont	Washington
	Wyoming
North Eastern Reporter	
Illinois	Southern Reporter
Indiana	Alabama
Massachusetts	Florida
New York	Louisiana
Ohio	Mississippi
North Western Reporter	
Iowa	South Eastern Reporter
Michigan	Georgia
Minnesota	North Carolina
Nebraska	South Carolina
North Dakota	Virginia
South Dakota	West Virginia
Wisconsin	
	South Western Reporter
Pacific Reporter	Arkansas
Alaska	Kentucky
Arizona	Missouri
California	Tennessee
Colorado	Texas

TABLE 2.6   The seven regional reporters and states for which appellate decisions are reported for each region. Note that these regions are not related to the federal circuits, and that their composition is arbitrary and is not established by law.

4. "Damages"—In civil cases, commonly money awarded by the court to a plaintiff as compensation for injuries suffered as a result of actions by the defendant. Sometimes a lawsuit will seek "equitable relief." Federal environmental laws do not provide grounds on which a court can award monetary damages to individuals.

5. "Criminal action"—Action for the violation of a law for which, if the defendant is found guilty, the state will punish the defendant through fines or imprisonment. The violation of some environmental laws is classified as a criminal act.

6. "Civil action"—Action for the violation of a law for which, if the defendant is found liable (responsible for injury), the court will order payment of damages to the plaintiff. Defendants are not subject to imprisonment in civil cases. Some cases may involve both criminal considerations and civil issues.

7. "Jurisdiction"—The authority of a court to hear and decide a case and to enforce its decision. Jurisdiction involves two elements: (1) personal jurisdiction, the authority of the

court over the individual defendant, and (2) subject matter jurisdiction, the authority of the court to hear cases involving the particular controversy. Generally, federal courts hear matters involving the Constitution or issues of federal law, and state courts hear matters of state law. Under certain conditions, federal courts may hear issues of state law, and state courts may hear issues of federal or constitutional law.

8. "Standing" (or "Standing to Sue")—To be a plaintiff—that is, to initiate a lawsuit— an individual must have standing with the court. This generally requires that the individual can show damages, or the potential of immediate damages or harm, if the court does not act. The parties to the lawsuit and subject matter of the dispute must also otherwise be within the jurisdiction of the court. In some instances, Congress has established standing to sue by statute. This statute allows an individual to initiate a lawsuit without demonstrating personal harm. Legislation such as the Clean Air Act includes such a provision so that a private citizen may bring suit to have the provisions of the law enforced.

9. "Ripeness"—A constitutional requirement, associated with the concept of standing, that refers to the issue brought before the court. Ripeness requires harm or the immediate threat of harm and requires that a decision by the court could resolve the issue. The Constitution prohibits courts from issuing advisory opinions or decisions on hypothetical issues.

10. "Exhaustion of (Administrative) Remedies"—A requirement that all available administrative procedures to resolve a problem to be resolved before a case will be hard by a court. This is an important concept in environmental issues, because many issues involve administrative rules and regulations.

11. "Formal and Informal Adjudication"—The two types of administrative hearings for disputes involving violation of agency rules, regulations, and standards. Formal hearings are more trial-like, with formal procedures and a detailed record or transcript maintained, which can be critical for appeal purposes. Generally, the defendant in administrative proceedings may request a formal hearing.

12. "Judgment"—The decision of the court, which includes the award of damages, if appropriate.

13. "Summary Judgment"—A decision by the court, prior to trial, based on a motion made by either party. The party making the motion claims that, even if all facts are interpreted in favor of the other party, the law requires the court to decide in favor of the party making the motion. When a court grants a motion for summary judgment, the case is completed, unless the decision is appealed. Generally, when basic facts are disputed, a motion for summary judgment will not be successful.

14. "Administrative Law Judge" (ALJ)—An official who presides at administrative hearings and has the authority to administer oaths, take testimony, rule on the admissibility of evidence, and determine facts. Individuals are also called hearing officers; they are not judges or members of the judiciary. Frequently, the administrative law judge at initial hearings is an employee of the agency making the claim of wrongdoing against the defendant.

Situations in Environmental Litigation

In matters of environmental litigation, several different situations may occur. Consider, for example, the situation in which the defendant is a utility company cited by the EPA for violations of the Clean Air Act by discharging more sulfur dioxide than allowed by its permit. A lower level administrative law judge (hearing officer) might preside over an initial hearing between the EPA and utility company. If the EPA presented adequate evidence to prove its charges, the ALJ would issue orders for the utility company to stop the excessive emissions and might also fine the company. The company could agree with the initial decision and comply with the orders, and the matter would be settled. Or the company could appeal to higher officers, in the EPA and ultimately to court, but the appeal must be based on a matter of law, not on the facts presented at the hearing. The appropriate court for appeal may be specified in the legislation, or by the Federal Administrative Procedure Act.

Actions for some violations start in court because the claimed wrongful act does not involve an agency, or because the law does not allow the agency to hear certain claims. In such cases, the action starts by filing a lawsuit in a court of appropriate jurisdiction. If the federal government is the plaintiff and the act is a violation of federal environmental law, the case would start in federal district court.

Private parties may be plaintiffs in actions based on alleged violations of environmental laws, rules, and regulations. Several major environmental acts specifically grant "private right of action" to individuals, by which the private citizen has standing to initiate a lawsuit to force compliance with a law without having first to show potential or actual personal damages or the threat of personal harm. Both the Clean Air Act and the Clean Water Act include a provision for private right of action. If the lawsuit is successful, the court will award equitable relief, but not damages, to the individual. In addition, private citizens, including lobbying and public interest organizations such as the Sierra Club, Greenpeace, and the National Resource Defense Council, can sue, but these organizations must establish standing by demonstrating that a claimed violation threatens the organization or its members. These organizations frequently sue only for equitable relief, including fines imposed against violators, but not for damages.

Litigation Under Common Law Claims

Violation of environmental laws may lead to civil litigation by private parties seeking compensation for damages suffered. Although the damage may have resulted from violation of federal law, because federal environmental laws do not provide a basis for individual, private claims of damage, most claims are brought under state common law causes of action. The "cause of action" is the statement of the principle of law on which the lawsuit is based. Such lawsuits are based on state laws (remember, the common law is generally a state source of law), and lawsuits are initiated in state courts, although federal courts may hear such cases. Most frequently, lawsuits claim liability arising from commission of one of the common law torts of nuisance, trespass, or negligence.

Each of these three torts involves specific, intentional actions that must be proved for the plaintiff to sustain any claim of damages. The plaintiff must prove actual damages or losses from the act. Note, however, that the plaintiff does not have to prove that the damages were intentional, only that the act that caused the damages was intentional.

Nuisance can be claimed when the defendant's actions are proved to deny the normal, peaceful use and enjoyment of the plaintiff's property. A second type of nuisance involves proof that the defendant's acts constitute a public nuisance that harms the plaintiff and at least a segment of the public at large. Noise and odor frequently provide the basis for claims of nuisance. This includes the noise and odor from public and private waste treatment and disposal facilities. The odor or noise can be, but does not have to be, the result of violation of environmental regulations to sustain the claim of nuisance.

Trespass requires the intentional "invasion" of the property of the plaintiff, and damage must be proved. The trespass does not require personal entry: Trespass claims may include smoke and waste or debris blowing onto private property. It may also include runoff waters, although many states have specific statutes to protect property owners, in addition to trespass claims.

Finally, some violations of environmental laws also involve the tort of negligence. A very common example is the misuse of pesticides, which violates federal law. If the misuse results in harm to the individual, a claim of negligence may be sustained and the defendant held liable for damages caused. Negligence does not require violation of the environmental law, but when the defendant can be proved to have violated the law, proof of negligence is easier to establish.

Constitutional Issues

Some aspects of environmental law have issues involving constitutional rights. With increasing frequency, private landowners claim that enforcement of the provisions of the Endangered Species Act or provisions for wetland protection specified in the Clean Water Act constitutes an unconstitutional taking of their private property. To date, courts have not agreed with these claims, but pressure is mounting to provide some relief. The legal precedent that no taking has occurred is under fire and subject to change in the future. Not even *Stare decisis* lasts forever.

Criminal Sanctions

A number of environmental statutes authorize criminal action against violators. In recent years, the federal government has increasingly sought to bring criminal actions against the most serious violators, which include massive fines and prison sentences. Corporate officers have been held liable for the most serious types of environmental violations that threaten health.

QUESTIONS AND CONCEPTS FOR DISCUSSION AND RESEARCH

1. Discuss how the "voice of the people" can be expressed and can affect environmental issues.
2. What limits the scope or extent of congressional legislative authority?
3. Briefly describe or discuss the basic structure of the United States court system, and trace how an environmental case would move through that system. Indicate also how court decisions are cited and where the decisions of the various courts are published.
4. Why is understanding how administrative rules are promulgated important for understanding environmental regulation today? What are the two major functions of agencies

regarding administrative rules? What must an agency do before a rule it proposes can have the force of law? Where are proposed rules first published? Where are final rules published and maintained for reference?

5. Briefly contrast federal rule making with state rule making in terms of hearings and legislative authority or oversight with respect to the implementation of the rule.

6. Develop a simple outline of the federal court system, and from this outline, discuss how the courts "make law."

REFERENCES AND SELECTED READING

Cigler, A. I., and B. A. Loomis. 1995. *Interest Group Politics.* Washington, DC: CQ Press.

Coggins, George Cameron, and Charles F. Wilkinson. 1987. *Federal Public Land and Resource Law.* 2d ed. Mineola, NY: The Foundation Press.

3

Risk Assessment and Management

Risk assessment and management are a continued source of controversy in the formulation of environmental policy and regulation. Although the concepts of assessment and management can be defined and discussed independently, ultimately they must merge in the expression of policy, laws, and regulations. Risk assessment is a major analytical tool in supporting environmental decision making, and it supports risk management decisions. Consideration of the variety of approaches to risk assessment and risk management reveals the complex factors that must be evaluated and helps explain the lack of a uniform approach, although many environmental issues share common elements.

Understanding basic issues related to risk assessment and management requires fundamental definition of each, even if these are subsequently modified. The shortest definitions state that assessment involves understanding the problem, and management involves doing something about it. Although conceptually useful, and amazingly brief, these definitions fail to reflect adequately the complexity of the subject.

A generally accepted definition of risk provides a reasonable starting point and reveals part of the problem: "RISK, the exposure to chance of injury or loss; a hazard or dangerous chance." Part of the problem arises from an apparent circular definition, the use of "hazard" and "danger" in the definition of risk. Some have suggested that concepts of hazard versus danger better suggest levels or magnitudes of potential harm or injury and should be separated from the concepts of risk and risk assessment. To others, this discussion exemplifies the type of semantic argument that tends to block agreements and needed progress.

A more detailed definition divides the concept of risk into two components: the chance of exposure to harm and the magnitude of harm suffered. Obviously, this approach requires weighing both the exposure element and the magnitude element: The most serious risk would be frequent exposure to serious harm, and the least would be rare exposure with minimal harm. Circumstances creating rare exposure coupled with grave harm or frequent exposure with minimal harm create assessment problems. Consider, for example, exposure to two natural forces, sun and lightning. Excluding considerations of prolonged exposure to sun and cancer risks, consider the assessment of sunburn harm (a mild but frequent exposure) compared with being struck by lightning, a rare, but generally fatal, event!

The concept of management involves two competing interests. Assuming that the common element in the basic concept is "doing something" about the problem, management involves a technical component that addresses what can be done and how can the risk be reduced (or managed). The second component cannot be ignored: the relative cost versus the benefit from the proposed remedial or preventive action. As a result, frequently risk management strongly reflects cost: benefit analysis.

Those who argue that assessment and management should be considered independently frequently depend on the notion that assessment is a technical process capable of precise measurement and analysis, whereas management is far more subjective. A general description or definition of assessment that reflects this contention describes risk assessment broadly as a scientific enterprise in which facts and assumptions are used to estimate the potential for adverse effects on human health or the environment that may result from exposure to specific pollutants or toxins. Management is distinguished as a decision-making process that involves such considerations as risk assessment, technological feasibility, economic considerations related to cost:benefit relationships, statutory considerations, public concerns, and other similar subjective factors. In this sense, risk management is distinguished from risk assessment, and management logically follows assessment.

Separation is not always simple, and many will agree that assessment is not always based on hard science, nor is management purely subjective. Nonetheless, justification exists to support a separation with the philosophy that assessment can be more objective than some management considerations.

Clearly, in the face of controversy, terms assume different meanings, which can block progress. Because of the diversity of circumstances and issues, some concepts of the assessment/management process seem to have evolved on a case-by-case basis. Significant portions of some major environmental laws seem to reflect this diversity, and even courts have not resolved this sensitive question, at least as it relates, for example, to the preparation of environmental impact statements. Analysis of some of the diverse factors that affect both assessment and management decisions will help explain the continued use of multiple standards.

Despite the confusion and disagreements, the EPA has established three general definitions associated with this complex subject (EPA 1989).

1. *Risk assessment* is "the qualitative and quantitative evaluation performed in an effort to define the risk posed to human health and/or the environment by the presence or potential presence and/or use of specific pollutants." This definition is reasonably precise, but it fails to resolve many problems because it includes the undefined concept of "risk" and because it applies to the "presence or potential presence of specific pollutants." Apparently, this definition excludes environmental problems not associated with specific pollutants.

2. *Risk management* is "the process of evaluating nonregulatory responses to risk and selecting among them. The selection process necessarily requires consideration of legal, economic, and social factors." This definition reflects the regulatory responsibilities of the EPA.

3. *Risk communication* is "the exchange of information about health or environmental risk between risk assessors, risk managers, the general public, news media, interest groups, etc." Congress has recognized the critical importance of risk communication, even though it can cause disturbances. Part of federal environmental legislation includes the Emergency Planning and Community Right to Know Act (42 USC 11001 to 11050), which, among other things, establishes requirements to inform the public about transporting and storing certain types of dangerous materials.

BASIC ISSUES AFFECTING RISK ASSESSMENT AND MANAGEMENT

Regardless of the name or description, we all face varied risks daily: Some are effectively unavoidable as a part of daily life, and others are far more a matter of personal choice. For example, consider the risk in commuting to and from work, school, or social engagements; the risk of an accident is ever present. Steps can be taken to reduce risk, by choice of mode of transportation, safety of equipment, and safety practices, but travel cannot be made risk free—and few would select the alternative life of the isolated recluse! In contrast, exposure to other types of risk are far more a matter of individual choice. One of the most commonly cited examples is the choice of smoking in the face of mounting evidence of the health hazard. The bottom line in terms of risk assessment is simple to state, but difficult to formulate: determination of an acceptable risk, or acceptable potential of harm. The briefest introspection yields the conclusion that no single acceptable level of risk exists for the varied types of environmental issues that exist today, although logical groups may reduce the options to a reasonable few.

Three Major Factors in the Perception of Environmental Risk

Consider first a major dichotomy regarding the nature or the object of the potential harm: human health versus resource conservation. In general, clearer risk-assessment standards have been established and adopted for factors affecting health than for the preservation of natural resources. The effects of many environmental factors affecting human health are subject to rigorous scientific quantification, which allows fairly precise predictions of the consequences of various levels of exposure. This quantification has immediate practical applications. The medical profession has established limits for exposure to x-rays, for example, and physicians, nurses, and technicians are monitored to ensure that safe limits are not exceeded. In spite of criticisms, standards for food purity and water quality help ensure the health and safety of all citizens and, in fact, the American food supply is the safest in the world.

A second major consideration in evaluating risk-assessment standards emerges from the basic intellectual approach of the evaluator. This distinction is definitely not clear cut, but some scholars have suggested a basic difference between scientists and social scientists. The position of the scientist is reflected in a definition of risk: "the estimation of the association between exposure to a substance and the incidence of some disease, based on scientific data" (Winner 1986). Note that this definition seems quite limited, and that it calls for decisions based on the use of scientific data. Further investigation of the scientific approach suggests that not all factors need be evaluated before decisions are made or action taken, but that decisions and/or actions should reflect the level of knowledge and facts available to ensure reasonable safety. On the other hand, the social scientist questions whether full risk assessment is possible, but suggests action should be deferred until all the facts are known.

The posture of the social scientist (Ruckelshaus 1983) suggests that acting on the "current level of information" (whatever that level may be) favors the *status quo,* which by definition means continued environmental degradation. The social scientist goes on to say that the basic concept of risk assessment is misleading. The general public has become complacent to the concept of risk, and some shock factors are needed, such as stress on concepts of hazard or even fear, to achieve a greater public response.

A third major area of concern regarding risk assessment that is receiving increasing attention focuses on the point or points at which the risk is assessed. Assessment may be critical at three stages, and the nature of the assessment and conclusions may change. First, environmental risk associated with the manufacture of the product must be assessed by determining what, if any, adverse effects manufacture has on the environment. For example, the manufacture of many types of plastics involves organic solvents that become potential pollutants. Even food products frequently yield large amounts of organic material that becomes a significant disposal problem, hence a pollutant. Second, the potential effects of the product in its intended use must be assessed for potential risk factors. Certainly this would include virtually all of the common pesticides: insecticides, herbicides, and similar products. Third, the risk effects associated with the spent product must be assessed, including toxic decomposition products as well as general disposal problems. The concern is serious because of the significant amount of packaging materials and single-use items commonly encountered in daily living. Disposal can become a major concern of risk assessment for a product with relatively slight manufacture or use risk. For example, the popular product paper diapers represent a serious waste disposal problem in the nation's overflowing landfills.

The Emphasis on Human Health Risk Assessment

Although widespread concern about the environment in general exists in the United States and throughout the world today, major emphasis in terms of environmental risk assessment has focused on threats to human health. Concern expressed about the environment and a strong emphasis on the negative environmental impact of pesticides have led to concern about pesticide residues in foods and in the water supply. With a major emphasis in the early 1970s, Congress responded to these concerns, and assessment of health hazards assumed center stage.

Government regulators, industry, and a wide spectrum of interest groups recognize a variety of categories of substances and activities that pose significant threats to the environment, hence that require the attention of risk assessment. Substances are classified as toxic or hazardous, and radioactive materials receive special attention. Activities that are of increasing concern, in addition to the manufacturing processes that produce or release toxic or hazardous materials, include activities that lead to soil erosion, siltation and urban runoff: mining and timbering, and urbanization in general.

Two general reasons can explain this emphasis on risk assessment: (1) risk related to the cancer-causing agents, and (2) risk associated with age and the ability to speak for or to protect one's interests. Few would argue that protecting human life is justifiable, particularly in terms of a major killer, such as cancer, with an additional focus on those who cannot readily care for themselves—the unborn, young children, and, to a lesser extent, the elderly. In some respects, the risk-assessment focus on potential carcinogenic and related compounds can be justified on grounds of the greatest good for the greatest number of people. In addition, the extensive, ongoing health-related research in the United States provides the type of solid scientific data from which reliable assessments can be formulated and effective risk management efforts initiated.

In terms of health issues, the major emphasis of risk assessment has been placed on air and water—quality of the nation's air and water, the materials that represent health hazards, and how these hazards can be reduced and the problems eliminated. These critical topics are discussed in detail in chapter 6 (air) and chapter 7 (water). In recent years, increased emphasis has been placed on assessing safety and environmental risks found in the workplace and in the home. Public schools have also been the target of close scrutiny, particularly with concern over asbestos, radon, and lead in drinking water.

Major Study Organizations

Risk assessment as a recognized branch of science has grown markedly in recent decades, with federal research funds supporting a wide variety of efforts. For example, the world-famous Lawrence Berkeley Laboratory at the University of California at Berkeley has explored methods to improve the scientific basis of risk assessment, including analysis of complex groups of risk factors: exposure, dose, metabolism of the substance, early and late indicators of effects, and adverse impacts on humans and on ecosystems. Research, with a significant emphasis on carcinogens, examined four general areas: characterization of exposure of human populations to environmental pollutants and radiation; ranking priorities for possible hazards; mechanisms of damage from subcellular components to the entire organism; and the effects of environmental pollutants on ecosystems and their restoration. The restoration aspects included a specific emphasis on the impact of sediments on San Francisco Bay. Other renowned research facilities have also joined the efforts in improving risk assessment.

The Brookhaven National Laboratory in Long Island, New York, has stressed a team approach to complex issues of improving the scientific basis of risk assessment. This giant, world-recognized research facility assembles teams of professionals from medicine, engineering, economics, and biology with the goal of establishing realistic risk assessment to avoid the misallocation of research funds. Among other general areas of emphasis, the Brookhaven Laboratory has emphasized risk assessment related to nuclear safety. Universities and industries have continued strong cooperative efforts to expand the realm of reasonable risk assessment.

Impact of Changing Technology on Legislation

The Federal Food, Drug, and Cosmetic Act has undergone numerous amendments. Among other functions, this act protects the quality of food sold in the United States, including regulating pesticide residues in processed foods. In 1958, partly in response to growing public concern over suggested misuse of agricultural chemicals, U.S. Congressman Delaney introduced an amendment to the act that effectively prohibited sale of food that had *any* detectable residue of a substance known to cause or suspected of causing cancer in humans or laboratory animals. This amendment did not consider the amount of residue or the amount of the substance that might prove harmful to humans; if a carcinogen was detected, the product could not legally be sold. The Delaney Amendment illustrates two significant issues regarding risk assessment: (1) the policy of *no* residue, without consideration of what might be detected, and (2) the issue of technology—what constitutes *no* detectable residue.

Since 1958, when Congress passed the Delaney Amendment, science and technology have made dramatic advances in the fields of toxicology and analytic chemistry. In 1958, chemical residues could be detected in parts per thousand, with some highly sophisticated determinations in parts per hundred thousand. Today's technology allows detection to the level of parts per million (.000001), and smaller amounts in many instances (parts per billion, .000000001, or less). Consequently, foods that in 1958 would have appeared to have no residues now are found to have prohibited residues, but at levels 10 to 100 times less than those anticipated by the original legislation.

In the summer of 1996, Congress passed legislation that amended both the Federal Insecticide, Fungicide, and Rodenticide Act (FIFRA) and the Federal Food, Drug, and Cosmetic Act. The amendments included repeal of the Delaney Amendment and incorporation of assessment considerations involving the different consumers and possibility of different levels of exposure and toxicity. These amendments are discussed in chapter 11.

Toxicology and Risk Assessment

In the science of risk assessment, a critical first step is determining the toxic level of a substance as it relates to humans or any other "target." However, determining a toxic level does not directly establish a limit for exposure to that substance. The merging of assessment and risk management occurs when the allowable exposure limit is set; this limit is intended to provided a wide margin of safety below the established toxic level of a substance.

Measures of Toxicity

Initial steps in scientific risk assessment frequently start with exposure tests, which involve feeding substances to test animals at various rates. The rates usually are established as a ratio of the weight of the dose to the weight of the test animal, commonly expressed as milligrams of material per kilogram of body weight. Two measures are used to express toxicity: (1) the LD50, the dose that leads to the death of 50 percent of the test animals; and (2) the maximum dose that yields no observable effect on test animals. A low value for either measure reflects high potential toxicity of the material. Usually several types of animals are used, and several traits are observed: Mice, rats, and rabbits are the most common test animals, and in addition to death rates, studies include the incidence of birth defects, fertility, and cancer or other tumor growth.

Margins of Safety

Regulatory agencies, most frequently the EPA, establish the margin of safety for known toxic levels of a substance by direct experiments and statistical techniques to determine the dose that yields no observed adverse effects on experimental animals (NOEL, the no observable effect level). The allowable exposure level (called the allowable daily intake, ADI) is established by dividing the NOEL level by a safety factor that ranges from 100 to 1,000. The calculation is based on the assumption that humans are ten times more sensitive to the material than the test animals used to determine the NOEL value. ADI is expressed in milligrams of the substances per kilogram of body weight per day (mg/kg/day).

In the case of a substance suspected of being oncogenic (tending to cause tumors), the EPA becomes more conservative: If exposure to a substance increases the lifetime risk of developing cancer by a factor of more than 1 in a million (1×10^{-6}), the EPA must regulate the substance to reduce the risk to below that level. Thus, the acceptable risk is 1:1,000,000. The story of the regulation of a pesticide, Alar, clearly illustrates the impact of this standard.

Impact of Public Pressure on Risk Assessment

In the years following World War II, public concern about the safe use of pesticides and other chemicals increased dramatically, as did federal regulation of pesticides. In addition to concern about the general impact of pesticides on the environment, much interest focused on assessing the potential danger to human health, particularly cancer, caused by pesticides or pesticide residues in food. Public interest focused on two aspects of risk assessment: the reliability of animal tests in establishing toxicity levels for humans and the fact that toxicity levels did not distinguish between sensitivity to toxic materials and diets of adults and children.

The National Resource Defense Council (NRDC), a very active private environmental lobbying organization, claimed that pesticide residue standards set by the EPA allowed too great a risk of cancer and that the standards failed to recognize differences in susceptibility and dietary consumption between adults and children, particularly for fresh fruits and vegetables. NRDC contended that children were at a greater risk than adults from pesticide residues on food. In a 1989 report based on a two-year study, the NRDC focused on a single product, Alar, a chemical used by apple growers to promote natural ripening of the fruit and to enhance its red color. It claimed that the residue permitted by existing EPA regulations represented an unacceptable risk level and demanded that the EPA ban the use of the chemical.

The NRDC claimed that the residue would result in 6,000 additional cases of cancer among school-age children during their life time. With an estimated national population of 240 million, this represented an increased incidence of cancer of one individual in 40,000. NRDC called on the EPA to follow its established guidelines of regulating a substance if it represents a risk of cancer increase of one in a million.

Both the EPA and the manufacturer disagreed with the NRDC. They noted that available statistics suggested that approximately 25 percent of the population would develop cancer during their life time. With a school-age population of approximately 22 million, this converts to 5.5 million cases of cancer. If the disputed risk assessment was correct, Alar, would increase the number from 5,500,000 to 5,506,000, an increase of .025 percent

(.00025). Both the manufacturer and the EPA insisted that this increase was effectively so small as to not justify regulation.

The news media, including one national broadcast network, and some well-known entertainers rallied in support of the NRDC demands for action. Public pressure mounted for EPA action to invoke its policy of regulating a substance if it represented a one-in-a-million or greater increase in the estimated risk of developing cancer. Before the EPA took formal action, the manufacturer withdrew the controversial product from the market. Apple growers claimed the controversy hurt their income, and the loss of Alar lowered the quality of the product demanded by consumers.

Removing the material from the market did not end the controversy. The EPA insisted that the NRDC estimated increase of 6,000 cases of cancer from Alar was based on out-dated data. In 1989, based on additional data, the EPA reduced the toxic standard of Alar tenfold. Subsequently, the EPA reduced that standard by half. According to these values, Alar did not represent a significant threat of cancer. Nonetheless, the manufacturer ceased producing it. Some contend that the NRDC did not report the newer EPA standards and supporting data because such factual material could have weakened the massive media support and subsequent public pressure to regulate pesticides more rigorously.

The Alar story reveals several very relevant points regarding risk assessment. Risk assessment is not static, but flexible and ongoing. As more is learned, standards can be modified. This is a position strongly supported by William Ruckelshaus (1983), a former administrator of the EPA. Risk assessment, at least for pesticides, can be based on very technical, repeatable procedures, and standards can be established that more than adequately protect the public. Issues such as Alar not withstanding, the American public enjoys one of the safest food supplies in the world.

The data on which the Alar story was based have been presented in the news media. In addition, they are summarized and discussed in several modern environmental science texts (Chiras 1994; Nebel and Wright 1993), and subsequent events have been reported in the technical literature (Marshall 1991).

The issue of Alar and concerns about pesticide residues have not yet been finitely resolved. The conflicting interests, opinions, and facts led in part to significant amendments to the laws regulating the pesticide industry and the use of pesticides, including the call for more technical data. Pesticides in the environment, including the regulation of residue in food, are discussed in chapter 11.

Risk Management Concerns

As assessment becomes more sophisticated, issues of risk management become more complex in some ways; the Delaney Amendment and 1996 additional amendments plainly illustrate this concept. The meaning of "no detectable carcinogens" has changed with increasing sophistication of analytical equipment and techniques. Management, like assessment, involves decisions at different stages of a problem. Assuming that the risk element can be adequately described, then the point of management may become a major issue: prior to exposure to prevent harm, or after exposure to remedy harm. In some instances the issue appears clear—the magnitude of the harm is great, and prevention is the only logical choice. Obviously, lethal materials must be treated in this manner, but even then the factor of the acceptable level of risk must be addressed: how many individuals realistically face a lethal risk.

With less-than-dire consequences, the prevention-versus-remedy controversy frequently assumes an economic posture. The decision is strongly affected by cost/benefit considerations: relative benefit compared with the costs of alternative management approaches. Part of the total research effort at the Lawrence Berkeley Laboratory focuses on cost:benefit analysis and identifying criteria to be used in setting priorities for work on potential hazards.

Health considerations raise significant issues. The ideal is to prevent exposure to harm, but the cost can be prohibitive. Thus, the issue becomes one of the cost of remedy and/or treatment versus the cost of prevention. The issue may seem relatively simple in terms of prohibiting the sale or discharge into the environment of a material that has been shown to be a harmful pollutant. The picture becomes clouded when the same harmful material has great benefits, such as the unquestioned benefits from using certain pesticides and fertilizers. Additional economic considerations emerge from the absolute prohibition of a widely used compound. For example, the prohibition of the use of lead additives in automobile gasoline led to the closing of manufacturing plants and created serious local economic hardships in communities in which the producers of the additive were major employers. Management involves far more subjective decisions of this nature than the more technical aspects of risk assessment.

ASSESSING LAND POLLUTION

Congress has recognized the massive problems associated with polluted lands resulting from storing and dumping a wide variety of dangerous pollutants. The story of the Love Canal characterizes this immense problem. In the last century, a developer sought to develop a canal connecting waterways around Niagara Falls, New York. The attempt failed, and several years later, the incomplete canals were thought to be ideal sites for dumping all categories of industrial wastes. After the dumping and the closing of the dumps, land was made available for development of homes and schools. The developers failed to appreciate warnings about the materials buried at the site. Ultimately, as buried storage containers decayed, toxic substances surfaced and caused serious health problems, leading ultimately to the closing of homes and schools and relocation of families. The Love Canal situation and other similar situations ultimately led Congress to take steps to clean up such hazardous sites. With respect to risk assessment, the point to recognize is that the laws fix blame for pollution and assign responsibilities for paying for cleanup efforts, efforts that can cost millions of dollars.

As a result, a new area of risk assessment has emerged, assessment of environmental risk associated with land. The assessment involves determinations as to whether any condition on the land represents a potential environmental risk; old dump sites, toxic storage areas, and underground storage tanks all represent potential sources of pollution for which a land buyer may be liable, according to law. Asbestos represents an additional concern in buildings. From a very practical standpoint, land risk assessment plays a critical role in the sale of land. Lenders are unwilling to finance the purchase of property if the buyers face potential cleanup costs. The economic basis of this concern is simple: The value of the property as collateral is reduced by the potential cost of cleanup. At times, the potential cleanup costs exceed the value of the land.

In terms of land risk assessment, three fairly distinct phases are recognized. Phase 1 involves examination of public land records and may include viewing the site to determine whether any obvious problems exist. Phase 2 represents a technically more active stage, actual land (soil) and water tests to determine the presence of pollutants. Phase 3 is the remedial stage, steps to correct the problems from identified pollutants. Risk assessment in this area is becoming a new technical career area in environmental science and resource conservation.

Phase 3 represents more than assessment. By analogy to health issues, this stage represents risk management too. In general, remediation is a growing element of environment concern, sharing the stage with efforts to prevent pollution or environmental degradation.

Remediation commonly requires sophisticated, expensive technology. Research is continuing to develop new and improved technologies. The diversity of technical disciplines reflects in part the magnitude of the remediation efforts under way in the United States. Efforts range from genetic engineering to developing microorganisms that will decompose oil spilled on land or in the ocean to engineering technologies to remove a variety of toxic materials from the soil, and include advanced technologies designed to minimize discharge of toxic leachate from landfill sites. In the area of resource conservation, efforts to restore wetlands and protect endangered species as well as the technology to reduce agriculturally related erosion must all be considered part of both remediation and preventive strategies.

Although work is far from complete, marked progress has been made in cleaning up some of the nation's rivers and lakes. For example, the Hudson River in New York is a success story, and the cleanup of the Chesapeake Bay, from its headwaters to the Atlantic Ocean, is an outstanding example of the efforts of concerned citizens. In both cases, massive cooperative efforts reduced the discharge of pollutants into the rivers. This includes sewage treatment and work on agricultural nonpoint source pollutants. Starting with only a handful of supporters, the Chesapeake Bay Foundation, an organization devoted to saving the bay, has become a leading voice in environmental remediation.

Even the quality of the air we breathe has been improved by the elimination of the use of lead as a fuel additive. Although many hazardous waste sites remain, significant steps have been taken to identify them, reduce or eliminate their growth, and, in several instances, clean them to the point of returning some sites to useful purposes.

RISK ASSESSMENT AND BIOTECHNOLOGY

Biotechnology represents great hope for improved quality of life. Biotechnological methods have yielded new products that are major advances in agricultural production, human and animal health, and medicine. At the same time, however, these technologies have raised serious questions in terms of environmental risk assessment. The questions all center on three areas of concern:

1. The basic biological nature of the product and its interaction with the environment;
2. Possible unique environmental problems associated with the manufacture of the product, particularly concerns associated with chance releases of the product into the environment; and

3. Issues related to the control of the product when it is released into the environment, including, for man-made life-forms such as new microorganisms, the destruction of the organism, should it become harmful.

These serious basic concerns lead to the question of whether the products of modern biotechnology require some unique approach to risk assessment. This issue has received extensive attention by leading scientists.

A Major Federal Report

Basic answers are suggested by Fiskel and Covello (1986) in a final report made to the Office of Science and Technology, Executive Office of the President. The report provides a solid, scientific basis for environmental risk-assessment policy formulation as it relates to biotechnology.

The report contains eight chapters, and the subjects of the chapters provide a rapid and accurate overview of the scope of the studies and application of the findings.

Chapter 1, The suitability and applicability of risk management methods for biological introductions: This chapter concentrates on two fundamental areas, the suitability of various management options with respect to the end products of biotechnology, introductions, or newly created life-forms.

Chapter 2, Methods for evaluating microorganism properties: This chapter provides basic scientific guidelines in terms of the study of the organisms without any direct consideration of risk assessment. Obviously, understanding how to study an organism is a prerequisite to assessing the risks it might create. This chapter recognizes not only that the new life-forms may present new risks, but also that new methods may be needed to assess those risks.

Chapter 3, Human exposure effects for genetically modified bacteria; and Chapter 4, Human exposure effects to viruses and effects of assessment: Note the separation of the analysis of bacteria in chapter 3 and viruses in chapter 4, which accurately reflects the differences in these two life-forms and the fact that the technical depth of the report distinguishes them.

Chapter 5, Ecological consequences of assessment: Effects of bioengineered organisms: The report addresses the complex issues of risk assessment in an ecosystem situation, not just in the controlled conditions of the research laboratory.

Chapter 6, Assessing the transport and fate of bioengineered organisms in the environment. This chapter addresses a commonly expressed serious public concern—what happens to new life-forms after they are released into the environment and how they can be monitored and controlled.

Chapter 7, Ecological structure and function analysis: This discussion considers a broader perspective than just that of the organism under investigation. It properly stresses the complexity of interactions among organisms with the inanimate, physical environment by considering the dynamic flux typical of most ecosystems. The fact that this type of material is included in the report clearly illustrates the depth of the complexity of risk assessment.

Chapter 8, Controlled testing and monitoring methods for microorganisms: For many materials, appropriate testing can be completed in the laboratory and the results safely applied to more general conditions. However, in the case of newly created or modified life-forms, a major consideration is the fate of the organism in the real environment, and this means the ultimate release of that organism into the environment. Assessment of that risk is a unique feature of risk assessment and biotechnology. With certain materials—potential toxins or otherwise potentially harmful substances—human exposure can be limited to the most controlled situations, but with bioengineered organisms, control may be lost with release, making assessment of that risk essential.

This report does not propose to provide answers to the complex questions identified. Instead, it isolates issues and approaches. Clearly it focuses on microorganisms, the prime product of much work in biotechnology today. It recognizes the issue, for example, of an organism that changes from beneficial to potentially harmful after being released into the environment. The report addresses issues related to the practical development of organisms for the biological control of agricultural pests, pathogens, weeds, and insects, which make this concern very real. After the pest is destroyed, what becomes of the initially beneficial organism? The same question occurs concerning proposed release of organisms that can neutralize or decompose certain chemicals, including petroleum products.

A Five-Step Approach

The report suggests a five-step approach to risk assessment each step of which requires basic research. Although listed separately, in many instances, these steps must be considered simultaneously, and interactions among them may further complicate decisions.

1. *Risk identification:* Studies to identify sources of potential harm.
2. *Risk source characterization:* Studies to determine the actual basis of the harm or nature of a toxic response.
3. *Exposure assessment:* Studies to determine the basis of exposure, or how humans are exposed to the potential harm.
4. *Dose response assessment:* Studies to determine the magnitude of exposure before harm occurs.
5. *Risk estimation:* Studies to estimate two types of harm, health and economic losses caused by the organism or by its control.

Multiple Assessments May Be Required

Given the fundamental steps in the assessment of risk associated with biotechnology, the next consideration examines the stages or phases of the biotechnology process at which risk must be assessed. Again, five assessment points are suggested:

1. Formation of the product, which may involve either the basic research creation or commercial manufacture of the altered life-form.
2. Release of the product into the environment.
3. Proliferation or reproduction of the life-form in the environment.

4. Establishment of the life-form in the environment.

5. The ultimate effects of the established life-form on the environment.

Obviously, serious thought has been devoted to the issues of risk assessment associated with biotechnology, and the advent of this technology has posed unique questions related to risk assessment. The management of risk cannot be better than the quality of the assessment of the risk itself.

ETHICAL CONSIDERATIONS

Although not an integral element of risk assessment, ethical considerations will play an increasingly important role in the overall regulation of biotechnology research, development, and practical applications. The most serious fundamental questions have been introduced concerning the ethics of "manufacturing" or creating new life-forms. Additional arguments continue to emerge regarding actual ownership of these discoveries and the liability for damages they might cause. Ethical considerations will have significant impact on the regulation of the products of modern biotechnology. Ultimately, in the formulation of policy, ethical considerations must be taken into account along with economic factors and risk-assessment analysis.

Animal Testing

Some view the use of animals in research as an ethical issue. Although alternative methods for some studies that have used animals are available, animal testing remains an essential component of risk assessment and other aspects of biological research.

Opposition to the use of animals takes two forms. The first is opposition on the basic philosophical grounds that animals have rights and that use of animals in any situation violates those rights and is not subject to technical resolution. Unfortunately, some extreme animal rights activists have weakened their stance by illegally disrupting research projects and facilities. The second form of opposition calls for humane treatment of animals used for research. Few would deny this as a reasonable posture, although some would claim that certain animal care standards formulated by regulatory agencies are excessive.

Opponents to animal testing also point to the fact that animal test results frequently are not directly transferable to humans. This argument has certain merit, but those opponents fail to recognize three essential facts. First, statistical methods allow reliable comparisons and applications to be made. Second, in terms of safety standards, regulatory agencies incorporate extensive safety factors to exposure and dose limits. Third, commonly the dose levels used in animal studies, when converted to human applications, represent exposures that are extremely unlikely to occur, if not impossible.

Animal testing will remain an essential element of risk assessment because it provides essential data to establish toxicity levels, a key to assessment.

RISK ASSESSMENT AND RESOURCE CONSERVATION

Science provides a strong technical and factual foundation for environmental risk assessment as it is applied to issues of toxic or harmful substances and human health. Consequently, the results of assessment activities become key elements in the formulation of risk management strategies. Unfortunately, science has not provided the same analytical basis for many issues related to the assessment of risk associated with damage to or loss of natural resources. A central problem appears to be the definition or identification and characterization of harm or damage, a key element of risk assessment.

Harm must be considered in two components: harm or damage to the environment or natural resource, and the harm such damage causes to humans. Some argue that unless an act represents measurable potential, direct harm to humans, it need be of little regulatory concern. The opposing argument insists that the natural environment must be preserved and protected for its own value.

Estimating the direct harm to the environment from a given act or a given substance in many instances is far simpler than estimating the impact of that harm on humans. The simplicity stems from the fact that the harm can be estimated following the general protocols recommended for assessing health risks. On the other hand, estimating human impact is more subjective. Consider the following examples.

- The Forest Service grants a permit to clear cut several hundred acres of virgin timber.
- A section of river is dammed for the development of a reclamation and power project.
- A designated primitive area is explored for commercial oil drilling.
- Acres of habitat for an endangered species are allowed to be cleared, or a wetland is allowed to be drained.

In each instance, many aspects of the actual harm to the environment can be estimated. With the forest, for example, the number of trees taken can be determined and the time for regrowth approximated. Even anticipated problems of runoff and erosion plus loss of wildlife habitat can be predicted.

Of course, the question remains concerning the harm these events cause humans. Some elements can be expressed in dollars, such as the value of trees or the cost of erosion control. Other aspects are not subject to economic analysis, such as habitat destruction, or simply the loss of beauty.

The same types of issues exist with respect to the other examples. Some harm can be assessed in terms of actual damage. Other aspects at least can be expressed in terms of estimated cost. Ultimately, some issues are essentially subjective, such as the preservation of wilderness or wild and scenic rivers.

For certain federal actions, the provisions of the National Environment Policy Act (NEPA) establish grounds for decision making. NEPA requires federal agencies to prepare environmental impact statements (EIS) for actions that significantly affect the human environment. Although the EIS is not required to examine all potentials, the law reflects the government policy that action affecting the environment must be taken on an informed basis. Unfortunately, NEPA does not obligate states or private parties, but it represents a long step in the direction of informed decision making that must characterize risk assessment and resulting risk management strategies.

RISK MANAGEMENT

Obviously, risk assessment must precede risk management. With respect to health-related environmental issues, risk can be assessed in fairly precise, quantitative terms; precise assessment leads to more effective and logical management strategies. As assessment becomes less precise, however, management strategies by necessity become more subjective. The assessment of risk associated with the management and protection of natural resources commonly includes significant subjective components, which make separation of the assessment and management functions less distinct. Regardless of the initial separation, assessment and management must merge in the formulation of management strategies.

Risk is part of life, and in some situations risk management has become no more than acceptance of certain risks. Unfortunately, the individual has little choice in exposure to many environmental risks. We all effectively breathe the same air and drink the same water; therefore, we all are exposed to environmental risks associated with air and water pollution.

In recent years, the government has modified its basic philosophy regarding the management of environmental risk. The initial major environmental legislation of the late 1960s and 1970s placed emphasis on compliance with legislated standards to minimize the effects of pollution. This policy resulted in an emphasis on remedying the effects of pollution. In 1990, Congress recognized this trend as less than optimum, and in the Pollution Control Act of 1990 directed that efforts should focus on prevention, not on remediation. Of course, this decision did not terminate the extensive environmental cleanup efforts under way or preclude initiation of new efforts. It did establish a new general direction for future efforts.

The risk management choice of prevention versus remedy is not simple, because it requires determining the relative risks of preventing the pollution and cleaning up versus preventing the pollution at the onset. In many situations, this decision becomes strongly influenced by economics: the cost and benefits of prevention versus costs and benefits of cleanup efforts. Frequently, prevention of air and water pollution requires major modifications of manufacturing systems, which lead to price increases to the consumer or the potential of factory closures and local unemployment. In this sense, risk management decisions affect who pays initially, although ultimately, costs are passed on to the consumer.

The Issue of Economics

Risk management represents a significant expense to manufactures and to consumers. As a result, economic considerations play a significant part in determining management strategies. Estimating cost effectiveness is a frequently employed, basic economic procedure for prioritizing risk management strategies. The analysis looks at combinations of alternatives to determine which combination yields the most effective return for funds spent. This does not mean the greatest return or the greatest reduction in pollution. This requires a balancing of interests: costs versus level of pollution control. The basic concept examines the cost of control of pollution versus the total costs of not controlling the pollution and considering all intermediate options. Economic analysis not only must weigh costs and benefits, but also must include the balance between health issues and impacts on natural resources. In 1981, in the face of the increasing regulation of industry and the expense of compliance with regulations, President Ronald Reagan, directed federal agencies, through an executive order, to include a cost:benefit analysis as part of proposals for new environmental regulations.

By this action, the government acknowledged that the cost must be a consideration in determining environmental quality. The cost of risk management occurs at several steps: costs of identifying problems (the cost of risk assessment); costs associated with policy development, including costs of EIS and economic analyses; research to identify "harm"; the need for and development of new technology to manage the risks; costs of implementing management strategies, which can include substantial modification of manufacturing facilities and significant new expenses in the construction of new manufacturing facilities or products; costs of banning a product as a pollutant in terms of the damage it causes; costs of remedy versus lost income to the manufacturer, and possibly lost jobs and resultant unemployment.

In earlier legislation, Congress had directed the elimination of certain pollutants. Experience has demonstrated that such sweeping steps are not only unreasonable, but highly impracticable, if not impossible as well, and in many instances not necessary. In terms of any economic analysis, placing a real value on certain aspects of the environment that pollution clearly damages remains a major challenge.

Concurrently with the analysis of expenses, benefits must be evaluated. Some are difficult, if not impossible, to evaluate accurately, such as the value of saving a human life or reducing the incidence of disease. Certain costs can be estimated, but great voids remain. The same type of problem arises with resource depletion: The value of certain aspects of natural resources can be estimated, but for other aspects, the value is personal, and highly subjective. With increasing national concern over health care costs, certainly health benefits will become more important factors in all aspects of risk analysis and formulation of risk management strategies.

CONCLUSIONS

Understanding the basic concepts of risk assessment and risk management provides a solid basis for understanding and evaluating environmental laws, regulations, and policies. Major environmental legislation as well as rules and policy reflect both the assessment and management strategy policies of Congress and regulatory agencies.

Separating the assessment aspect from management is conceptually helpful but, ultimately, management must reflect the assessment of the risk. Risk assessment for many health-related issues can be accomplished on a factual, technical basis because harm and its causes can be clearly defined scientifically. For many natural resource considerations, definitions of harm appear to be more subjective. Nonetheless, efforts should continue to minimize subjectivity. The type of logical development employed in the analysis of risk assessment and management as they relate to biotechnology could yield fruitful results for resource considerations.

QUESTIONS AND CONCEPTS FOR DISCUSSION AND RESEARCH

1. Distinguish between risk assessment and risk management, then formulate arguments that the same criteria can (or cannot) be used for health-related environmental issues and issues related to natural resource conservation or protection.

2. Formulate arguments for and against the idea that risk assessment can and should be separated from risk management.

3. What issues, if any, are unique to biotechnology as it relates risk assessment and management and the environment?

4. How important should cost:benefit analysis be in risk management decisions? Should such considerations be uniform for all environmental issues?

5. What part does toxicology play in risk management decisions? How and why has its role changed in recent years?

6. In what, if any, risk management deliberations might an EIS be significant?

REFERENCES AND SELECTED READING

Chiras, Daniel D. 1994. *Environmental Science Action for a Sustainable Future.* 4th ed. Menlo Park, CA: Benjamin/Cummings.

Fiskel, Joseph, and Vincent Covello, eds. 1986. *Biotechnology and Risk Assessment: Issues and Methods for Environmental Introductions.* New York: Pergamon Press.

Marshall, E. 1991. A is for Apple, Alar, and . . . Alarmism. *Science* 254:20–22.

Nebel, Bernard J., and Richard T. Wright. 1993. *Environmental Science: The Way the World Works.* Englewood Cliffs, NJ: Prentice Hall.

Ruckelshaus, William D. 1983. Science, Risk, and Public Policy. *Science* 221:54–59.

U.S. Environmental Protection Agency. December 1989. *Glossary of Environmental Terms and Acronym List.* EPA 19k–100z. Washington, DC.

Winner, Langdon. 1986. Risk: Another Name for Danger. *Science for the People.* May/June, 1986.

PART TWO

Natural Resource Regulation

4

Land Resources and Environmental Policy

Land and the resources associated with it—timber and grassland, minerals of all kinds, water, and wildlife including fish and game—constitute the majority of the nation's natural resources. Such resources represent a significant portion of the environment subject to laws and regulations. In the United States, land and its component resources have been subject to some form of regulation since the earliest English and European settlers arrived nearly four hundred years ago. Although early regulations addressed ownership, they also had an impact on "land use" and therefore reflect the earliest conservation/natural resource regulation in America. The pattern of regulation of land is typical of the regulation of most resources and of the environment in general: As a resource becomes scarce, or threatened, regulations increase. The pattern of land regulation in the United States reflects the impact of decreasing supplies coupled with increasing regulation. In addition to its historic interest, this pattern can be found in most other aspects of environmental regulation in the United States today.

THE IMPACT OF POPULATION GROWTH

The growing population imposes increasing and frequently conflicting demands on the nation's land and related natural resources. Conflicting demands involve a variety of interests and issues. Protecting or preserving lands to ensure the nation's continued agricultural productivity is a high priority that frequently involves conflicts with urban growth, development, and industrialization.

Preserving the land commonly includes preserving the natural resources associated with it, which involves complex relationships. Controversies over harvesting timber provide

73

an excellent example of such conflicting interests: Moderate conservationists have called for protecting forests by carefully regulated timber harvests to protect timber productivity. The issue frequently focuses on the amount of timber to be harvested. Timber interests point to the needs for timber and employment associated with timber harvest. Other conservation interests seek to prohibit timber harvest in certain areas, citing uniqueness of a specific forest area and destruction of wildlife habitat as reasons. Both reasons are related to protecting biodiversity. Some would seek protection on the basis of conserving wilderness for the sake of wilderness. Hunters may join either group to the extent of protecting wildlife habitat, but some preservationists are adamantly opposed to hunting! The same general types of concerns arise over the impact of mining, natural gas, and oil exploration activities.

Land development cannot be separated from other environmental concerns: Increased water conservation and water pollution, air pollution, and the generation of solid waste and need to dispose of it all are associated with population growth, which is the fundamental force affecting increased demands on natural resources such as land.

Clearly land is a valuable resource, and the value may differ depending on the individual's perspective of appropriate or best use. Controversy frequently arises over environmental regulations that limit land use to protect or preserve some element of the land. Environmental laws and policies affecting its use and development logically are part of the broad picture of environmental regulation.

ISSUES RELATED TO PUBLIC VERSUS PRIVATE OWNERSHIP

The laws, rules, regulations, and policies affecting land use reflect more than the complexity of the resource itself. The relationship between land as a resource and environmental regulation must consider two classes of land, privately owned land and public land—land owned by the federal government or by other governmental entities, states, counties, and other recognized, local governmental subunits.

Although state law regulates the vast majority of real estate sales and the Constitution significantly restricts the authority of the federal government over privately owned land, a variety of elements of federal environmental law and policy directly or indirectly affect the rights of private landowners. In addition, state laws and local rules and regulations with significant environmental implications also affect landowners' rights, as do a variety of legally binding, environmentally significant private agreements. Understanding the basic concepts of land ownership provides the necessary foundation to understand this frequently overlooked, very practical aspect of environmental regulation.

Much of the environmental regulation of the land resource is federal regulation of federally owned lands. In every state, the federal government owns some land; in some states, the federal government is a major landowner. A significant portion of the federal environmental regulations related to land use involve forest-management policy. Many involve management of the nation's rangeland resources, and mining faces continued federal environmental regulation. Obviously, the laws and policies related to the management of the national parks and monuments include significant attention to the environment.

The historic acquisition of the federal land resources and the subsequent distribution of these resources have enormous environmental implications with a continuing impact on much of the nation today, and indeed are felt worldwide. The acquisition and distribution of land resources by the federal government provide a clear example of the evolution of environmental policy. The status of land use also provides a tangible case for the application of the analysis involving posing the four previously mentioned questions: Where are we? How did we get here? Where should we go? How should we get there?

LAND OWNERSHIP

Basic Concepts of Land Ownership

Understanding the basic concepts of ownership will enhance understanding of many aspects of land management policy and provide a foundation for applying the concepts of ownership interests to other resources and environmental issues. Consider first the basic idea of *ownership,* which is practically defined by ownership rights. Ownership rights include the rights to possess property, to manage that property, and to transfer (or convey) ownership of that property. In some instances, ownership may include responsibilities to protect certain property. Ownership is more than simple possession; management and the authority to transfer are critical aspects to ownership.

For all practical purposes, property law in terms of real estate sales in the United States is entirely state law, although the right to own property is protected by the Constitution. The federal government is a major landowner; thus, federal land policy affects significant areas of land—national forests, national parks, and thousands of acres of the western range.

Concepts of Real Estate Law

At one time, ownership of real property was limited to royalty. The Crown awarded certain rights in real property to individuals in recognition of their service to the Crown. The ultimate reward was to be granted title to land in what now is recognized as ownership in "fee simple absolute" (FSA). Ownership in FSA is full ownership of real estate in perpetuity (forever). This ownership allows the title holder (owner) to use, manage, subdivide, and transfer the land. Transfer can be by sale, gift, or even after death of the owner by will, and if the owner dies without leaving a will, the state will distribute the land to the owner's heirs.

Today, when an individual claims ownership of land, generally the claim is assumed to be fee simple ownership. Proof of ownership is generally in the form of a deed, which identifies the seller and buyer of property and provides an accurate description of the land. Land ownership remains a basis of the American dream, and certainly was a driving force in both the original colonization and the settlement of the country.

RESTRICTIONS ON OWNERSHIP RIGHTS

The concept of ownership in FSA suggests the right to use land any way the owner wishes. However, this idea is not entirely true. Many forces limit land use, including a variety of environmental considerations. Restrictions on land use trace to many sources.

Federal Laws and Regulations

As previously mentioned, real estate law is generally state law, but the Constitution protects the citizen's right to own property and prohibits the government from taking property from anyone without cause and compensation to the individual from whom the property was taken. Nonetheless, a variety of federal laws, several of which constitute major environmental legislation, may greatly restrict the individual's right to use property, even when that property is owned in fee simple absolute.

For example, Congress enacted the Endangered Species Act, 16 USC 1531 *et seq.,* to protect a variety of animal and plant species from extinction. In addition to protecting the individuals, the law protects the habitat critical to their survival. Owners of such "critical habitat" cannot use their land in a manner that destroys the critical habitat. Frequently, this restriction has stopped timber harvesting and mining activities on private property. A second common example focuses on wetlands. Federal law prohibits landowners from draining or otherwise disrupting wetlands without first securing a federal permit. The provisions of the permit may greatly restrict what the owner is ultimately allowed to do with the land. In the extreme case, the permit can be denied, and the owner prohibited from using the land.

The impact of the Endangered Species Act and Section 404 of the Clean Water Act has led many landowners to claim that the governmental restrictions amount to an unconstitutional taking of their land. To date, however, courts have not agreed with this contention. The basic judicial interpretation of the Constitution with respect to "taking" remains that the action of the government must totally divest the owner of all value of the land in question.

State and Local Laws and Regulations

State governments also exercise powers that can restrict land use. In some coastal states, for example, state laws greatly restrict building along beaches to protect the beach line from erosion. In addition, laws related to septic tank installations and wells can limit land use, and even building permits can effectively limit land uses, frequently on an environmental basis, such as very restrictive conditions limiting permits to build animal waste disposal lagoons and similar activities.

Local zoning ordinances and local and regional land-use planning regulations can limit how an owner can use land held in FSA. Zoning frequently is done at the community (city or town) level and generally limits land use in terms of business versus residential uses and location on multiple family dwellings. It also restricts such things as the size and placement of signs and required parking spaces. Zoning should be considered a source of environmental regulation because it can regulate the environment of the residential and business community.

Like zoning, land-use plans developed by governmental entities with the authority to enforce them must also be viewed as potential restrictions on land use that have environmental implications. Planning includes such environmental considerations as housing density, required green spaces in land developments, road siting, and infrastructure concerns such as schools, water supplies, and traffic management.

In addition, in some states, land-use planning considerations may allow a state or local agency to deny certain types of permits. Such authority has restricted land use by limiting permits for livestock waste-treatment facilities, hence limiting where such facilities can be located. States have reviewed this issue, and several now are making such rules a matter of state law, thereby reducing what appears to be excessive discretionary authority of the agencies.

Private Restrictions

In some situations, an individual may actually own the right to use property held in FSA by another. This right is held in the form of an easement or right-of-way, interests in the property that allow another person or persons specified use of the property. Frequently easements exist when the property is purchased; sale of the property does not extinguish the rights of the person holding the easement rights. For example, easements are commonly granted to utility companies for utility service lines across property, either on poles or underground. Roadways and drainage ditches represent other forms of easements. Such easements may restrict the absolute use of the land by the owner, but the land is still held in FSA.

Many states recognize a special easement, the *conservation easement,* which the landowner gives to a public interest organization, such as the Nature Conservancy, to conserve some environmentally sensitive or unique feature of the land—for example, to protect a particular scenic vista, to provide wildlife habitat, or to restrict grazing to provide winter feed for wildlife. The landowner retains title to the land, and the provisions of the easement restrict the use of the land, just as they would for any other easement.

Additional private restrictions that affect land use and that have significant potential to affect the environment are related to financing purchases of property. Credit institutions, through restrictions imposed in mortgages, can greatly affect the manner in which borrowers use land. Restrictions, from an environmental perspective, are imposed to protect the lender's interest in the property that the borrower has pledged as collateral. The basic concept of a mortgage coupled with today's policy of landowners' liability for pollutants on their property explains this potential limitation.

Few property buyers, either commercial or residential, pay cash for property; most transactions are financed and the land is pledged as collateral. Through the provisions of a mortgage, buyers agree that if they fail to repay a loan, the lender can take title to the property. Generally, a mortgage grants certain rights to the lender to protect the lender's interest in the property. These rights may include the right to inspect the property and the requirement that the borrower maintain the property in reasonable condition, and may limit removal of products, such as timber, without specific permission of the lender.

New Environmental Liabilities

Federal law now says that the owner of property is responsible for cleaning up hazardous materials or wastes stored or disposed of on that property. To protect the value of collateral, lenders now, as a provision of the mortgage, frequently require borrowers to refrain from storing or dumping hazardous materials on the property. Thus provisions of a mortgage can significantly limit how an owner can use the land. Some may consider this a federal restriction because the cause is federal law, but the impact is through the private lender and through agreements with the borrower/landowner. The same issue exists concerning property with certain types of underground storage tanks that may become sources of pollution (see chapter 9).

ADDITIONAL LAND REGULATION CONCEPTS

Several additional terms and concepts are important to understanding the history of the regulation of public lands in the United States. These common terms assume unusual definitions and meanings when used in the context of land regulation and ownership. The following terms all relate primarily to public land, land initially owned by the federal or state government.

- **"Entry on the land,"** or merely "entry," recognizes the concept of "squatters' rights," which is the right of an individual to take possession or repossession of land by entering on it in a peaceful manner. Critical aspects are the actual entry on the land, not claiming it from a distance, and the concept of a peaceful claim of possession. In the early history of the United States, the vast majority of land owned by the federal government was open to entry.
- **"Withdrawal,"** or "withdrawal from entry," is the opposite of entry. This legislated or limited executive action declares that certain land is not available or open to entry. Withdrawal preserves title of the land for the United States. **"Reservation"** is similar to the concept of withdrawal, with one major difference: Withdrawal applies to land available for entry; whereas reservation applies to land not available and means that the government effectively reserves title to the land. The reservation can be temporary or permanent.
- **"Eminent domain,"** or the government's right or power of eminent domain, is the authority of the government to take property for public use, or to force the sale of property. However, the government cannot take private property, even in its exercise of its power of eminent domain, without justly compensating the owner.

FEDERAL ACQUISITION AND OWNERSHIP OF LAND

The federal government owns approximately 730 million acres of land, or about one-third of the land area of the United States. With relatively minor exceptions, reference to public lands is reference to this enormous land holding. The majority of this land is in the western states, with Alaska the leading state. The United States Constitution empowers Congress to manage the property of the United States, which provides more than adequate authority for the massive legislation affecting public lands. It also allows the Congress to buy, sell, or trade land. The land is held as national forests, national parks and monuments, and thousands of acres of rangeland in the West. In addition, relatively small areas are owned for the business of the nation, everything from federal office buildings to military bases, shipyards, federal prisons, and post offices.

By the time of the first settlements in Virginia in 1607 and the Pilgrims in Massachusetts in 1620, the extent of the North American continent had been fairly well described. France, England, Spain, Russia, and the Netherlands all had explored various parts of what is now the United States and claimed portions of the North American continent. When the Constitution was ratified, France, Spain, and Russia claimed title to part of the lands in North America, including Alaska, and the United States claimed title to lands between the Allegheny Mountains and the Mississippi River. This land all traces to claims of ownership associated with the original colonies and to ownership concessions made by some colonies to the new government of the United States as a condition of ratification.

The Discovery Doctrine

The traditional story of the colonies about settlement of the North American continent and founding of the United States fails to address a basic question that has affected the character of the nation since its founding: the basis on which the people who settled the continent or the governments who authorized such settlements claimed title to the land. The Discovery Doctrine provided the basic justification for settlement, although its fairness is questionable.

The land was not vacant, waiting for settlement: It supported a diverse population of Native Americans. The initial settlers in the United States claimed title under the authority of the English Crown, and frequently in the name of the Crown. Similar claims were made by explorers for other nations. These settlers effectively ignored the "title" of the native inhabitants. In addition, some of the land was acquired by a combination of conquest of other nations represented in the New World and purchase from these nations. Of course, these "owners" had no more title than did the original settlers in Virginia or Massachusetts.

Native Americans generally treated the land as a common resource, without individual ownership. At one time, apparently, no need existed to regulate land use or to establish individual ownership. Then, the Europeans arrived, invoking a doctrine or philosophy that they believed justified their settlement and assumption of ownership: the Discovery Doctrine.

This doctrine, invoked in philosophy by all who took title to land from its native inhabitants, cast the Europeans in the role of superiors to the natives and claimed that the natives lived on the land, but did not and effectively could not own it! It implied further that the settling nation did some great service to the natives by bringing European civilization to them. Many would claim that all title to lands in the United States must trace to Native Americans.

A Surprising Decision

The philosophy of the Discovery Doctrine has been directly expressed and adopted by the Supreme Court in a decision regarding land ownership. This decision incorporates a surprising position expressed by the Court in 1823.

Chief Justice Marshall delivered the opinion of the Court. The facts are quite simple: Johnson purchased land directly from leaders of an Indian tribe in what is now Illinois. Apparently no dispute arose over payment; to all concerned, it was a "fair deal." Subsequently, M'Intosh, through negotiations with the federal government, purchased the same land and received a federal patent for the land. The suit followed to determine actual ownership. The Court reviewed in some detail the basic premises of the Discovery Doctrine and the philosophy that natives were inhabitants of the land but did not own it. On that basis, the Court awarded title of the land to M'Intosh, noting that because the natives did not own the land, they could not have sold it to Johnson. According to the Court's application of the Discovery Doctrine, because M'Intosh had negotiated with the federal government, which was in theory acting on behalf of the Native Americans, his purchase was the only valid purchase. Then the Court characterized the natives as inferior and perpetually under the protection of the United States government! See *Johnson v. M'Intosh,* 21 US 543 (1823).

With respect to land, clearly the advent of the need to formally establish ownership signaled the initiation of increasing regulation of this natural resource. In addition, the variety of regulations, acts, and limitations on acquired lands rapidly added to the body of resource regulations establishing who could own land and how could title be secured.

Public Land States and the Acquisition of Public Lands

Title to the thirteen original colonies—New Hampshire, Massachusetts, Rhode Island, Connecticut, New York, New Jersey, Pennsylvania, Delaware, Maryland, Virginia, North Carolina, South Carolina, and Georgia—generally reflects direct acquisition of land by application of the Discovery Doctrine. Each colony existed as a specific entity before the birth of the nation. Of the thirteen original colonies, seven were created by specific royal grants and six by independent, private groups seeking various types of freedom.

In addition to the land claimed by the original colonies, the new nation acquired title to land by purchase, international treaties, or conquest. Ultimately, ownership by the federal government extended from the Atlantic to the Pacific Ocean and north to south from the border with Mexico to the established Canadian border. Much of this acquisition came from purchases.

The Louisiana Purchase in 1803 represents the first major land acquisition by the federal government. This involved the purchase of 523 million acres of land from France for three cents an acre. The purchase included much of the rich agricultural lands of what now are the Great Plains states, and it extended through the Red River Valley the length of the Mississippi River to New Orleans. In 1867, Alaska was purchased from Russia for $7.2 million. At the time, the mineral resources of the territory were unknown.

Treaties have played a comparable role in federal land acquisition. Between 1817 and 1819, the United States acquired title to all of Florida from Spain. Part of this involved conquest, and part reflected Spain's inability to contend with continued resistance of Native Americans in Florida. In 1840, the northwestern border of the United States was established by the Oregon Compromise, a treaty with Great Britain. The Treaty of Guadalupe-Hidalgo in 1848 settled the disputed southwestern border with Mexico and included sale of most of the Southwest to the United States for $15 million.

Prior to this treaty, Texas, which at the time existed as an independent republic, was annexed in 1845. Subsequent to annexation, Texas sold some 79 million acres of its western lands to the United States. This land ultimately became part of the states of New Mexico, Oklahoma, Wyoming, Colorado, and Kansas.

Agreements and concessions among the colonies extended federal land ownership. Several colonies ceded land to the federal government, and that land ultimately became portions of several states. For example, land ceded by Georgia became Alabama and Mississippi. Tennessee was carved from lands originally part of North Carolina, and the Great

Lakes states all trace title to lands of the original colonies. The general pattern of land acquisition is described in Figure 4.1.

The origin of land title based on acquisition determines whether land within a state is considered to be part of the public domain, owned by the federal government and therefore subject to federal management. States created from the original thirteen colonies are not public domain states. Land initially belonged to an independent colony. States formed from lands acquired by purchase or treaty, except for Texas and Hawaii, are public land states. States created from lands ceded by the original colonies to the United States vary in the extent of public domain land. For example Tennessee and Kentucky, formed from lands initially included in North Carolina, have no public domain lands. Neither Maine nor Vermont are public domain states. Both states formed by the cession of lands for Georgia to the United States have public domain land. The Great Lakes states, formed in part by cession from North Carolina to the United States, also have public domain land.

Although the federal government owns lands in every state, title might not trace to a public domain basis. Federal land ownership varies greatly among states, from nearly 88 percent in Alaska to about 0.33 percent in Connecticut. The government has secured title to

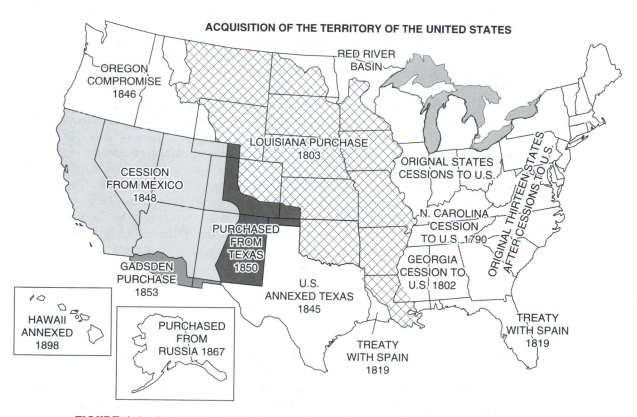

FIGURE 4.1 Acquisition of the territory that now comprises the United States. Drawn from BLM data.

land by purchase, including exercise of its power of eminent domain. Clearly, an early, if unwritten, policy or philosophy of the United States was to secure title to all lands, from coast to coast in the North American continent. Ultimately, this doctrine found expression in the Manifest Destiny, the belief that Destiny demanded that the United States should expand its sphere of social, economic, and political influence across the continent.

The Power of Eminent Domain

The government can require private interests to sell land, but the land subsequently must be used for the public good. To force a sale, the government exercises its right of eminent domain. In fact, through its exercise of eminent domain authority, the government can require the sale of property to private parties, but the land use still must be for the public good; for example, land needed for public utilities.

A single case in 1896 finitely recognized the government's power of eminent domain. The Constitution does not directly grant either the federal or state governments the right of eminent domain, but the right is at least strongly inferred by the Fifth Amendment, which guarantees that no person shall be deprived, "of life, liberty, or property, without due process of law" and continues, "nor shall private property be taken for public use without just compensation." Clearly, the Founding Fathers contemplated the exercise of eminent domain and, equally clearly, they intended to protect the individual's property rights by limiting the exercise of this authority.

A single case in 1896 finitely recognized the government's power of eminent domain. The facts of the case are relatively simple, and the implications comparatively great. *U.S. v. Gettysburg Elec. Ry. Co.* 160 U.S. 668 (1896).

The railroad company owned land in and around the historic Gettysburg battlefield. Following the Civil War, the government sought to establish a national military park that would include land owned by the railroad company. When the railroad company resisted sale of the land, the government sought to condemn the land and force the sale. The issue ultimately reached the Supreme Court, where the Court considered whether the proposed use (a national military park) represented a kind of public use or public interest that would justify allowing condemnation, or the exercise of the power of eminent domain. The Court found that the proposed use adequately established a public use and that the government had the right to condemn the land. The Court reviewed the sources of governmental power and noted that much authority existed by *implication* in the Constitution. In making its ruling, the Supreme Court found the power of eminent domain to be implied; following this case, that power has not been successfully challenged.

FEDERAL DISTRIBUTION OF LAND

As a result of the extent of colonial land claims, the new nation was "land rich," but in many ways "cash poor." Title to land was used to pay debts of the Revolutionary War, and the sale of public land was considered as a source of income for the infant nation. Prior to ratification of the Constitution, the Congress of Confederation enacted the Land Ordinance Act of 1785. This act introduced the grid survey pattern, which divides land into rectangular townships composed of thirty-six sections one mile square each (an area of 640 acres), arranged in a six-by-six grid and numbered consistently from the upper right to the lower left section. In addition to the grid survey, the act also made public land available without limit for a dollar an acre.

Federal Land Policy: Early Environmental Policy

The initial government land policy favored establishing the family farm and supported settlement westward, into the wilderness with the reward to settlers of title to land. It even accepted squatters' rights to land they settled. The rate of growth and settlement outpaced the rate of surveying and mapping the nation's lands. As a result, in many instances, the government owned unidentified land; and potentially patents failed to describe adequately land conveyed to private title, resulting in the possibility of multiple claims to the same land or related problems with titles, land descriptions, and boundaries.

Grants to States at Statehood

States Admitted from the Public Domain

Ohio, which was admitted to the Union in 1803, was the first state created from the public domain. Congress sought to formulate a system whereby other anticipated "public land" states would be admitted to the Union on equal footing. After heated debate, to support the Doctrine of Equal Footing and to help ensure that all new public land states enjoyed comparable, but not necessarily equal, resources, Congress granted new states four percent of the public (federal) land for public schools. Effectively, this allowed the states to sell the land and use the proceeds to establish a public school system. In addition, Congress gave the new states five percent of the proceeds from the sale of federally owned land and gave them the right to lease all salt springs. The federal government first applied this pattern of land distribution to Ohio. Subsequently, the government applied the same basic distribution to the admission of Louisiana, Indiana, Illinois, Alabama, Missouri, Michigan, Arkansas, Florida, and Iowa. Later admissions included land for other uses as well.

Land grants to states were not without complications. Much of the land granted had not yet been surveyed, yet the federal government granted specific sections within each township. In the past fifty years, much of the West remained unsurveyed. As a result, specific land granted to states for public schools was previously occupied, and states then had to accept alternative choices of land as their "school land," land to be sold for the support of public schools. Selection of alternative lands for schools created several problems with environmental overtones, some of which have been resolved only in recent years. The following case that established the *In lieu* doctrine reflects recent resolution of these issues.

The *In Lieu* Doctrine

The selection of land *In lieu* of the specified sections led to litigation in Utah. Utah was admitted to the Union in 1896 as a public land state and therefore eligible for federal land grants. School sections were occupied, so the state selected from the public domain (open rangeland administered by the Department of the Interior, Bureau of Land Management) valuable oil shale land in place of the designated, but occupied, sections. The federal government refused to grant title and a suit followed. Ultimately, the Supreme Court held that although the law entitled Utah to land, selection must be of comparable land *In lieu* of the occupied land. Utah did not secure title to the land with the valuable oil shale resource. Although the issue does not arise frequently, this case established the standard of selecting alternative parcels of land in the form of the Doctrine of *In lieu* Selection. See *Andrus (Sec. of Interior) v. Utah,* 446 US 500 (1980).

Other Grants to States

The federal government has recognized the importance and economic significance of land ownership to the states and has conveyed land to the states through a variety of acts. In 1841, for example, the federal government granted 500,000 acres of land to each public land state, less prior "gifts." In 1850, Congress passed the Swampland Act, which gave title to swamplands to the individual states. This, of course, included wetlands, which now are a prime target for federal protection.

Swampland Giveaway

The Swampland Act followed an initial limited transfer of "worthless swampland" from the federal government to the state of Louisiana. Congress initially intended that a relatively limited amount of land would be transferred, some 5 to 6 million acres. As a result of fraud and misrepresentation by the state officials under pressure from private interests, more than 80 million acres were transferred to several states. Officials wrongly classified valuable land as swamps, including some 80,000 acres of prime agricultural land that, with the aid of state officials, were wrongfully transferred to large, private farming interests in California. As a result of this type of abuse, Congress ultimately terminated the giveaway of swamplands. However, Congress did not stop programs transferring title to land to the states and to private entities. Today, that type of land is protected as environmentally fragile wetlands.

Grants to States and to Individuals

The Homestead Act

In 1862, Congress passed three acts involving distribution of public lands, the impact of which forever changed the face of the nation. The first, the Homestead Act (43 USC 161 *et seq.*), allowed for the transfer of public land to individuals. Initially, this act allowed for a quarter section (160 acres) plus another quarter section to a married couple. Congress amended the initial act, recognizing that in many areas 160 acres (or even 320 acres) was not adequate to earn a living. Although many homesteads failed, and in many instances land barons accumulated vast expanses of land from disenchanted homesteaders, the Homestead Act truly opened the West to settlement by all, and made land ownership available to any person willing to work the land. Provisions of the Federal Land Policy Management Act passed in 1976, 42 USC 1701 *et seq.,* terminated the last vestiges of homesteading. This represents a vast turnaround in federal policy, from the giveaway represented by the Homestead Act to a policy of federal ownership expressed by FLPMA.

The Railroad Act

As the nation grew, the need for a communications and a transportation link became increasingly apparent. In 1862, Congress passed the Rail Road Act (12 Stat. 498, July 1862), which funded the building of the first transcontinental railroad. Grants of public land provided the basic financial incentive. The act provided a 400-foot-wide right-of-way, plus granted twenty odd-number sections of land in a 40-mile-wide band from the center of the right-of-way for every mile of track laid. The initial intent was that the railroads would sell the land for $1.25 per acre to finance the development and to encourage settlement. The outcome was the establishment of numerous enormous landholdings in the western United States. As a result of land trades with other interests, timber and agriculture, the pattern of land ownership today continues to reflect the impact of the act.

The Morril Act

Congress recognized a similar need for postsecondary education and the value of education to the general public. By grants to states at statehood, Congress provided support for public schools. Several of the original colonies boasted outstanding private colleges and universities. Through the provisions of the Morril Act of 1862, Congress took a giant step toward making college education available to the population at large. Congress granted land to the public domain states, the proceeds from the sale of which would be used to establish and support colleges of agriculture and the mechanic arts. Some of the nation's leading universities trace their roots to this act; in addition, subsequent related legislation established the research arm for agriculture, the Agriculture Experiment Station, and the extended learning arm, the Agricultural Extension Service. The institutions formed as a result of this act, and a subsequent act in 1890 to support the traditionally Black institutions, led to a system of colleges and universities known worldwide as land grant colleges. These are now world-famous comprehensive universities, today serving far more than the needs of agriculture.

The Homestead Act, the Railroad Act, and the Morril Act all involved distribution of the nation's land resources, and as such reflect land policy, and changes in land policy. Each has exerted a significant impact on the environment. For example, the Homestead Act led to the initial settlement of the Great Plains, and unfortunately, some of the serious soil erosion problems today trace to inappropriate land uses from destruction of native vegetation in an attempt to farm land that simply was not suitable for farming. The Railroad Act and related land exchanges among private parties and with the federal government have affected major patterns of land ownership and continue to affect timbering and conservation as well as issues related to wildlife habitat protection. The Morril Act and the subsequent emergence of the world's strongest and most extensive system of higher education have provided both the educated individuals essential to address today's environmental problems and the sites for much of the research in both technology and policy. The impact of these three acts far exceeds the initial intent of the legislation.

Special Interest Groups

Distribution of public land did not stop with grants to states and the acts just discussed; other special interests also benefited from the distribution policies of the government. Mining interests, for instance, have been beneficiaries of federal land policy, and the continuing policy has been the subject of public criticism.

Mineral Resources

The Congress of Confederation recognized the value of the nation's mineral resources. Although lands were open to entry, the federal government reserved, or claimed title, to one-third of the precious metals on public lands regardless of ultimate ownership of the land. With ratification of the Constitution, this reservation became ineffective. Congress essentially ignored mineral rights and the regulation of mining on public lands from 1807, when it passed legislation to allow leasing of lead mines in Missouri, Indiana, and Illinois to 1872. Various leasing laws passed from 1807 to 1846 proved to be ineffective, but did establish congressional power to lease public land and to regulate mining activities on public land. In terms of practical regulation of mining activities, the law of the mining camp prevailed, and in spite of stories to the contrary, this law proved, for the miners, to be effective.

In 1872, Congress reentered the picture with the General Mining Law (30 USC 22 to 39). In part, Congress acted in response to pressure as more conflicts over mining rights and land policy arose. This act, known popularly as the Hard Rock Mining Act, remains in force today. The 1872 act consolidated two earlier acts and set down the basis for establishing a mining claim and ultimately, by working the claim, for the miner to patent the title to it. With the death of homesteading in 1976 as part of FLPMA, the Hard Rock Mining Act represents the only way a private citizen now can claim title to public land. This illustrates a remarkable reversal of federal land policy that started with massive availability of public lands to the policy of the government now maintaining control. The evolution of policy suggests passing from a period of unregulated plenty, through a period of increasing demand, to regulation and now to control commonly by market force factors. Some policies that limit land distribution reflect more general government interest than market considerations *per se*.

The Public Trust Doctrine

Congress expected, and to some extent directed, that much of the land given to states would be sold and the proceeds used for various purposes, such as establishing colleges in the case of the Morril Act. However, in some instances, states were forbidden to sell specific parcels or types of public land because of the value of the land to the public at large. Such land is held by the state in the public trust. Although the Public Trust Doctrine is not widely invoked, courts have applied it to the sale of public land and to the state's authority to regulate wildlife and game animals. The doctrine stems from an 1892 Illinois case decided by the Supreme Court.

The facts can be summarized as follows. When Illinois was admitted to the Union, land ownership included the "bed and banks" of Lake Michigan bordering Illinois. The state, under rather questionable circumstances, granted a large portion of Chicago's waterfront property to the Illinois Central Railroad, a private business interest. Ultimately the state attorney general brought suit to revoke the grant. The Court had to decide whether the legislature could deprive the state of current and all future control of the land (lake bed and bottom) and overlying water. The Court viewed this land as unique and not the same type of property that the state normally would sell. It then decided the state held title to the land "in the public trust" so that the people of the state could enjoy the benefits of the property, which in this situation included navigation along the lake, fishing, and recreational activities. *Illinois Central Railroad Co. v. Illinois,* 146 U.S. 387, 1892.

Thus, this case gave birth to the Public Trust Doctrine, which imposes limits on the sale of resources of common interest and value to the people of a state. The Public Trust Doctrine has also been applied to the authority of a state to manage wildlife and restrict shipment out of state of legally taken game animals. See *Greer v. Connecticut.* 161 U.S. 519, 1896.

Obviously, for this doctrine to apply, a government entity must exercise ownership authority over some object or resource. No precedent exists, but the question occurs that given the extensive control certain governmental agencies exercise, or attempt to exercise, over various aspects of the environment, quasi-ownership could be inferred. If this position is accepted, then the government agency should be obligated to manage the resource following the tenets of the Public Trust Doctrine. In most instances, this is probably done, but a question could be raised about breaching this doctrine, such as when the government allows the sale by auction of air pollution credits, which, under very specific conditions, allows a business to exceed air quality restrictions.

REVERSAL OF THE GIVEAWAY POLICY

A superficial survey of the history of land acquisition and distribution suggests that the United States experienced a period first of acquisition, followed by a fairly extensive period of seemingly unabridged disposal, leading to the current policy of federal retention of title to lands. To be certain, acquisition had to precede distribution, which plainly it did. Without a doubt, from ratification of the Constitution to well into this century, federal policy favored land distribution to varied nonfederal interests, including private parties. Clearly, the federal government recognized the importance of land as a resource to public land states as expressed in the Equal Footing Doctrine. Nonetheless, even as the nation acquired land, certain land was withdrawn from entry by presidential order (executive order) or agency action. That is, private citizens could not secure patents on certain lands.

Initial Withdrawals

Protecting Interests in Timber

Initial withdrawals involved specific forest lands of unique value for the essential ships' timbers they produced. (Recall that the generic term "withdrawal" refers to a statute, executive order, or administrative order that changes the designated status of a parcel of land from available for entry to unavailable. It is generally considered to be a negative act, prohibiting certain land uses without specifying future uses.) The young nation recognized the value of timber assets, although, in some ways, those encouraging westward expansion viewed the forests as an enemy to be tamed by harvesting, or merely by clearing. Generally, the policy had allowed settlers to harvest timber for any necessary purpose. Although commercial harvest of timber constituted trespass, the government did little to stem the tide of timber harvest from the public lands until the close of the nineteenth century.

The National Parks and Forests

Following the Civil War, the voice of conservation became stronger, and Congress acted to establish greater control over the nation's timber resources. At the same time, environmentally sensitive organizations came to life. For example, the Sierra Club, currently a significant voice for conservation and environmental protection, was founded in 1892. Earlier, in 1872, because of its beauty, abundant wildlife, and unique geothermal features, what is now known as Yellowstone National Park was set aside as a "national pleasuring ground." Subsequently, President Theodore Roosevelt, an ardent outdoorsman and conservationist, by Executive Order authorized by Congress set aside or withdrew lands that became the foundation of the National Forests.

The First National Park

The executive withdrawal of Yellowstone marked the start of the modern era of federal land management, but a later event, passage of the General Revision Act of 1891 (16 USC 471 *et seq.*), represents greater impact and policy formulation and as such must be considered to be of greater significance to both federal land policy and to the management and preservation of the nation's forest resources. This act can be viewed as a basic environmental conservation act.

The act authorized the president to reserve millions of acres of public lands (effectively to withdraw them from public entry), which provided the resources now identified as the nation's national forests and national parks. In addition, the act repealed laws that had allowed relatively unregulated exploitation of the nation's timber resources by private interests. The Organic Act, as it is commonly called, was unique in that it granted the president the specific authority to "set apart or reserve lands"; yet, the Constitution vests in Congress the authority to manage the property of the United States. Prior to the Organic Act, the president had assumed the authority to withdraw or reserve lands by executive order as part of his executive authority or executive privilege. Passage of FLPMA in 1976 severely restricted both the assumed authority and that granted by the Organic Act for the president to reserve lands. The pattern of regulation of public lands—in this case, public lands that generally included valuable timber resources—reflects the trend of increasing the level of federal regulation of natural resources, and of the environment in general. For all practical purposes, the only legislated power available to the president to restrict entry to public lands is through the Antiquities Act.

Recent Presidential Withdrawal

In September 1996, the president, exercising his authority under provisions of the Antiquities Act (16 USC 431 *et seq.*), converted 1.7 million acres of "public land" in Utah into a national monument. This action met with mixed reactions. Environmentalists and conservationists hailed it as a brave environmental decision. The new national monument is rich in coal and is located in an area with high unemployment. Many local and state officials were less impressed. They criticized the action because it will prohibit coal mining, which will have a negative economic impact on communities in southern Utah and potentially throughout the state. The Antiquities Act authorizes such executive action to reserve land that qualifies as historic landmarks, historic and prehistoric structures, and other objects of historic or scientific interest on government (public) land.

In addition to limiting the distribution of land resources, the government has even acted to return or secure title to specific resources that are of unique national importance or value. In a variety of acts, Congress has authorized an agency to secure property for specific purposes. For example, although not well budgeted, the Endangered Species Act, 16 USC 1531 *et seq.,* authorizes the purchase of critical habitat.

THE EVOLUTION OF LAND RESOURCE MANAGEMENT POLICY

As a policy, the pattern of ownership of public land is fairly clear: from the Discovery Doctrine to conquest and purchase, to an era of open giveaway and, as land became scarce, a return to emphasis on federal retention of title to public lands. During this period, the management policy of the public lands evolved with strong environmental implications. With respect to freely available land in the United States, demand now clearly exceeds supply, and partially in response to this situation, the land resources are subject to increasing regulations.

The initial posture of resource management apparently was to exploit resources. The emphasis on granting ownership clearly focused on using the land and its resources. Even early forest management seemed to ignore possible damage. Of course, the set-aside of Yellowstone represents the first major protection step. This was followed by the Organic Act, which authorized the national forests. Following this, a series of acts addressed the wise management of the forests. All initially focused on the forest resource, as Congress mandated in the early legislation. However, the basic philosophy changed with time, and management became more complex.

MUSY as a Policy

The stated management policy now is one that will foster multiple use and sustained yield. This policy precisely reflects the Multiple-Use, Sustained-Yield Act of 1960. Although MUSY provided the support for uniform management of the nation's forests, the rangelands lacked such strengths. In 1976, Congress passed the Federal Land Policy Management Act, which empowered the United States Department of the Interior to manage the range resources of the nation with the same authority the U.S. Forest Service enjoys in the management of the national forests. This brought the same policy of multiple use/sustained yield to these lands as that adopted for the forests. For the nation, management has become a total systems approach and the interests of all users, from the timber and livestock interests to conservationists, hunters, and fishermen, are considered. Planning has taken new dimensions as the policy moves to the twenty-first century. In addition, the concerns of water quality and wildlife protection expressed in the Endangered Species Act have now become part of the management of these enormous land resources. The policy evolution has been from no management—because none apparently was needed—to recognition of damage and a response with extensive planning and broad regulation. To some extent, elements of the management process suggest that the final stage in the evolution of environmental policy, as it relates to natural resources, is controlled not by market considerations, but by less tangible factors.

CONCLUSIONS

Land represents one of the fundamental natural resources of the human environment. The sale and management of land is subject to extensive regulations, and historically governments, initially ruling families, controlled the ownership and transfer of land title. Current land policies in the United States reflect a virtually complete circle, from an initial policy of freely granting title to public lands to the government's now retaining title to its lands and, in some, instances seeking to restore title to lands formerly owned.

Many factors determine the value of land, and land-management policy has reflected this value. Agricultural uses set an initial basis for land value, and even today, agricultural zoning—laws that require land to be retained in agricultural uses—reflects the continued importance of this use. Timber, minerals, and grazing rights all contribute to land value, and all have played a role in the evolution of land-management policy in the United States. Water rights associated with the use of water are part of land management and ownership and are subject mainly to state laws. Riparian rights (the rights of owners of land on the banks of water courses related to the use of the water) run with the title to the land; appropriations can be sold or otherwise transferred. Groundwater is subject to less current regulation, but regulatory efforts are increasing.

Land management policy is a visible form of environmental regulation. With respect to public lands, the policy has evolved from one of land devoted to special interests (timber and mining are major examples) to the uniform adoption of management for multiple uses and sustained yield. This more complex management philosophy reflects the continuing evolution of environmental policy as it relates to the fundamental resource, land.

Clearly land is a fundamental resource to the nation. The bounty of land enjoyed by the United States represents a great wealth and strength because it is the foundation of the world's strongest agricultural system. The nation's interests are served by land management policies that protect its land resources.

QUESTIONS AND CONCEPTS FOR DISCUSSION AND RESEARCH

1. Discuss land as a natural resource and how and why it is—or should be—regulated by environmental laws.

2. Define or describe the concept of "land ownership" in FSA, and discuss the factors related to environmental issues that might limit absolute use of land owned in FSA.

3. Trace the acquisition of land by the United States from pre-Colonial days to the present.

4. Trace the land-acquisition and distribution policies of the United States and describe with examples how these policies have changed over time.

5. Cite and describe the major provisions of the significant legislation affecting federal land-use policy and management.

REFERENCES AND SELECTED READING

Coggins, George Cameron, and Charles F. Wilkinson. 1987. *Federal Public Land and Resource Law.* 2d ed. Mineola, NY: The Foundation Press.

5

The Evolution and Growth of Environmental Law and Policy

Environmental regulation started with the regulation of critical natural resources. Land is an obvious example, and resources associated with the land follow a similar pattern. In the early days of the United States, separating regulation of timber and mineral resources from that of the land was difficult, if not impossible. The growth of regulation of other resources may appear more obvious, in part because the regulation is more specific. The evolution of regulations related to health issues, commonly the regulation of the numerous forms of pollution, may appear simpler to trace because the focus ultimately is narrower, and the historic time frame generally much shorter. However, the narrow focus may be misleading. Examination of many of the major environmental acts reveals an initial legislative pattern of attempting immediately to resolve all issues, followed by a lengthy series of amendments that ultimately address manageable aspects of the initial problem.

The pattern of regulation of natural resources such as land is relatively easy to trace, based on the assumption that as the resource becomes scarce, regulation will increase. Although not as obvious, the same type of forces explain the evolution of most environmental regulations. Availability of the resource may not appear to be the issue, but reduction in the quality of the resource, or increased threat of harm, becomes the issue that explains increased regulation. For some factors, the early stages of the loss or reduction in quality are frequently not obvious. In addition, as suggested in chapter 3, concerns arise as a result of more sophisticated techniques to measure or describe environmental quality. This explains, in part, the sudden emphasis on a specific facet of the environment, such as the increased regulation of lead in the environment.

Medical science has long recognized potential harm from exposure to lead because of its toxic properties. Potential exposure to lead has included air pollution caused in large part by additives in gasolines, various sources in drinking water, and even food containers and utensils. Recently, lead in paint has become a serious concern in private housing. Rules effective in the fall of 1996 require home sellers to inform prospective buyers of potential lead hazards from paint, based on the age of the house and the chance that lead-based paint had been used. The new rules reflect several facts. First, technical advances have shown that the relatively small amounts of lead in paint can be harmful, particularly to small children. Second, exposure takes many forms, from flakes of old paint to lead vapor when old paint is removed, and the problems associated with disposal of building materials covered with lead-based paints. Similar concerns arise about asbestos in buildings, but to date the federal government has promulgated no asbestos regulations specifically affecting the sale of private homes.

MAJOR FACTORS IN THE GROWTH OF ENVIRONMENTALISM

Concern over the environment does not trace to a single date, event, or person. Nonetheless, several benchmarks provide a framework for discussion. Policies reflecting land resources and management, including withdrawal or reservation of land, provide a basic pattern of regulation from late in the eighteenth century to the present. The history of resource management of land parallels the growth of the nation, and is a continuing story.

The Impact of War

Technology

Many of the current environmental problems, and much of the resulting environmental policy and regulations, stem from the technology developed to support the efforts of World War II and events during and immediately following the war, although some legislative action followed more than a decade later. The war effort yielded numerous valuable products, many of which have led to matters of environmental concern: products ranging from pesticides and other agricultural chemicals to plastics and related synthetic compounds. The use of plastics between 1928 and 1958 jumped from about 4 million pounds per year to about 4 billion pounds per year (R. Testin, personal communication, January 1997). This use resulted in two sources of pollution: pollution from the manufacturing processes and pollution in the form of tons of waste that flooded landfills with discarded nonbiodegradable materials. In addition, nuclear power became a reality, and the medical use of radioactive materials skyrocketed, yielding problems of the disposal of nuclear waste.

The Population Explosion

Population growth, the World War II baby boom, represents perhaps the biggest single factor in environmental degradation. As population increases, the potential for environmental degradation increases. Increasing population places more pressure on finite natural resources—space, air, water—and increases demands for goods, the production of which further degrades the environment.

By the early 1950s, smog, a product of massive increases in automobile use linked with urban growth, became a serious problem around Los Angeles, California. The resulting deterioration of air quality and impact on health precipitated the initial federal clean-air legislation. Of course, the problems of smog, or loss of air quality, are not confined to the use of automobiles in Los Angeles; they reflect a more general symptom of urbanization and industrialization.

The News Media

The impact of mass media, particularly television, on the relatively sudden emergence of environmental concern and subsequent explosion of environmental regulation cannot be ignored. In the immediate post-World War II era, TV became a way of life, and today few events worldwide cannot reach the living rooms of America nearly instantly. The media expose the general public to major environmental problems and issues and serve a valuable educational function. Media exposure and public interest in recent years have brought many environmental issues into the political arena. The public now judges candidates for public office at all levels on their stance on environmental issues. The major party platforms have included specific environmental planks.

Social Unrest

Major events since 1950 clearly reflect media attention. From the late 1960s to the mid-1970s, the nation faced a variety of serious socioeconomic issues. These issues ranged from racial issues (related to school integration and economic and social-assistance programs such as the food stamp program), to the nation's economy (unemployment, job opportunities, and inflation), and to massive public opposition to the war in Vietnam. Activists asserted that the government's priorities failed to address critical domestic issues. These voices of criticism put increasing pressure on the government to act to protect the environment. Protest marches, political campaigns, and related activities became part of the daily media fare for TV, newspapers, and radio.

Three Strong Voices

Rachel Carson

Technology developed during World War II led to the development of an amazing array of chemical pesticides. Few can deny the impact they had on necessary food production to support the war effort and on higher crop yields and superior crop quality after World War II. Unfortunately, the chemicals that benefited crop production presented serious issues related to both food safety and environmental degradation. A single individual played the predominate role in bringing these issues to public attention, and federal laws and rules today reflect her concerns.

In 1962, Rachel Carson, a marine biologist from Pennsylvania, published *Silent Spring,* a book that met with immediate public interest. From her work and independent study, Carson developed a deep concern for damage to marine life and birds that apparently was the result of excessive and unwise use of pesticides. In *Silent Spring* she discussed the accumulation of toxic pesticide residues in the food chains of many forms of wildlife. She

catalogued apparent declines in populations of common birds and damage to their reproduction. Although her work appeared to some as an indictment of all agricultural chemicals
and those who used them, a more realistic interpretation is that she recognized the toxic nature of the newly available, very popular pesticides and had the courage to forcefully call
attention to potential harm. She called for restrictions on the use of pesticides to limit the
accumulation of toxic residues in the environment and thereby protect both food and
wildlife. She called for mandatory programs to educate users about the proper and safe
use of pesticides and about the potential toxic effects of excessive use on the environment.
Carson also encouraged minimum use of the least toxic pesticides available, with emphasis on developing alternatives to the general use of pesticides.

   Although others expressed similar concerns that influenced the development of federal laws, rules, and regulations, the voice of Rachel Carson, through *Silent Spring,* provided the catalyst and backbone for current federal regulation of pesticides. Through her
writing, she stimulated widespread interest in other environmental issues and problems,
particularly those associated with natural resource conservation and food safety, and her
adamant stance to minimize the use of pesticides certainly encouraged continuing national
research efforts in the technical field of biological control of agricultural pests.

Paul Ehrlich

Shortly after Carson's popular book exploded on the public, Paul Ehrlich, a respected population biologist and recognized research scientist, published *The Population Bomb.* In this
book, Ehrlich warned of imminent exhaustion of essential natural resources as a result of
uncontrolled population growth. He predicted that the planet would be unable to feed the
exploding population and that the rampant growth could not be slowed adequately in time
to avoid disaster. The idea of zero population growth (ZPG) rapidly emerged as a public response to Ehrlich's predictions. Although the dire predictions suggested by *The Population
Bomb* have failed to materialize, Ehrlich's writing generated massive public concern about
depletion of resources and focused attention on the undeniable fact that people cause environmental degradation. Although less active today, organizations supporting ZPG continue to stress limiting family size to ease the deterioration of the environment.

Gaylord Nelson and Earth Day

The drive for legislative action during this period of heightened environmental awareness
lacked a key element for success—an effective, dedicated political spokesperson. In spite
of growing public concern about the deterioration of many facets of the environment and
extensive media attention to environmental issues, environmental issues had not received
significant legislative attention, and environmentalists apparently could not identify an effective spokesperson or political friend in Washington. In the post-World War II era,
through the Korean War, and into the dissident period of the anti-Vietnam era of the mid-
1960s, Congress simply had not recognized the environment in general as a major concern.
Change waited on the political horizon.

   With one exception, Congress considered the deteriorating condition of the environment a political "nonissue." Senator Gaylord Nelson of Wisconsin saw the need to protect
the environment for future generations and sought to stimulate political and legislative action. He realized that effective protection of the environment required legislative commit-

ment and action. Although he successfully convinced President John F. Kennedy and other national leaders to undertake a national conservation tour in the fall of 1963, the tour failed to stimulate the desired political interest he realized was needed to generate significant legislation. As a result, he sought to develop interest in the public sector that in turn could pressure politicians. This effort succeeded beyond his greatest expectations.

Peace rallies, protest marches, and sit-ins characterized the mid-1960s protest of the Vietnam War and general dissatisfaction with the government, particularly in the eyes of America's youth. Building on the concepts of group activities, Nelson conceived the idea of a national environmental teach-in day, an event similar to the antiwar teach-ins. In September 1969 he announced this event for a day to be scheduled in the spring of 1970. The idea received an overwhelming positive response from across the nation. The event is now annually celebrated worldwide as Earth Day.

Participation in Earth Day events on April 20, 1970, more than achieved Nelson's goal of stimulating interest in environmental issues. Estimates show that over 20 million people (10 percent of the American population) participated in peaceful Earth Day demonstrations across the nation. The nation's youth were involved through the educational system—ten thousand elementary and high schools participated as well as some two thousand colleges and universities. In the face of the amazing response to the concept of Earth Day, Congress could no longer ignore the environment as a major political concern.

The concept of Earth Day has continued to thrive. In 1990, more than 200 million people in 141 countries celebrated the twentieth anniversary of Earth Day. The silver anniversary of Earth Day on April 20, 1995, saw a continually growing international commitment to environmental protection, much wider public interest in environmental issues, a public more broadly informed about environmental issues, and an impressive list of legislative and administrative actions taken since 1970.

RESOURCE MANAGEMENT

Although Earth Day brought great attention to the need for federal action to protect the environment, the federal government formulated significant resource conservation and management policy in the last century and has continued policy development into current legislation. The more visible, more recent (post-World War II) legislation has focused more attention on health-related pollution issues than on resource conservation, but Congress has certainly not ignored the management and protection of natural resources. The majority of legislation intended to manage the nation's lands or otherwise protect natural resources is found in two titles of the *United States Code:* Title 16, Conservation, and Title 43, Public Land.

Forest Management

Although predated by the formation of Yellowstone National Park in 1872, the General Revision Act of 1891 stands as the benchmark for comprehensive management of federal lands. This act set the tone for a new federal land policy—federal retention of title—instead of the prevalent policy of land giveaway. It empowered the president to set aside public land and repealed both the Preemption Act and the Timber Cutting Act, which had led to abuse of federal lands by private interests. The provisions of the General Revision Act resulted in massive areas of federal lands ultimately becoming national forests or national parks. The Organic Act, passed in June 1897 16 USC 475, *et seq.,* including amendments, defined the purpose and basic management of lands set aside as national forests. The act specifies, "No national forest shall be established, except to improve and protect the forest within the boundaries, or for the purpose of securing favorable conditions of water flow, and to furnish a continuous supply of timber for the use and necessities of the citizens of the United States." The Organic Act also places the administration of the national forests under the Secretary of Agriculture. The basic policy of the Organic Act has witnessed a gradual, but very significant, philosophical change that has significant environmental implications.

In 1944, Congress acted to specify that the national forests would be managed to ensure a sustained yield (16 USC 583). Although on its face, this move does not reflect a significant departure from the philosophy suggested by the Organic Act, clearly it requires conservation, not just timber harvest, to be a basis of management. Far more significant changes followed.

In June 1960, Congress significantly modified the management philosophy and applicable technologies through the imposition of the provisions of the Multiple-Use, Sustained Yield Act, MUSY, 16 USC 528–533. This new policy stated that national forests "are established and shall be administered for outdoor recreation, range, timber, watershed, and fish and wildlife purposes." Clearly the philosophy of MUSY presented significant new environmental issues to forest management. No longer was the forest to be viewed and managed exclusively as a source of timber.

Wilderness Preservation

Following the significant policy change reflected in the provisions of MUSY, Congress recognized the rampant deterioration of much of the nation's natural resources and the critical need to preserve shrinking, priceless, nonrenewable natural resources. As a result, in 1964, Congress passed the Wilderness Act, which created the National Wilderness Preservation System. The act established wilderness areas "to ensure that an increasing population, accompanied by expanding settlement and growing mechanization, does not occupy and modify all areas, leaving no lands in their natural condition." Congress further expressed its policy in terms of the purpose of the act, which was to secure for the people "the benefits of an enduring resource of wilderness." 16 USC 1131(a). In addition, Congress defined its concept of wilderness: "A wilderness, in contrast with those areas where man and his works dominate the landscape, is hereby recognized as an area where the earth and the community of life are untrammeled by man, where man is a visitor who does not remain."

Federal land policy clearly has evolved to include preservation of resources for future generations in the face of rapid population growth and the related deterioration of the varied resources. The Wilderness Act attempts to preserve a unique, extremely varied, and diminishing natural resource, the wilderness. However, as reasonable as this may seem, preservation efforts and regulations that restricted the use of public lands have been challenged on several fronts.

To satisfy the legislative intent of Congress, the Forest Service has established and enforces strict regulations in areas designated as wilderness. Generally, these regulations include the prohibition of operating motor vehicles in designated areas. Courts have sustained these strict regulations, as a 1965 Idaho case illustrates. *McMichael v. United States,* 355 F.2d 283 (1965, Ninth Cir).

The facts of *McMichael v. United States* are fairly simple. The Forest Service designated an area in the Boise (Idaho) National Forest as a primitive area. This designation prohibited the use of motor vehicles, and notices explaining the prohibition and rules were posted in the area. Federal officials cited two cyclists for operating recreational motor vehicles in the restricted area. The cyclists did not deny knowing of the rule, and they argued that the Forest Service could not restrict the use of the national forests.

They cited the Organic Act of 1897, referring to the stated policy that "No forest shall be established except to improve and protect the forest within" 16 USC 475. They contended that this statement established the purpose and use of the national forests and that no legislative authority existed for identifying primitive areas in the national forest system or provided a basis for prohibiting their actions. However, the court took a decidedly different view.

Without direct reference to the Wilderness Act, the court first found that fire protection, an effort clearly within the scope of authority under the Organic Act, justified limiting the use of vehicles. Next, the court cited MUSY and found it allowed special-use designations, such as wilderness or primitive areas. In a complete vindication of the Forest Service, and much to the joy of conservation/wilderness interests, the Ninth Circuit sustained the actions and policies of the Forest Service regarding legislative authority to designate areas for special uses.

Additional Preservation

Following MUSY and the enactment of the Wilderness Act, Congress recognized the need to act to protect a variety of special uses to ensure the implementation of the multiple-use concept and philosophy. Most of the legislation reflects congressional awareness of the impact of population growth on limited natural resources and a legislative intent to protect those resources and make them available to future generations while providing for regulated current use.

Following the Wilderness Act, Congress acted to protect specific uses and aspects of the nation's natural resources and, in 1968, passed the National Trails Act. This act focuses on four related goals or purposes: preservation of, public access to, travel within, and enjoyment and appreciation of the open outdoor areas and historic resources of the nation. 16 USC 1241. Congress further directed that the trails should be primarily near the urban areas of the nation, with secondary emphasis on scenic and historic travel routes of the nation located in more remote areas.

Congress specified the first two trails in the initial act: the Appalachian Trail, which covers over 2,000 miles along the Appalachian Mountains, from Mount Katahdin in Maine to Springer Mountain, Georgia, and the 2,300-mile Pacific Crest Trail from Mexico to the Canadian border in Washington. Subsequent amendments recognize nineteen specific trails, from the 1,000-mile historic Pony Express Historic Trail from Saint Joseph, Missouri, to Sacramento, California, to the famous Santa Fe Trail in the Southwest and the Potomac Heritage National Trail near Washington, D.C. The act includes provisions for additions and encourages maximum state participation in the trails program. Other acts continued to reflect this policy of preservation of special environments or of the environment for special uses and the need to provide environmental sanctuaries for an increasingly crowded population.

Congress recognized certain unique and irreplaceable features of America's rivers at the same time it recognized the need for the trails program. In the Wild and Scenic Rivers Act, 16 USC 1271 *et seq.,* passed on the same date as the Trails Act, Congress declared, "certain selected rivers of the Nation which, with their immediate environment, possess outstandingly remarkable scenic, recreational, geological, fish and wildlife, historic, cultural, or similar values shall be preserved in free flowing condition, and that they and their immediate environment shall be protected for the benefit and enjoyment of present and future generations." 16 USC 1271. In this legislation, Congress recognized the need to modify the policy of damming the nation's rivers. Clearly, Congress recognized environmental values that are not simply expressed in economic terms.

The Wild and Scenic Rivers Act requires congressional action to add a river or section of a river to the protected list, and it invites the governor of each state to nominate rivers for inclusion. Currently over 140 specific rivers and sections of rivers, with numerous individual, specific segments described, are protected by provisions of this legislation.

Specific regulations for these resources have been formulated as a result of each of these acts. The rules and regulations are found in the *Code of Federal Regulations,* starting at 43 CFR 8000 and continuing to 43 CFR 8370.

The provisions of MUSY, the Wilderness Act, the National Trails Act, and the Wild and Scenic Rivers Act illustrate the evolution of special regulation of environmental resources and reflect an increasing awareness of Congress of the need for and value of resources beyond economic considerations. Recall that initial resource regulation on timber and minerals reflected specific national or commercial interests.

The Range Resources

Much of the popular history of the western United States as told in the movies and novels involves either disputes over mineral rights or range grazing rights. Many of the disputes portrayed romantically by today's media in fact reflect serious controversies, many of which the government has resolved, but some of which continue. Mineral rights remain under the provisions of the Hard Rock Mining Act of 1872, 30 USC 22 *et seq.,* and many controversies reflect the application of state property law, and the "Law of the Mining Camp." Rangelands have been the recent target of increasing regulation.

The nation's range resources are concentrated in the West and are administered by the Bureau of Land Management (BLM), a unit of the Department of the Interior. Until fairly recently, BLM had relatively little authority to regulate range use effectively. Consequently, range conditions have deteriorated markedly as a result of constant overgrazing of the range.

The Concept of the Commons

The story of overgrazing the western range provides a nearly perfect modern-day example of "The Tragedy of the Commons." The basic story of the "tragedy" is simple, and the message clear and environmentally to the point: When a limited resource is subject to unregulated community use, slight overuse by any one individual causes little apparent damage. Unfortunately, the damage is cumulative—a little damage caused by each of a large number of individuals can destroy the resource for all.

Historically, the major controversies involved competition for use of the range resource, frequently between cattle and sheep producers. With limited federal guidance, state laws and state courts heard and decided many of these controversies involving federal lands. A 1918 Idaho beef/sheep controversy provides a classic example. *Omachevarria v. Idaho,* 246 US 343 (1918).

In the absence of enforced federal regulation of the use of public grazing lands, Idaho passed a law seriously restricting grazing sheep on public land. Cattlemen insisted sheep destroyed the range. Cattle interests succeeded in passing a state law that effectively prohibited grazing sheep on land previously grazed by cattle. *Omachevarria* challenged the law. The Court upheld this law that effectively excluded sheep producers from Idaho's public rangeland. The Court agreed with Idaho: "The police power of the State extends over federal public domain, at least when there is no legislation by Congress." Sixteen years later, Congress took its first major step to exercise federal control of the western rangelands by enacting the Taylor Grazing Act of 1934, 43 USC 315, *et seq.*

The law directed the Secretary of the Interior to establish grazing districts and authorized issuing grazing permits. It specified that preference be given to local landowners and allowed fencing the public land and the development of wells on the public land. However, the law failed to empower the Secretary of the Interior with adequate enforcement authority, favoring local advisory committees representing livestock interests. Thus, range deterioration continued as a result of continued overuse, although the government had acted to initiate control of the grazing lands.

FLPMA

In 1976, Congress addressed the need to exercise uniform management of the public lands through the provisions of the Federal Land Policy Management Act, FLPMA, 43 USC 1701–1784. This act represents several significant changes in federal land policy. It affirmed the emerging congressional policy that the federal government should retain title to public lands. It terminated acquiring title to public lands by homesteading, called for an inventory of the nation's public land resources, and specified that the government should receive fair market value for the use of the lands, a policy that allowed significant increases in fees charged by BLM for grazing permits, and it granted the Secretary of the Interior the same scope of authority over BLM land as granted to the Secretary of Agriculture for the management of the national forests. FLPMA also adopted the provisions of MUSY in terms of a multiple-use philosophy. Initially, livestock producers and state leaders did not willingly accept the newly asserted federal control of the nation's rangelands.

The Sagebrush Rebellion

In 1979, Senator Orrin Hatch of Utah introduced legislation to convey title to most of the range to the individual states. The state of Nevada also considered a bill to assume title to this land within its borders. The controversy became known as the Sagebrush Rebellion and focused on what the states perceived as inflexible federal management as a result of FLPMA. Ultimately, the federal district court decided the Nevada issue. *Nevada Ex Rel. Nevada State Board of Agriculture v. United States,* 512 F.Supp. 166, aff'd 699 F.2d 486 (9th Cir 1983).

Litigation started in April 1978, following the enactment of FLPMA. By notice published in the *Federal Register*, the Secretary of the Interior placed a moratorium on entry to all BLM lands in Nevada under the Homestead Act and the Desert Lands Act. Nevada argued that the federal government held the land in the public trust, could not deny entry to it, and in fact must convey it to state ownership. Nevada also argued that FLPMA violated its Tenth Amendment rights and the "equal footing doctrine" applied to all public land states on admission to the Union. Ultimately the Court refuted all arguments and found fully in favor of the government. Although the decision effectively ended the rebellion, it did not satisfy many interests.

Wildlife Management and Protection

By tradition, state governments exercise control over wildlife, fish, and game management. This common law concept traces to the rights of landlords to control hunting on their estates. This authority transferred to state governments in the United States, and a case late in the nineteenth century confirmed the policy. *Greer v. Connecticut,* 161 US 519 (1896).

The Court upheld a state law that prohibited shipping game birds out of state even when they were legally hunted. *Greer* challenged the law on the basis that it violated the Commerce Clause of the Constitution. The Court said, "Aside from the authority of the state, derived from the common law ownership of game, and the trust for the benefit of its people, which the state exercises in relation thereto; there is another view of the power of the state in regard to the property in game which is equally conclusive. The right to preserve game which flows from the undoubted existence in the State of a police power to that end, which may be nonetheless effectively called into play, because by doing so, interstate commerce may be remotely and indirectly affected." In its decision, the Court looked to numerous sources of law to strongly endorse the power of the state to manage wildlife resources. Regardless of this position, the right to manage is far from absolute, and states rights appear to be diminishing.

Federal intervention of wildlife management appears to be reasonable in certain cases. Situations involving interstate issues may be encountered, for example, with migratory waterfowl, and similar situations in which management involves international agreements. In recent years, federal control has reached further than these cases.

Wild Horses and Burros

In parts of the southwestern United States, wild horses and burros, the offspring of once-domestic livestock, roam freely on public and private land. Under favorable conditions, populations of these ancestors to domestic stock have increased to the point of damaging the range, or at least of competing with cattle for limited feed. Stock producers looked on them as a nuisance, and sought to reduce their numbers. Massive popular pressure forced politicians to act to protect these animals.

In December 1971, Congress passed the Wild and Free-Roaming Horses and Burros Act, 16 USC 1331–1440. This law described the wild and free-roaming horses and burros as of cultural and historic significance, to be protected from branding, harassment, and death. The act considered the animals part of the natural system of public lands and brought them under the protection of the federal government. It prohibited harming the animals, regardless of where they were found—on public or private lands—and required state cooperation in their management. Livestock interests opposed the law.

The opposition in New Mexico reached the courts, when that state sought to impose its own management strategy on the roaming beasts: *Klepp, Secretary of the Interior v. New Mexico,* 426 US 529 (1976). When New Mexico refused to cooperate in protecting the animals as required by law, the litigation ensued. The Court found that the wild horses and burros were property of the United States and that Congress had the absolute power, granted by the Constitution, to regulate the property of the nation. This appears to represent a significant departure from the policy stated by the courts regarding wildlife management authority as expressed in *Greer v. Connecticut.* One fact distinguishes the Wild Horses and Burros case from Greer: Greer clearly considered regulation of game animals. In the New Mexico case, the animals were not even wild animals, let alone game; they were feral animals—wild offspring of what had been domestic animals. Nonetheless, that case also suggests that the United States owns parts of the environment (natural resources) other than land. In recent years, the Congress, in the interest of protecting resources, has enacted additional protective legislation.

The Endangered Species Act

In 1964, prior to enactment of the Endangered Species Act, the Department of the Interior conducted a study of rare and endangered species of North American wildlife. The study revealed serious problems, which led ultimately to enactment of the Endangered Species Act, perhaps the best known and most controversial legislation protecting all forms of wildlife, including plants. The results of the 1964 study, and the subsequent increasing awareness of environmental degradation and depletion of natural resources—including the shocking recognition of the destruction of critical habitat for many species of animals and plants and the resulting rapid race toward extinction—demanded congressional action. Demands for protection came from two poles: protection merely for the sake of maintaining nature, and protection of species of potential, but unknown, value, frequently with the implication of medicinal value of plant species.

Congress responded with dramatic legislation in the provisions of the Endangered Species Act, 16 USC 1531, *et seq.,* passed in December 1973. In the act, Congress found, "various species of fish, wildlife, and plants in the United States have been rendered extinct as a consequence of economic growth and development untempered by adequate concern and conservation." This act recognizes various values of species—esthetic, ecological, educational, recreational, and scientific. 16 USC 1536.

The Endangered Species Act (ESA) is complex and powerful. The act clearly states its intent to identify endangered species and to protect them and the environment on which they depend. It recognizes two categories of species; the more serious are species facing extinction, designated as endangered, and the less serious are threatened species.

Provisions of the ESA

Nine major provisions provide a logical overview of the scope of the act:

1. Provisions for determining whether a species is endangered and for establishing an endangered species list.

2. Authorization to acquire land that is identified as critical habitat for an endangered species.

3. Requiring cooperation among states and between states and the federal government.

4. Requiring full cooperation among federal agencies coupled with the policy that the provisions of the act take precedence over any other conflicting legislation.

5. Encouraging international cooperation to protect endangered species, which includes the cooperation of the Secretary of Commerce in enforcing provisions of rules prohibiting import of products of endangered species, such as skins or hides.

6. Encouraging cooperation with the Western Hemisphere Convention.

7. Provisions for significant penalties for violations of the act.

8. Establishment of an endangered species committee.

9. Specification of what constitutes a prohibited action, focused on the concept of "taking."

Actions included in the description of the prohibited "taking" provide a clear perspective of the intended scope of regulation authorized by Congress. "No taking" of a representative of an endangered species means the absolute prohibition of the following: taking, harassing, pursuing, hunting, shooting, wounding, killing, trapping, or capturing. The Endangered Species Act includes protection of critical habitat on public and private lands to help ensure protection of designated species. The issue of the required protection of critical habitat on private land has raised a serious constitutional question. Because steps necessary to protect the habitat commonly restrict land use, owners have claimed that such restrictions amount to an unconstitutional taking of their property according to the Fifth Amendment.

Although some states have considered compensation for lost value, currently the courts have not considered such restrictions to constitute a taking, and the government has not compensated owners. This situation represents one of the major criticisms of the Endangered Species Act, and it is subject to review and congressional amendment at any time. It has become a political issue.

Endangered Species

The practical heart of the act is the list of endangered species. In the summer of 1996, the lists of threatened and endangered species included the following:

	animals	plants
endangered	320	434
threatened	430	526

See 50 CFR 17.11 and 17.12 for the current lists of endangered and threatened species.

The act specifies how species can be added to the list and requires the formulation of a recovery plan for each species listed as endangered. 16 USC 1533(f). The goal is that by following the recovery plan, species will ultimately be removed from the list. Some recovery plans have met with marked success: The whooping crane, the California condor, and the piping plover, a beach inhabitant, are recovering from near extinction. Efforts to reintroduce the gray wolf to Yellowstone National Park and the recovery of grizzly bear populations illustrate the potential positive impact of the act. The law requires implementation of the recovery plan, with priority given to those plans deemed by qualified professionals to have the greatest potential for success.

Judicial Interpretation of the ESA

The wording of the act suggests the most serious congressional intent regarding protecting endangered species and their critical habitat. In one highly significant case, the Court declared that Congress indeed intended this act to take precedence over all other actions. *Tennessee Valley Authority v. Hill,* 473 US 153 (1978). The facts in *Hill* are fairly simple.

Years prior to enactment of the Endangered Species Act, Congress funded, and the Tennessee Valley Authority initiated construction of, a major dam project on the Little Tennessee River near Knoxville, Tennessee. Funding for the dam project continued following enactment of the Endangered Species Act. A variety of interests opposed development of the project, but various efforts to stop it failed throughout the planning and development stages. Nearly all construction was completed and the floodgates were to be closed to flood the planned reservoir, when a scientist from the University of Tennessee identified representatives of an endangered fish species, the snail darter, in an area to be changed by the anticipated flooding. Although scientists demonstrated that the fish could be transplanted successfully and, in fact, were found in other areas, and despite the arguments that Congress had funded the project *after* enacting the Endangered Species Act and therefore must have intended the completion of the project, notwithstanding the endangered species, the Court prohibited closing the floodgates.

The Court recognized all the issues raised concerning funding and related matters, but it declared the congressional intent to be clear: This act was to take precedence over all others. The Court noted that the act did not require it to balance interests in applying the provisions of the act. The Court found a clear mandate; therefore, to protect the snail darter, the floodgates could not be closed, thereby preserving critical habitat of an endangered species, a species of undemonstrated economic significance.

Congress did not amend the Endangered Species Act as a result of this decision, but it did pass special legislation specifically authorizing flooding, in spite of the provisions of the Endangered Species Act. Thus, the Court's interpretation of the act remains, and its provisions are to be given preference over all other federal legislation.

CONGRESSIONAL STATEMENTS OF ENVIRONMENTAL POLICY

MUSY and FLPMA represent statements of policy, not substantive law that prohibits or requires specific acts. Such laws commonly provide the basis for formulation of rules by regulatory agencies and may indicate to courts the general intent of Congress to guide their decision making. By contrast, the Wild and Free-Roaming Horses and Burros Act and the Endangered Species Act both express policy, but they clearly express substantive law. To protect certain resources, specific acts are prohibited or required.

The National Environmental Policy Act

Purpose

The National Environmental Policy Act of 1969, NEPA, which became law in January 1970, represents one of the broadest, yet one of the most concise, statements of congressional concern over the environment. NEPA, 42 USC 4321–4370, is relatively short and provides general policy guidelines to the federal government. Congress clearly expressed its purpose in the act:

> To declare a national policy which will encourage productive and enjoyable harmony between man and his environment; to promote efforts which will prevent or eliminate damage to the environment and biosphere and stimulate the health and welfare of man; to enrich the understanding of the ecological systems and natural resources important to the Nation; and to establish a Council on Environmental Quality, 42 USC 4231.

In NEPA, Congress further explained the basis of many of its environmental concerns in the expression of a national environmental policy:

> The Congress, recognizing the profound impact of man's activities on the interrelation of all components of the natural environment, particularly the profound influences of population growth, high density urbanization, industrial expansion, resource exploitation, and new and expanding technological advances and recognizing further the critical importance of restoring and maintaining environmental quality to the overall welfare and development of man, declares it to be the continuing policy of the Federal Government, in cooperation with State and local governments, and other concerned public and private organizations, to use all practicable means and measures including financial and technical assistance, in a manner calculated to foster and promote the general welfare, to create and maintain conditions under which man and nature can exist in productive harmony, and fulfill the social, economic, and other requirements of present and future generations of Americans, 42 USC 4331.

The scope of these two introductory sections of NEPA reflects the depth of congressional concern about the environment. Congress recognized a national problem and also saw the need for cooperation among all interested parties. Actions of the Council on Environmental Quality called for by NEPA led directly to the establishment of the Environmental Protection Agency, the federal government's major environmental policy and enforcement agency.

The Environmental Impact Statement Requirement

One short section of NEPA expresses a key general policy provision with specific impact on activities of the federal government, the requirement to prepare an environmental impact statement, EIS, expressed in 423 USC 4332(C). This section, which applies to actions of the federal government states,

> The Congress authorizes and directs that, to the fullest extent possible: (1) the policies, regulations, and public laws of the United States shall be interpreted and administered in accordance with the provisions set forth in this chapter, and (2) all agencies of the Federal Government shall . . . (C) include in every recommendation or report on proposals for legislation and other major Federal actions significantly affecting the quality of the human environment, a detailed statement by the responsible official on—(i) the environmental impact of the proposed actions, (ii) any adverse environmental effects which cannot be avoided should the proposal be implemented, (iii) alternatives to the proposed action, (iv) the relationship between

local short-term use of man's environment and the maintenance and enhancement of long term productivity, and (v) any irreversible and irretrievable commitments of resources which would be involved if the proposed action should be implemented.

NEPA represents a federal policy commitment to environmental protection and calls for interpretation of laws in accordance with the provisions of the act: The policies of NEPA should be followed to the "fullest extent possible." This provides significant room for judicial interpretation. However, the Supreme Court found no room for interpretation of the application of the Endangered Species Act in *Hill*.

The Limits of NEPA

NEPA applies only to actions of the federal government, and it does not oblige the government to follow recommendations formulated by the EIS or suggested by required opportunities for public input to the EIS. The policy effectively requires the government to act with knowledge of the potential environmental consequences of a proposed plan. The five broad items to be considered suggest a serious examination, but the law does not require examination of all possible consequences, or even analysis of the worst-case scenario. NEPA, particularly the EIS requirement, has been subject to litigation and interpretation by the courts.

Challenging the Provisions of NEPA

Litigation related to the EIS requirement has taken two forms: challenges as to when an EIS is required and challenges concerning the adequacy of the EIS prepared by the government agency. The first challenge involves three considerations: (1) defining federal action, (2) defining the concept of "major" action, and (3) characterizing "significant" environmental impact. The federal element is fairly well established: It involves direct federal projects as well as other projects for which some type of federal permit is required, such as a permit to construct a nuclear power plant, or an activity requiring a federal license. Defining the limits of "major" action is more subjective and has generated more controversies. The current standard focuses on the commitment of resources, either monetary or otherwise. Commitment of funds is a major action, but budget development and strict planning activities have not uniformly been subject to the EIS requirement of NEPA. The final consideration, defining "significant environmental impact," presents even more difficulty.

The first hurdle is defining the human environment. NEPA seeks to assure all citizens of a safe and healthful environment. From this statement, clearly the provisions of NEPA must apply to the total environment, not just to the natural environment. Social and economic environmental consequences may be included in the determination of the environmental significance and impact of proposed government actions in addition to the impact on the natural environmental and resources. The definition of significant impact is subject to dispute too. Congressional intent is not clear, but obviously harm or potential harm to human health represents a "significant impact."

Conceptually, every governmental action has some potential to affect the human environment. The interpretation of NEPA has focused on reasonable, direct effects on any element of the human environment. The general issue of when an EIS is required has been fairly well settled. The accepted existing standards favor preparation of an EIS, although agencies required to prepare the statements protest the time, expense, and effort involved.

The affected public is invited to review and comment on the EIS for any specific project, which leads to the second major challenge to NEPA, adequacy of the EIS. When circumstances require an EIS, competing interests frequently dispute both the adequacy of the study leading to the EIS and the actions and alternatives suggested as a result of the study and the EIS. NEPA offers general guidelines for what constitutes an EIS, but lacks specific requirements. The act specifies five basic requirements to be included in an environmental impact statement. Controversy continues to arise over at least three of the criteria: characterization of the environmental impact of the proposed action, identification of unavoidable environmental effects, and alternatives to the proposed action.

Minimum Specifications for an EIS.   EIS requirements as formulated by the EPA have been published in the *Code of Federal Regulations;* see 40 CFR 1508.1 *et seq.* for the general rules describing an adequate EIS.

- The concept of "significantly" is defined as "including context and intensity." 40 CFR 1508.27.
- "Context" includes all of society as well as local and regional factors.
- "Intensity" is equated with "severity." With respect to intensity, the rules recognize a $3 \times 3 \times 3$ system of analysis involving actions, alternatives, and impacts. 40 CFR 1508.25.

The regulations do not require all types of actions, alternatives, or impacts to be addressed in an acceptable EIS. Elsewhere, the regulations provide ten measures of intensity of use that should be considered in formulating certain environmental impact statements. These are summarized as follows:

1. beneficial and adverse effects
2. degree of effect on human health
3. unique characteristics of geographic area, including factors such as proximity to historic areas or to prime farm land
4. degree to which effects on the quality of the human environment are likely to be controversial
5. degree of uncertainty of effects on the human environment
6. degree to which action or use would establish a precedent
7. relation of action to other individual actions that individually might be insignificant
8. impact on sites listed on, or eligible to be listed on, the Historic Sites Register
9. impact on endangered species
10. possible violations of federal or state laws

Although the Supreme Court did not address all issues, it has characterized aspects of an acceptable EIS under the requirements of NEPA. *F. Dale Robertson, Chief of the For-*

est Service, et al., Petitioners v. Methow Valley Citizens Council, et al., 490 US 342 (1989). The issue involved the Forest Service granting a special-use permit to develop a ski area on U.S. Forest Service land.

Scope of the EIS. Little disagreement existed concerning the requirement of an EIS. The project involved the federal government (the Forest Service) granting a permit to significantly change a portion of a national forest that could be considered part of the human environment. Controversy erupted over the adequacy of the EIS prepared by the Forest Service.

Ultimately the Supreme Court addressed two basic questions regarding the adequacy of an EIS: whether an EIS must include a fully developed plan, and whether it must present a worst-case analysis of potential harm. The EIS prepared by the Forest Service included five alternatives, ranging from no development to a plan that anticipated installation of sixteen ski lifts serving over ten thousand skiers per day. The studies included impacts on water, soil, vegetation, wildlife, as well as on land use and transportation, and considered the economic impact of the proposed development. However, none of the studies fully explored the impact off the site. Ultimately, the Forest Service recommended the second option, sixteen ski lifts serving up to 8,200 skiers daily. Opponents claimed that the EIS failed to include the worst possible consequences of the approved plan. The Court decided NEPA did not require a worst-case analysis, and the Court interpreted the EIS requirements of NEPA saying,

> The sweeping policy goals announced in Section 101 of NEPA are thus realized through a set of "action forcing" procedures that require that agencies take a hard look at environmental consequences . . . and that provide for broad dissemination of relevant environmental information. Although these procedures are almost certain to affect the agency's substantive decision, it is now well settled that NEPA itself does not mandate particular results, but simply prescribes the necessary process. Agencies are not constrained by NEPA from deciding other values outweigh environmental goals. *Methow Valley Citizens Council et al.,* 490 US 332 at 350.

The Court further declared that agencies must be allowed to interpret their own regulations. In the case of natural resources, an appropriate EIS does not require a worst-case analysis. In other circumstances, lower courts have required a worst-case analysis.

Opponents to the use of herbicides on rangeland insisted that an EIS required to secure permits to spray must include a worst-case analysis because of the alleged carcinogenic properties of the spray. The Court agreed, noting that the admission by the BLM that no level of spray could be perfectly safe obligated the agency to complete a worst-case analysis. *Save Our Ecosystem v. Clark,* 747 F.2d 1240 (9th Cir 1984).

Rules promulgated by the Council on Environmental Quality set the standard for the requirement of a worst-case analysis, although the criteria at times are not clear. According to the 40 CFR 1502.22(b) promulgated in 1982, a worst-case analysis is required when an agency is faced with incomplete or uncertain facts.

The Current Situation. The situation today remains unclear. The 1989 U.S. Supreme Court decision in the ski area permit case establishes the precedent that NEPA does not always require a worst-case analysis; it does not preclude the earlier decisions and rules. One fact is clear: NEPA represents a statement of policy, not substantive law. Even the recommendations derived from the most rigorous EIS do not bind an agency to a course of action. The philosophy is that with the EIS, the agency will make an informed, therefore a wise, decision. Many would challenge this position!

The Pollution Prevention Act of 1990

In recent years, Congress has indicated, through policy statements, a shift in emphasis in terms of pollution control. The Pollution Control Act of 1990, 42 USC 13101–13109, is a brief statement of this change in philosophy. Like NEPA, this act makes a statement of policy, in addition to substantive law, and it provides a basis for establishing congressional intent and the subsequent interpretation of laws.

The first section reflects congressional concern and a change in policy. In the statement of "findings," Congress notes that the United States annually produces billions of tons of pollution and spends millions of dollars controlling the pollution. It continues, noting that significant opportunities exist for industry to reduce or prevent pollution at its source and then admits that "opportunities for source reduction are often not realized because existing regulations, and the industrial resources they require for compliance, focus on treatment and disposal, rather than source reduction; existing regulations do not emphasize multi-media management of pollution; and businesses need information and technical assistance to overcome institutional barriers to the adoption of source reduction practices." 42 USC 13101(a). With these findings, Congress set a new policy direction for pollution control.

The policy stated in the 1990 act requires source reduction as the nation's primary attack on pollution: "The Congress hereby declares it to be the national policy of the United States that pollution should be prevented or reduced at its source whenever feasible." The policy continues that unpreventable pollutants should be recycled whenever feasible, and that the remainder that cannot be recycled should be disposed of in an environmentally safe manner. The act sets a priority for treating all types of pollutants: prevent, recycle, then dispose.

CURRENT LAND MANAGEMENT POLICY

The regulation of natural resources in the United States recognizes several complementary points. Land, or space, is no longer freely available and competition for varied uses can be intense. Placing a value on "undeveloped" land in traditional terms is difficult, but logic demands that environmentally fragile and unique areas be protected from unrestricted development. Governments at all levels have joined the federal government in efforts to limit development, including the purchase of lands to be retained as "wilderness." Problems of damage from overuse have extended to the national parks, and some parks have resorted to limiting visitor access to damaged or deteriorating areas. This includes requiring reservations for camping, limiting length of stays, and restricting motor vehicle access to many areas, and encouraging commercial camp areas adjacent to, but outside of, park property.

Ecosystem Management

The basic policy of multiple use/sustained yield has evolved now to encompass ecosystem management. This management policy requires consideration of the impact of an activity on an entire ecosystem, not just the target resource of the activity. For example, by federal (U.S. Forest Service) permits, timber harvest is allowed in the national forests. Determining the impact of a proposed timber harvest now must include consideration of effects on the interests of varied users of the forests, in addition to timber interests—hunters, campers, other recreational users, and preservationists. The impact analysis must also include consideration of longer-term effects—potential runoff from roads, siltation of rivers, lakes, and streams, and disruption of wildlife, particularly during mating seasons. These requirements are in addition to full compliance with the provisions of the Endangered Species Act. These factors and the multitudes of interactions among them now must be included, for example, in forest management plans required by federal forest management legislation and grazing allocation decisions for western rangelands managed by the Bureau of Land Management. These additional complexities add new dimensions to environmental impact statements required by NEPA as part of the timber harvest permitting or the grazing permitting process.

The Extended Effects of Land Management Policy

Land management also addresses other major environmental concerns. Protecting all forms of habitat also contributes to protecting biodiversity, an issue that includes two interrelated elements: protecting genetic diversity within populations of a single species and protecting the diversity of a species within a given community or ecosystem. Protecting genetic diversity protects the species against sudden environmental changes, such as the occurrence of a new disease. Protecting diversity within the community is essential to protecting the delicate natural food chain on which all steps are interdependent. Protection must extend to plants as well as animals, including insects, and must include the world of microbial life because of the critical role microbes of all classifications play in the natural recycling of energy through the food chain and decomposition of organic matter.

The Impact of Forest Protection on Air Quality

In the United States, the Clean Air Act expresses most efforts to protect quality of the nation's ambient air, which include steps to protect against the excessive accumulation of greenhouse gases. Protection of the nation's forests contributes to reducing the accumulation in the atmosphere of carbon dioxide, one of the greenhouse gases.

Through the biologically complex process of photosynthesis, green plants take in carbon dioxide and combine it with oxygen derived from splitting water molecules to form carbohydrates. Obviously, the greater the mass of green plants, the greater the photosynthetic activity. Concern over the destruction of rain forests involves two issues: the loss of massive photosynthetic capacity and the associated reduction in the removal of carbon dioxide from the atmosphere and the loss of biodiversity inherent in these natural areas. Although the scale is reduced, grasslands and other large areas also may significantly affect the carbon dioxide content of the air.

Mineral Exploration

Mineral exploration, including petroleum and natural gas exploration, represents multiple, continuing threats to the environment. In addition to the direct effects of mining or drilling, activities related to mining represent environmental threats. Most mining activities include developing roads and the associated problems of erosion, silt in streams, rivers, and lakes, and dust. Moreover, human activity may disrupt the habitat of wildlife, particularly during mating seasons. Some mining activities involve the discharge of toxic substances into surface waters, and heavy machinery is a source of many forms of pollution, much of which is associated with the consumption of fossil fuels.

Early federal policy encouraged mining and the exploitation of the nation's mineral wealth. Efforts have received favorable legislative action, and the Hard Rock Mining Act continues to provide the basic regulation of the industry. Other environmental regulations, including the Clean Water Act, make special allowances for mining activities. In recent years, Congress has come under increased pressure to review the provisions of the Hard Rock Mining Act and the status of mining on the public lands. Increased emphasis on resource preservation, public opposition, and the provisions of NEPA regarding granting permits on public land all suggest the need for more stringent regulations in the future. In part, these changes will be tied to the continued development of forest-management plans mandated by federal law and more uniform management of the extensive western rangelands by BLM under the authority of FLPMA.

A Matter of Population Growth

In the final analysis, a growing population imposes increasing demands on all types of natural resources, the supplies of which no longer can be considered limitless. These resources are conveniently combined under the umbrella of "land resources," and their management cannot be separated from that of the land. As resources become more scarce, greater restrictions must be anticipated. Policy changes reflect the growing demands and decreasing supplies. Many changes are regularly reported, such as the growing restrictions on timber harvest on public lands. The termination of homesteading by FLPMA certainly illustrates that demand for land exceeded supply. Other restrictions may be less apparent, but they protect the environment too.

Steps to reduce damage from overuse and regulations to restrict access to and use of sensitive areas in several national parks reflect the impact of population growth and are a unique example of supply exceeding demand. New regulations and policies include requiring reservations for camping, limiting stays for campers, limiting private vehicle traffic in parks, and even encouraging the development of private camp facilities outside of park property.

At all governmental levels, land and resource use is being limited. This is seen in simple things, such as permit requirements to cut firewood and even to cut a Christmas tree on national forest lands. Land use will be increasingly subject to permits and restrictions, and the permitting process for federal activities will trigger the EIS requirements of NEPA. The EIS will become an essential element of risk assessment and management for natural resources and the environment. It will have to consider numerous factors, many of which are subjective. Finally, NEPA and its EIS requirement apply only to federal actions, although some states have enacted an equivalent to NEPA with EIS requirements for state actions. This provides the opportunity for public input not otherwise available. Pressure will increase for all states to move in this direction as public interest in the environment and conservation continues to grow.

CONCLUSIONS

Environmental laws and regulations have evolved significantly in the history of the United States. This evolution includes both natural resources and health-related pollution. For land and related resources, the policy has changed from giveaway and exploitation to retention of title by the federal government and protection of resources. In addition to the policy of multiple use and sustained yield, land-use policy recognizes the importance of protecting certain aspects of the natural environment, and the government has even assumed and exercised ownership control of parts of the natural environment other than the land. Many of the laws and subsequent regulations are vague, but some express clear mandates. Courts have recognized the absolute protection of endangered species under the Endangered Species Act, and in spite of issues regarding the adequacy of EIS, NEPA clearly requires that the federal government act with knowledge in its projects affecting the human environment. In a clear statement concerning pollution, the federal government has said that prevention is the path of the future. In doing this, the government did not give up its massive regulatory efforts involving air, water, and the management of all types of waste. These are topics of the following chapters.

QUESTIONS AND CONCEPTS FOR DISCUSSION AND RESEARCH

1. Discuss the impact of World War II on the growth of both environmental issues and problems and environmental policy and laws.

2. Describe the impact of the writings and work of Rachel Carson, Paul Ehrlich, and Gaylord Nelson on the growth of environmentalism in the 1960s and 1970s.

3. In terms of the evolution of environmental policy, describe the impact of the following: the Organic Act, MUSY, FLPMA, Wilderness Act, National Trails Act, and the Sagebrush Rebellion.

4. What is the major feature of NEPA?

5. What are the major issues related to environmental impact statements? How have these issues been resolved?

6. What major policy change is expressed in the Pollution Prevention Act of 1990?

REFERENCES AND SELECTED READING

Carson, Rachel. 1962. *Silent Spring*. Boston: Houghton Mifflin.
Ehrlich, Paul. 1971. *The Population Bomb*. New York: Ballantine Books.

Graham, Frank, Jr. 1995. Earth Day 25 Years. *National Geographic* 187 (4) (April): 123–138.

Kubasek, Nancy K., and Gary S. Silverman. 1994. *Environmental Law.* Englewood Cliffs, NJ: Prentice Hall.

Newton, Lisa H., and Catherine K. Dillingham. 1994. *Watersheds: Classic Cases in Environmental Ethics.* Belmont, CA: Wadsworth.

U.S. Environmental Protection Agency. December 1989. *Glossary of Environmental Terms and Acronym List.* EPA 19K-1002. Washington, DC.

PART THREE

Pollution Control

6

Clean Air and Air Quality Considerations

INTRODUCTION

Clean air is not only desirable, but indeed essential for health. Although logically associated with today's industrial society, concern over deteriorating air quality and government regulations to promote clean air date from the thirteenth century.

Historical Perspective

By the thirteenth century, most of the available wood in and around London had been consumed, and the use of coal had increased dramatically. This use led to an equally dramatic increase in air pollution, which included more noxious materials such as sulfur dioxide, a source of acid rain and a currently recognized serious air pollutant. Odor from the pollutants became a problem that led to one of the earliest air quality laws—the prohibition of burning coal in London, enacted in 1273. Although not rigorously enforced, this law reflects the historic concern for control of the "annoyances" of air pollution.

Worldwide, the problem of deteriorating air quality is associated with two factors—urbanization, the concentration of housing and human activities, and industrialization, particularly manufacturing that requires the use of energy.

Table 6.1 illustrates the range of air pollutants affecting human health and natural resources, identifies sources of the various pollutants, and describes the most common damaging effects. The category "toxic pollutants" includes a wide array of industrial emissions, the control of which is mandated by legislation and many of which are specifically identified in the legislation or CFR.

Pollutant	Sources	Effects
Ozone. A colorless gas that is the major constituent of photo-chemical smog at the earth's surface. In the upper atmosphere (stratosphere), however, ozone is beneficial, protecting us from the sun's harmful rays.	Ozone is formed in the lower atmosphere as a result of chemical reactions between oxygen, volatile organic compounds, and nitrogen oxides in the presence of sunlight, especially during hot weather. Sources of such harmful pollutants include vehicles, factories, landfills, industrial solvents, and numerous small sources such as gas stations, farm and lawn equipment, etc.	Ozone causes significant health and environmental problems at the earth's surface, where we live. It can irritate the respiratory tract, produce impaired lung function such as inability to take a deep breath, and cause throat irritation, chest pain, cough, lung inflammation, and possible susceptibility to lung infection. Smog components may aggravate existing respiratory conditions like asthma. It can also reduce yield of agricultural crops and injure forests and other vegetation. Ozone is the most injurious pollutant to plant life.
Carbon Monoxide. Odorless and colorless gas emitted in the exhaust of motor vehicles and other kinds of engines where there is incomplete fossil fuel combustion.	Automobiles, buses, trucks, small engines, and some industrial processes. High concentrations can be found in confined spaces like parking garages, poorly ventilated tunnels, or along roadsides during periods of heavy traffic.	Reduces the ability of blood to deliver oxygen to vital tissues, affecting primarily the cardiovascular and nervous systems. Lower concentrations have been shown to adversely affect individuals with heart disease (e.g., angina) and to decrease maximal exercise performance in young, healthy men. Higher concentrations can cause symptoms such as dizziness, headaches, and fatigue.
Nitrogen Dioxide. Light brown gas at lower concentrations; in higher concentrations becomes an important component of unpleasant-looking brown, urban haze.	Result of burning fuels in utilities, industrial boilers, cars, and trucks.	One of the major pollutants that causes smog and acid rain. Can harm humans and vegetation when concentrations are sufficiently high. In children, may cause increased respiratory illness such as chest colds and coughing with phlegm. For asthmatics, can cause increased breathing difficulty.
Particulate Matter. Solid matter or liquid droplets from smoke, dust, fly ash, and condensing vapors that can be suspended in the air for long periods of time.	Industrial processes, smelters, automobiles, burning industrial fuels, woodsmoke, dust from paved and unpaved roads, construction, and agricultural ground breaking.	These microscopic particles can affect breathing and respiratory symptoms, causing increased respiratory disease and lung damage and possibly premature death. Children, the elderly, and people suffering from heart or lung disease (like asthma) are especially at risk. Also damages paint, soils clothing, and reduces visibility.

116

Pollutant	Sources	Effects
Sulfur Dioxide. Colorless gas, odorless at low concentrations but pungent at very high concentrations.	Emitted largely from industrial, institutional, utility, and apartment-house furnaces and boilers, as well as petroleum refineries, smelters, paper mills, and chemical plants.	One of the major pollutants that causes smog. Can also, at high concentrations, affect human health, especially among asthmatics (who are particularly sensitive to respiratory tract problems and breathing difficulties that SO_2 can induce). Can also harm vegetation and metals. The pollutants it produces can impair visibility and acidify lakes and streams.
Lead. Lead and lead compounds can adversely affect human health through either ingestion of lead-contaminated soil, dust, paint, etc., or direct inhalation. This is particularly a risk for young children, whose normal hand-to-mouth activities can result in greater ingestion of lead-contaminated soils and dusts.	Transportation sources using lead in their fuels, coal combustion, smelters, car battery plants, and combustion of garbage containing lead products.	Elevated lead levels can adversely affect mental development and performance, kidney function, and blood chemistry. Young children are particularly at risk due to their greater chance of ingesting lead and the increased sensitivity of young tissues and organs to lead.
Toxic Air Pollutants. Includes pollutants such as arsenic, asbestos, and benzene.	Chemical plants, industrial processes, motor vehicle emissions and fuels, and building materials.	Known or suspected to cause cancer, respiratory effects, birth defects, and reproductive and other serious health effects. Some can cause death or serious injury if accidentally released in large amounts.
Stratospheric Ozone Depleters. Chemicals such as chloro-fluorocarbons (CFCs), halons, carbon tetrachloride, and methyl chloroform that are used in refrigerants and other industrial processes. These chemicals last a long time in the air, rising to the upper atmosphere where they destroy the protective ozone layer that screens out harmful ultraviolet (UV) radiation before it reaches the earth's surface.	Industrial household refrigeration, cooling and cleaning processes, car and home air conditioners, some fire extinguishers, and plastic foam products.	Increased exposure to UV radiation could potentially cause an increase in skin cancer, increased cataract cases, suppression of the human immune response system, and environmental damage.
Greenhouse Gases. Gases that build up in the atmosphere that may induce global climate change—or the "greenhouse effect." They include carbon dioxide, methane, and nitrous oxide.	The main man-made source of carbon dioxide emissions is fossil fuel combustion for energy-use and transportation. Methane comes from landfills, cud-chewing livestock, coal mines, and rice paddies. Nitrous oxide results from industrial processes, such as nylon fabrication.	The extent of the effects of climate change on human health and the environment is still uncertain, but could include increased global temperature, increased severity and frequency of storms and other "weather extremes," melting of the polar ice cap, and sea-level rise.

TABLE 6.1 Summary of air pollutants with sources and effects. From *What You Can Do To Reduce Air Pollution*, EPA 450-K-92-002. U.S. Environmental Protection Agency. October, 1992.

State Initiatives

States established the initial air-quality regulations. In the face of virtually exploding industrialization in the 1880s, Illinois and Ohio, followed by New York and Pennsylvania, passed legislation limiting smokestack emissions. In 1890, Ohio limited the emission from stacks associated with steam boilers, a common source of industrial power. To some extent, limiting stack emissions led to taller stacks to disperse emissions, a practice still used in some areas. This practice led to an early pollution control philosophy—dilution of the pollutant—rather than reduction of the amount of pollutant produced.

As the nation grew, courts differed in their attitudes about pollution. Some courts insisted on a balancing between the "annoyance" of industrial air pollution and the economic benefits of industrial growth. Others found in favor of industry, and suggested private parties could move away from the polluter more easily than the polluter could move. The common law tort of nuisance provided a basis for early litigation involving air pollution.

Industrialization led to concentrations of people and, indirectly, to cars. As the number of cars increased, pollution from engine emissions—smog—became an increasing problem. In association with unique geographic and climatic features that restrict the flow of air from the central areas, smog in Los Angeles, California, became a vicious problem in the mid-1950s and led to the earliest federal air quality legislation. Increasingly, medical experts have come to recognize smog as a serious health threat.

The Impact of Smog

Although many would trace smog and the current extensive efforts to reduce this common pollutant of metropolitan areas to Los Angeles in the early 1950s, the term "smog" was coined in the early 1900s to describe the obnoxious mixture of smoke, fog, and other air pollutants and generally referred to any combination of smoke and fog. It now has a more precise definition. According to the EPA, smog is an air pollutant associated with oxidants (compounds that oxidize materials), and most smog is characterized as photochemical smog, which is smog caused by chemical reactions of various pollutants emitted from different sources. The most common chemicals include oxides of nitrogen and hydrocarbons, byproducts of the combustion of fossil fuels.

In addition to the physical irritation and common symptoms ranging from eye irritation to sore throats and similar minor problems, some scientists now conclude that smog and related air pollutants play a role in heart and lung disease conditions, and may contribute to asthma. Even the minute amounts of heavy metals and organic substances contained in smog can lead to neurological damage. The compounds comprising smog have been characterized as a carcinogen. In addition, air pollutants may harm more than humans.

General Effects of Air Pollution

Pollutants damage vegetation to the extent that in some areas ornamental plantings along streets and highways cannot survive. Pollutants such as smog may force the migration of wildlife capable of moving, but this is difficult to demonstrate because migration is also associated with increased concentrations of people and the related loss of habitat.

Certain pollutants, especially the oxides of sulfur and nitrogen, naturally yield acids that, over time, damage buildings and monuments. In addition, some scientists insist that these toxic compounds have resulted in "killing" lakes and streams, rendering them unfit to sustain animal, and in some instances plant, life.

Pollutants move with the flow of air. As a result, damage may occur many miles from the source of the pollution, and may be the result of exposure to small amounts over prolonged periods of time. Most of the "distance damage" has reportedly been the result of acid rain falling hundreds or thousands of miles from the site of the sulfur or nitrogen emission.

AIR QUALITY REGULATIONS

Early Regulations

Although air quality deterioration involved other materials and issues, by the mid-1950s, the federal government recognized smog as a serious problem and also recognized the need for some type of nationwide management/control effort. Initial efforts failed to remedy the problems.

The Air Pollution Control Act of 1955 represents Congress's first efforts to address the deterioration of air quality as a national problem. This act authorized federal funds for air pollution control research and authorized the surgeon general to investigate complaints raised by the states. Five years later, the Motor Vehicle Control Act of 1960 recognized automobiles as major sources of pollution and authorized research related to the effects of motor vehicles on air quality. Neither act proved to be effective in remedying the air pollution problems that were approaching crisis proportions: They failed to limit polluters or reduce pollution and failed to set standards to reduce pollution or prevent further air quality deterioration. The federal government saw its role as passive: to study and identify problems and to assist states, but not to regulate activities or set standards.

Initial Active Steps in Federal Air Quality Regulation

The Clean Air Act of 1963 continued much of the basic fact-finding policies of the earlier acts; however, it suggested a change in philosophy. The absence of any mandate to reduce air pollution represents the greatest deficiency of the Clean Air Act of 1963. The federal government continued to assume a passive role, but the act reflected increasing congressional concern about air quality and a willingness on the part of Congress to address this complex problem.

The Clean Air Act opened the door for federal action by authorizing the surgeon general to investigate problems on the request of state or local governments, or by his own initiative, and by authorizing the federal government to initiate independent studies addressing an expanded scope of potential problems. In addition, the act expanded the assistance to states authorized by its predecessor, the 1955 act. Although not mandated, the act allowed the federal government to address the abatement of specific problems, which initiated active remediation of air pollution at the federal level. Unfortunately, the act provided no basis for enforcement of abatement recommendations, nor did it establish any criteria or air quality standards on which to base abatement activities.

In 1965, Congress took a more dramatic step triggered by its increasing awareness of the negative impact of motor vehicles on air quality. The Motor Vehicle Air Pollution Control Act of 1965 represents a significant change toward active regulation to reduce air pollution for at least one source that Congress had previously identified as a serious problem: This act authorized the Secretary of the Department of Health, Education, and Welfare (HEW) to set motor vehicle emission standards. The target was simple—reduce the emission of pollutants from motor vehicles. Although potentially effective and logical in its intent, the act suffered from several weaknesses that limited its overall impact. The major weakness arose from the failure to establish enforceable standards. Congress effectively said this in subsequent legislation, and clearly stated it in hearings.

First, the act did not place the highest priority on emission reduction; it instead protected manufacturers by requiring the adoption of "feasible" steps to reduce pollution. The demands of the most vocal environmentalists would have required the most extensive efforts, disregarding simple feasibility and practicality considerations as well as economic considerations. Unfortunately, the concept of feasibility led to minimal steps, based on industrial interpretations of the definition of the term.

Second, the act included "economic considerations" in establishing feasibility. Both economic and feasibility criteria are seen in current regulations, and they represent sources of continued conflict between environmental and industrial interests. Related standards applied to other types of control include application of the "best available technology" (BAT). Economic considerations and practicability remain elements of many regulatory standards.

The conflicts related to standards for control reflect the reality of complex issues associated with risk assessment and management. Even in the early stages of air quality regulation, technology existed to detect minute amounts of pollutants. In addition, in terms of technical possibility, technology existed to effectively eliminate or drastically reduce many pollutants. In recent years, technology has advanced further, but the basic question of the reasonable limit to pollution reduction has not been answered. This question goes beyond technology, and is at the center of many issues when emphasis moves from risk assessment to risk management and considers actions of protecting and restoring the environment.

In some cases, the answer will ultimately be found in economic terms, the amount society is willing to pay for environment of a certain quality. Unfortunately, Congress has not been consistent in recognizing economics as a factor in setting environmental quality standards. For air quality, for example, economic factors are considered, but for protecting endangered species, economic factors are ignored.

Congress acted on more than vehicle-related air quality deterioration. The Air Quality Act of 1967 amended the 1963 Clean Air Act and reflected important changes in the regulatory philosophy and evolving legislative philosophy or policies. The introduction of air quality standards, which provide the basis for air quality control, represented the major change in the 1967 Air Quality Act. This act provided the basis for establishing air quality standards for ambient air, which allowed the identification of air quality regions—those that satisfied and those that failed to satisfy various standards.

The act suffered from two major weaknesses. First, it directed individual states to adopt air quality standards, and second, it lacked significant federal enforcement authority.

The act called for basic enforcement through committees and negotiation, but these provisions failed to provide adequate authority to address serious issues of interstate air pollution and continuing conflicts among diverse interests.

ONE GIANT FEDERAL STEP FOR AIR QUALITY IMPROVEMENT

Much of the Congressional action addressing air quality concerns and problems originated in the 1960s and the era of extensive popular pressure to "clean up" many components of the environment and increase efforts to protect vanishing natural resources. The exact impact of these efforts on legislation cannot be measured, but significant impact cannot be denied. This clearly is the case with the evolution of air quality legislation. After a series of apparently well-intentioned, but less than fully effective, steps, in 1970, the year of the birth of Earth Day, Congress took one enormous step toward remedying existing air quality problems and preventing future problems by enacting the Clean Air Act of 1970.

The Clean Air Act of 1970, 42 USC 7401 *et seq.,* represented a new focus on the serious problem of air quality and air pollution. Unlike other congressional actions, the Clean Air Act (CAA) did not ignore or repeal prior legislation; it included the heart of earlier air quality legislation and reflected massive congressional effort devoted to a complex subject and problem area.

The CAA now is found in Title 42 of the *United States Code,* The Public Health and Welfare. The act moves air quality legislation from Chapter 15B, the initial Air Pollution Act, to Chapter 85, Air Pollution Prevention and Control, and addresses the widest spectrum of air quality issues.

The CAA is an enormous and complex act, made even more complex by subsequent amendments; merely reviewing the size of the act reflects its comprehensive nature. The act itself extends from 42 USC 7401 to 7671q, covering 274 pages in the *United States Code,* excluding eight pages of index to Chapter 85. The CAA comprises over 170 sections and subsections covering effectively every aspect of air quality regulation.

Content of the Clean Air Act of 1970

A survey of the subject matter of the subchapters comprising Chapter 85 provides a manageable introduction to the scope of this gigantic body of legislation. The Clean Air Act of 1970 is divided into seven subchapters of varying length and general interest. Subchapter I, Programs and Activities, provides a general overview of the intent of the act and is the basis for the regulation of industrial air pollution. Subchapter II focuses on the regulation of vehicle-based air pollution. Subchapter III, however, seems to be out of place: It contains general provisions of the act and the basis for administering them. Subchapter IV—Noise Pollution—is a relatively short but important section, which Congress treated as part of air pollution. The fifth subchapter is designated Subchapter IVA, and it addresses the controversial subject of acid rain, or acid deposition in general. Subchapter V considers issues related to the wide range of permits authorized by the act. Subchapter VI, which replaces Subchapter I(c), is devoted to stratospheric ozone protection, a subject of controversy and significant concern to certain major environmental scientists.

Administration of the Clean Air Act, Subchapter III

Subchapter III, sections 7601 through 7621, provides the statutory basis for the administration of the act. Typical of many complex bodies of legislation, the general administrative provisions begin with a series of specific definitions that add clarity to the act. The administrator is defined as the administrator of the Environmental Protection Agency. This definition establishes the policy that Congress has placed the administration and enforcement of the provisions of the act under the authority of the EPA. The act broadly defines "air pollutant" to include

> any air pollution agent or combination of such agents, including any physical, chemical, biological, radioactive (including source material, special nuclear material, and byproduct material) substance or matter which is emitted or otherwise enters the ambient air. Such material includes precursors to the formation of any air pollutant, to the extent the Administrator has identified such precursor or precursors for the particular purpose for which the term "air pollution" is used.

At first reading, this definition appears long and cumbersome, but careful scrutiny suggests that Congress intended to include the widest scope of substances possible under the regulatory authority of the act and intended that the technical expertise of the EPA would be employed to identify specific pollutants. This breadth of intent is confirmed in the statement in definitions (42 USC 7602[g]) that says all language that refers to welfare includes effects on soil, water, crops, vegetation, man-made materials, animals, wildlife, weather, visibility, and climate changes as well as property damage, economic losses, and personal comfort and well-being.

Other terms that provide general understanding of the act include "stationary source," described as any source of air pollution other than vehicles. This clearly suggests the act considers two distinct sources of pollution, stationary and mobile sources. In addition, the act defines a "major stationary source" as one that emits 100 tons or more of any pollutant per year. Several other subchapters also include appropriate definitions for the subject matter they present. In addition, definitions provided by Congress offer technical guidelines and frequently reflect policy or legislative intent.

The Clean Air Act specifically grants the individual private citizen the right to sue to have the provisions of the act enforced without first showing that a violation caused the individual some form of damages. This right is for *injunctive relief,* a court order requiring someone to perform a certain act, or refrain from performing a certain act, such as polluting the air in a way prohibited by the act.

Congress clearly recognized competing economic interests in the provisions of the Clean Air Act. In spite of the obvious need for air quality protection and improvement, Congress also reacted to the economic realities of imposing standards and rules on industries in the United States. Thus, the force of the act is cushioned by specified economic considerations.

In a major policy statement, the Act, 42 USC 7617, directs the administrator to complete a detailed economic impact assessment of proposed air quality standards or regulations prior to publishing any notice of proposed rule making as required by the Administrative Procedure Act. The assessment must include at least the following factors:

1. the cost of compliance with the proposed rules, regulations, or standards;
2. the potential effects of the proposed rules or standards on inflation or economic recession;
3. the potential effects of the rules or standards on competition, particularly as related to small businesses;
4. the effects of the rules and standards on consumer costs; and
5. the impact of the proposed rules and standards on energy costs.

The act does not require the administrator to give highest priority to these considerations, but it clearly directs and allows them to be included in decision making. To this extent, the assessment required under the provisions of the Clean Air Act carries the same obligations as the response of any federal agency to the findings expressed by an environmental impact statement mandated by NEPA.

National Air Quality Standards, Subchapter I

Subchapter I establishes much of the regulatory basis for the entire CAA. This subchapter, entitled Programs and Activities, initially comprised four parts, A, B, C, and D. Congress repealed Part B, Ozone Protection, and subsequently included this complex issue as Subchapter VI, Stratospheric Ozone Protection. Subchapter I includes regulatory authorizations affecting the two major groups or sources of pollution—stationary and mobile sources—and establishes the general regulatory framework for air pollution prevention and control. It specifically provides for the regulation of emissions from stationary (industrial) sources.

The title of Part A, Air Quality and Emission Limitations, identifies the subject matter of the legislation, but does not really express the extent of the regulatory authority granted by Congress or the basic policies on which regulation shall be based. In the first section, 42 USC 7401, Congress explained the basis for its actions in terms of its "Findings of facts," a statement that justifies congressional action and the powers authorized under the provisions of the act.

Congress cited four general points in its statement of the facts on which the CAA is based. First, Congress recognized the impact on air quality of a growing population expanding in metropolitan areas that frequently cross state borders. Next, Congress considered the growth in the complexity of sources and types of air pollutants, including the increasing use of motor vehicles, that threaten health, agriculture, and transportation. In the third finding of facts, Congress expressed a basic policy: "air pollution prevention . . . and air pollution control at its source is the primary responsibility of the states and local government." Finally, Congress recognized the problem as so great as to require federal leadership and assistance to develop air pollution prevention and control programs. The statement of state responsibility remains a constant issue because the federal government requires states to comply with numerous rules and regulations (in many environmental areas in addition to air), but it fails to provide adequate support for states to comply with the requirements.

A Statement of Purpose

In addition to this general finding of facts, Congress expressed its general purpose for the CAA in Part A of the first subchapter. Like the "Findings of facts," the "Declaration of purpose" provides an overview of the breadth of congressional concern and the broad scope of regulatory authorization intended by the provisions of the CAA to be granted to the administrator. The initial purpose recognizes two general objectives to protect and enhance air quality: (1) to promote human health and welfare, and (2) to promote the nation's productive capacity. The act calls for a balance between health and welfare and industrial growth. The second major purpose calls for a national research effort focused on the control and prevention of air pollution. The third purpose, in keeping with the policy that the states must assume primary responsibility for air quality control, calls for federal assistance to the states to formulate and implement air quality control programs. The final major thrust calls for regional air quality control efforts.

Basic Provisions for Regulating Air Quality

The provisions of the CAA apply to ambient air. This term is repeatedly defined in the act, but in the simplest sense, it is outdoor air, air to which the general public has access.

Six sections in Part A of Subchapter I comprise the heart of the regulatory authority and basic regulations of the Clean Air Act; this includes 42 USC 7407 through 7412. These six sections effectively address the congressional findings of fact and implement the declared purpose of Congress. The sections appear redundant because in several instances one section identifies pollutants and another requires formulation of standards to control those pollutants. In addition, the initial pollutants considered by Congress appear to receive special treatment in terms of air quality consideration, but this is not the case.

Section 42 USC 7407, Air Quality Control Regions, affirms the congressional finding of fact that the individual states must assume responsibility for air quality control. Congress then mandates that each state meet this responsibility "by submitting an implementation plan for such State which will specify the manner in which national primary and secondary ambient air quality standards will be achieved and maintained within each air quality control region in such state." This section requires the states to meet uniform national ambient air quality standards, but allows the individual states, through the provision of an approved State Implementation Plan (SIP), to specify how the national standards will be achieved and maintained.

To carry out its SIP, the act requires each state to identify air quality control regions and to determine whether the region is or is not in compliance with primary and secondary ambient air quality standards established for specific pollutants. "Attainment regions" meet the established ambient air quality standards, whereas "nonattainment regions" fail to meet the established standards for one or more pollutants. Thus a given region may be an attainment region for one pollutant and a nonattainment region for another.

The statutory authority and directive to establish national primary and secondary ambient air quality standards appear in 42 USC 7409. The primary standards must focus on protection of human health, such that the attainment and maintenance of the standard will protect human health and allow an adequate margin of safety; the standard must be more than a minimum health safety standard. The attainment and maintenance of the secondary standards must protect public welfare from known or suspected harm from the pollutant. In addition, the secondary standards must protect the environment from harm from these pollutants.

Criteria Pollutants

The EPA has established primary and secondary national ambient air quality standards for six pollutants: sulfur dioxide, particulate matter (such as dust), carbon monoxide, ozone, oxides of nitrogen (more than just nitrogen dioxide specified by Congress in the act), and lead. The EPA considers these "criteria pollutants," because the law required the agency to develop health (science) based standards as a foundation for setting permissible atmospheric levels.

Human Health Effects of Criteria Pollutants

Medical science has documented harm caused by pollutants to nearly all essential body systems and parts. The National Association of Physicians for the Environment (NAPE) has reported extensively on specific types of pollutants and the harm they cause to various systems and parts of the human body. The following involve only criteria pollutants:

1. Lungs are damaged by nitrogen oxides and dust. Nitrogen oxides are products primarily of the combustion of fossil fuels and fertilizers. Particulate matter comes from smoke, as well as windblown dust and dirt. Asbestos comes from a variety of uses in older buildings, including insulation, and it is known to cause severe lung damage with long-term exposures.
2. All six criteria pollutants can damage the upper respiratory system, nose, throat, and sinuses.
3. Ozone increases the severity of asthma attacks if it does not actually trigger attacks.
4. Carbon monoxide limits the essential oxygen exchange function of blood; exposure has the effect of suffocation.
5. Lead, asbestos, and ozone all have been linked to heart disease.
6. Lead can severely damage the central nervous system; even low rates of exposure can cause behavioral changes. Young children and pregnant women are most susceptible to harm.
7. The immune system can be damaged by ozone.
8. The male reproductive system can be damaged by exposure to lead, which can also cause kidney damage.
9. Eyes are damaged by dust and particulate matter.
10. Because it affects the nature and amount of ultraviolet light reaching the earth's surface, ozone may be considered a secondary cause of most forms of skin cancer.

Understanding the type of harm a pollutant causes frequently provides a basis for prevention or remediation of the harm. For pollutants, the best solution seems to be to help minimize exposure by reducing the source of exposure. Although not fully effective, significant and effective steps have been taken to reduce many pollutants. The task is far from complete, and pollution remains a serious health threat.

The Requirement for State Plans

Implementation responsibilities of the ambient air quality effort imposed on the states by 42 USC 7407 and 7409 are detailed in 42 USC 7410, which provides the details and requirements of the mandated state implementation plan. This section requires first that states formulate a state plan that complies with the law and is acceptable to the administrator. Plainly stated, states must comply with the standards published in the appropriate CFR, such as 40 CFR 50.1. Exact methods of compliance are left to the states, and some flexibility in time is allowed, so long as the three-year deadline is satisfied and good faith efforts are initiated.

A Criticism of the CAA

The ambient air quality efforts have met with a variety of criticisms. One common criticism centers on the fact that nonattainment regions differ dramatically regarding the extent of their deviation from the established standards. Commonly the deviation reflects basic differences among regions in terms of existing industry and other natural factors that affect the concentration of a regulated pollutant. For example, a twenty-four-hour average ozone concentration standard applied nationwide might be violated only a few hours on only a very few days per year in an eastern Montana community, whereas the same standard might be regularly breached in a large, industrialized, otherwise significantly polluted metropolitan area. Critics suggest that nonattainment in the "Montana" situation does not represent the serious condition reflected in the "industrial" area and that the standards fail to recognize these very relevant differences. These criticisms may have merit, but ultimately either some type of uniform standard must be established or every situation must be treated separately, and adequate resources are not available for that specialized level of regulation.

Criteria pollutants provide the basis of classifying a region as "attainment" or "nonattainment" with respect to air quality. Based on this classification, the CAA provides the authority to regulate the emission into ambient air of an enormous array of hazardous pollutants. The primary regulatory emphasis is on major sources of pollution, but the act does not ignore small-scale polluters from its regulatory scheme. Moreover, stricter emission limitations are imposed on nonattainment than on attainment regions. The subject of emission permits and permitting regulations is covered in Subchapter V of the act.

STATIONARY SOURCES OF POLLUTION

The act directs the administrator to publish and periodically revise a list of air pollutants, "emission of which, in his judgment, cause or contribute to air pollution which may endanger public health or welfare", 42 USC 7408(a)(1)(A). The law further requires that air quality criteria be developed for pollutants on this list.

The CAA imposes specific definitions, technical restrictions, and guidelines to aid the administrator in determining the pollutants to be included on the list. For any listed pollutant, the CAA requires the administrator to utilize the latest scientific technology to anticipate potential damage and to consider specific factors in determining standards for emission limits. These include everything from variable factors, such as climatic conditions that might affect the nature or damage caused by the pollutant, to potential interactions with other pollutants in the air.

The final two critical sections of Part A, 7411 and 7412, narrow the focus of the part to industrial sources of pollution, or "stationary sources." Section 7411 sets the regulatory framework for "new stationary sources" of pollution. This section includes several definitions that are critical to understanding the impact of the law it expresses and reflects the basic policy formulated by Congress.

1. "Standard of performance" refers to the level of emission control that can be achieved using the best system of emission reduction, considering not only air quality but also costs, energy use, and the impact on other environmental effects. This definition again reflects the fact that Congress anticipated that the administrator would balance certain conflicting interests, such as air quality and cost.

2. "Stationary source" is any building, structure, facility, or installation that emits or may emit air pollutants. Obviously, given this definition, Congress intended to create the broadest scope of regulatory authority possible under the act.

3. "New source" is defined as any stationary source of pollution whose construction or modification began after publication of the regulations.

Section 7411 requires the administrator to identify stationary sources of air pollution and categories of such sources. After identifying these sources, the administrator must formulate and publish rules establishing standards of performance for various pollutants within a category. This grouping of sources into categories allows similar sources to be regulated in the same manner while recognizing differences between categories that justify different standards.

The categories and emission standards promulgated under this section appear in detailed rules published in 40 CFR 60, *et seq.,* which encompasses 784 parts divided into 75 subparts. Of these subparts, all but three are devoted to the regulation of specific categories of stationary sources of air pollution, including standards for designated "criteria" pollutants. The categories covered in the subparts represent virtually every facet of manufacturing and processing in the United States today. The standards and guidelines range from those for petroleum refineries (Subpart J) and small industrial-commercial-institutional steam-generating units (Subpart Dc) to those volatile organic compounds emitted by synthetic organic chemical manufacturing industry (SOCMI) reactor processes (Subpart RRR) and magnetic tape coating facilities (Subpart SSS). For each of these categories, the CFR provides specific guidelines or standards of performance to comply with the act.

In some ways, Section 7412, Hazardous air pollutants, represents the simplest portion of the act, and in other ways it is the most detailed. This section defines hazardous air pollutants to be regulated under the provisions of the act, provides a series of definitions, and contains an initial list of pollutants to be regulated. The law requires that, as far as possible, these pollutants be consistent with the categories established under 42 USC 7411. This section specifies that no pollutant listed can be emitted at a level greater than the established standard, which provides the basis of enforcement of the emission standards established by the act. The section also allows states to establish standards more rigorous than those set out by 42 USC 7412.

Required Compliance with State Implementation Plans

The CAA requires compliance with the SIP within each state, and provides enforcement authority that includes civil penalties of up to $25,000 per day for violations by any major source polluters and criminal penalties for serious, intentional violations. Violations of emission standards set for hazardous pollutants are also subject to penalties. However, the act provides for exceptions to avoid economic local hardship. For instance, the law favors use of local fuels and allows deviations from the air quality standards, if compliance with emission standards would prevent the use of such fuels and would lead to local economic hardship. This is another example of the balancing the act requires and the continuing policy of Congress to consider more than environmental issues: clean air considerations versus "local" economic issues.

Preventing Air Quality Deterioration

The provisions of Part A of Subchapter I represent only a fraction of the regulatory authority authorized by Congress. Congress expressed additional concerns and the basis for more extensive regulation in its declaration of policy for Part C (Congress repealed Part B and reenacted it as Subchapter VI). Part C expresses the intent of Congress to ensure no further deterioration of air quality in the United States. The congressional declaration of purpose targets five concerns:

1. Protect public health and welfare from actual or potential adverse effects of air pollution beyond the provisions of ambient air standard attainment;
2. Protect and enhance ambient air quality of national parks and similar federal facilities;
3. Ensure economic growth consistent with maintaining air quality;
4. Ensure that emissions of pollutants from one state will not interfere with the implementation of the plan in any other state; and
5. Ensure the most careful and thorough consideration of requests to allow increased air pollution.

Each state must include in its implementation plan steps to ensure that air quality will not further deteriorate significantly.

Part C designates the entire United States as either Class I or Class II with respect to application of its provisions. Class I areas are limited to international parks, wilderness areas (larger than 5,000 acres), national memorial parks larger than 5,000 acres, and national parks larger than 6,000 acres. Class II includes all attainment areas and areas that are otherwise unclassified. Obviously, nonattainment areas are considered and efforts are directed to the improvement of air quality in such areas, not merely to its protection. The distinction between Class I and II is reflected in allowable increases in levels of various pollutants. Class I areas receive greater protection, a policy that is in keeping with the basic policy of protecting these areas while recognizing the increased need for and use of such areas.

In addition to the SIP required by 42 USC 7410 in response to the general provisions of Section 7407, Part D, 42 USC 7501, requires each state to formulate and implement a plan that specifies how that state will make "reasonable further progress" in achieving attainment status for regions designated as nonattainment regions. The plan must show how the state will achieve attainment conditions by the applicable date set by the administrator. Attainment must be achieved as rapidly as possible, and within at least five years from the date of designation of the region as a nonattainment region. The plan must include the following provisions:

1. Implement all reasonably available control measures as quickly as practicable. Note that the concepts of "reasonably available" and "practicable" give the administrator great latitude in deciding whether a plan is acceptable and adequate. However, such administrative latitude frequently is the basis for disputes.

2. Provide for "reasonable further progress," which is defined as "annual incremental reductions in emissions of the relevant air pollutant as are required by this part or may reasonably be required by the Administrator for the purpose of insuring attainment of the applicable national ambient air quality standard by the applicable date."

3. Include a comprehensive inventory of all sources of air pollution.

4. Identify and quantify the emission of any pollutants to be allowed under the plan.

5. Obtain permits to construct and operate new or modified major stationary sources.

6. Include enforceable emission limitations, economic incentives, and other control measures.

7. Comply with 42 USC 7410(a)(2)—the requirement for a SIP—which includes provisions for enforceable emission limitations and monitoring techniques.

8. The administrator may allow a state to use equivalent modeling, emission inventory, and planning procedures.

9. Develop contingency measures should the plan fail to make the required "reasonable further progress."

Provisions are made to revise plans found to be inadequate and for modifications if air quality standards are relaxed.

APPLICATIONS OF TECHNOLOGY

The EPA has established detailed air pollution emission standards for nearly every type of industry. These are the standards to attain or maintain for compliance with the CAA. Technology plays the key role in industrial compliance with these standards.

Removing Particulate Matter

"Particulate matter" is a general term for solid or liquid particles found in the atmosphere. Currently, air pollution standards for particulate matter are based on PM-10, the fraction of particles ten micrometers or less in diameter. The primary standard to be attained is an annual average of such particles of fifty micrograms per cubic meter of air, or less.

Over 80 percent of the particulate matter considered to be an air pollutant occurs as "fugitive dust," dust generated by agricultural activities and construction and dust from unpaved roads. Nonagricultural activities, fuel combustion, transportation, and industrial processing share equally in about 6 percent of the particulate pollution; fires and other natural causes account for the remainder. The prohibition of burning garbage in open dumps and limits on the use of wood burning stoves have contributed significantly to the reduction in particulate matter.

Three principles have been applied to devices used to remove particulate matter from industrial exhaust systems.

1. Exhaust gases are discharged by swirling them through a cone or funnel-like structure. Centrifugal force pushes the particulate matter to the perimeter of the device, where the accumulated particles can be collected.
2. Electrostatic separation involves applying an electrical charge to particulate matter; the particles are collected on a plate of the opposite charge and gathered for disposal.
3. In some instances, a "simple" filter system is used: Discharge air is passed through a room-sized vacuum cleaner bag, and particulate material is filtered from the air and retained in the "bag."

Unfortunately, cleaning the air produces another environmental problem: The collected "dust" is frequently high in toxic materials, such as heavy metals, that require special considerations for safe disposal. Thus, an effort to clean the environment produces an additional problem, but at least the particulate pollutants are removed from the air and under control for safe disposal.

These physical/mechanical methods, however, are not effective for many air pollutants. A variety of other devices have been developed, and the law requires continued efforts to develop effective technology.

Removing Sulfur Dioxide

Sulfur dioxide can be removed from the air by using "scrubbers" that take advantage of basic chemical properties of the pollutant. Air polluted with sulfur dioxide is passed through a scrubber, a fine spray solution of lime. The pollutant reacts with the calcium and precipitates as nontoxic calcium sulfate. The chemistry may appear simple, but sophisticated equipment is required to handle the materials and regulate quantities treated.

Ozone Control

Unlike other pollutants, ozone, the most widespread of the criteria pollutants, is not produced directly by an industry. It instead is the product of interactions among other pollutants, particularly nitrogen oxides, which are produced by the combustion of fossil fuel, and volatile organic compounds, which are also products of combustion as well as by-products of chemical and petroleum industrial manufacturing activities. Efforts to minimize these pollutants directly affect ozone as well. The most significant progress has been made in efforts to develop clean fuel for automobiles, but the severity of the ozone problem demands continued efforts. The technical details of automotive and petroleum engineering efforts to reduce emissions of nitrogen oxides and volatile compounds are beyond the limited technical scope of this discussion. An important fact to note is the requirements for continued improvement in technology so that air quality can be restored without limiting industrial productivity.

Success in Reducing Lead Pollution

Technology linked with regulations can reduce air pollution effectively. The reductions in atmospheric lead illustrate this point clearly. The regulation was fairly simple: prohibition of the use of lead fuel additives. Technology yielded cleaner fuels and efficient engines that do not require lead. That same inventive technology can provide solutions for other, equally serious problems.

A Unique Example of Technology

Part of the technology to improve air quality involves increasing energy efficiency, thereby decreasing consumption and the emission of pollutants. Technology is industry specific, and some efforts to improve energy efficiency have yielded other forms of air quality improvement. Some programs sponsored by the United States Department of Energy (DOE) address fuel economy and clearly are part of a total effort to improve air quality. Consider a dramatic example involving a small industry.

Fabricating glass products, decorative bottles and other containers, windows, TV tubes, fiber optic materials, and insulation, requires high energy inputs. Processes for many products require furnace temperatures of 2800 F (about 1500 C). Generating this level of heat requires large amounts of fuel, electricity, or both. Consuming the fuel releases a variety of pollutants, including smog-causing nitrogen oxides.

A glass-manufacturing industry developed a new type of furnace that reduced pollutants and increased energy efficiency. The heart of the process is conceptually simple: Use pure oxygen rather than air (about 80 percent nitrogen and 19 percent oxygen) to burn the fuel. This conversion eliminated the major source of nitrogen, and the oxygen system burned the fuel more efficiently. The process produced amazing environmental results: Nitrogen oxide and carbon monoxide emissions reduced 80 percent, particulate matter emissions reduced 25 percent, natural gas consumption reduced up to 15 percent, and electrical consumption cut by up to 25 percent.

This process was commercially initiated in 1996 and has spread worldwide in the glass-manufacturing industry. It received the USDOE 1996 Best in Category: Industrial Technology Award.

Developing technology and implementing regulations cannot be approached in a vacuum. Technology is expensive, and the expenses ultimately are passed on to the consumer and/or the taxpayer. Hard issues still must be addressed in establishing the level of pollution that is acceptable.

EMISSION STANDARDS FOR MOVING SOURCES

Automobile Emission Control

Subchapter II considers specific standards for pollutants generated by motor vehicles. These standards are tied to Subchapter I in three ways: (1) the general concern about air pollution expressed by Congress; (2) the congressional call for research for clean fuels; and (3) the general air quality criteria expressed in Subchapter I, 42 USC 4708(1), that include both stationary and mobile sources of air pollution. Passenger cars and small trucks receive much of the attention of this subchapter, although not the entire focus. Two groups of standards are authorized by this subchapter: standards for engines and separate standards for fuels (gasoline, with major emphasis on gasoline additives). The major pollutants from moving sources include hydrocarbons (products from burning fossil fuel, such as gasoline), nitrogen oxides (which contribute to smog), carbon monoxide, and particulate matter. Fuel additives, such as tetra ethyl lead, represent a major source of lead as an air pollutant. This portion of the act calls for engine testing, and the CFR provides specific engineering standards under which individual tests must be completed.

Part A, the majority of this subchapter, is devoted to motor vehicles. This part authorizes the administrator to establish emission standards for new vehicles and engines. These standards address reducing emissions of hydrocarbons, carbon monoxide, and nitrogen oxides and present timetables for achieving emission reductions. However, provisions that allow time extensions to meet these standards have been cited as a major weakness of this portion of the act. As a result of these provisions, many of the specific standards set for 1995–96 have not been fully satisfied. Nonetheless, implementation of the standards has led to measurable improvement in air quality in numerous metropolitan areas.

Part of the improvement is directly attributable to the requirements for pollution control devices on all new cars in the United States coupled with penalties for removing these controls. Individual states must require the federally prescribed devices, and they are free to require additional control devices. California has set the trend in requiring auto emission control devices that exceed federal standards.

In addition to reducing emissions by improving engines and emission controls, this subchapter seeks to reduce pollutants by improving fuels and by limiting the use of fuel additives that contribute to air pollution. Perhaps the most significant aspect of this effort is the prohibition of the use of lead as an additive to gasoline. At one time, additives containing lead were common elements of premium grade gasoline and enhanced engine performance. Unfortunately, burning such fuel released thousands of tons of lead compounds into the atmosphere annually. For years, the medical profession has recognized health hazards from exposure to lead. The health benefits of reducing emissions of this well-documented, widespread, dangerous substance cannot be denied. The act addresses this issue directly. The sale of gasoline with lead additives is prohibited; moreover, the manufacture and sale of engines requiring leaded gasoline is illegal and subject to significant penalties. These provisions of the law have been extremely successful.

Figure 6.1 illustrates the impact on humans of prohibiting the sale of fuels containing lead. Although many pollutants have been reduced in the past two decades, the decrease in lead measured in ambient air is the most dramatic and is explained by the provisions of the act. Other pollutants have not received such rigorous attention, but they are not as readily identifiable with a single source, such as leaded gasoline. This figure clearly illustrates that progress can be made in pollution control with appropriate regulations properly enforced.

In addition to prohibiting additives containing lead and regulating other fuel additives to reduce pollutants, this subchapter calls for improvement in the basic nature of gasoline to reduce further the emission of dangerous pollutants. This emphasis popularly is known as the clean fuel effort or initiative. Provisions of the act support research on fuels, and other provisions require development of cleaner-burning fuels. Specific pollutants targeted for reduction include benzene, 1,3 butadine, polycyclic organic matter, acetal aldehyde, and

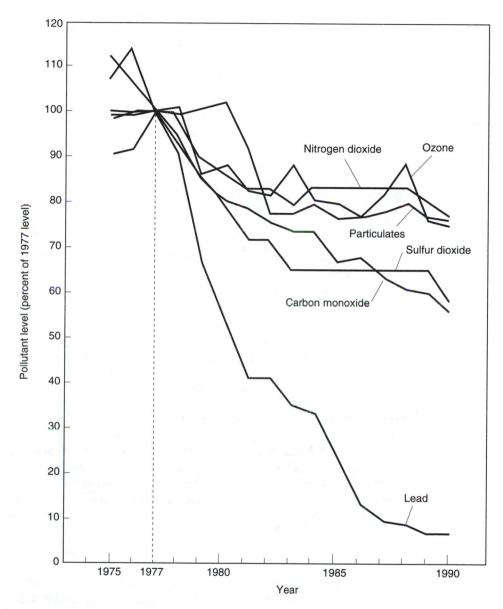

FIGURE 6.1 Changes in the level of six air pollutants expressed as the percent of the 1977 level. The marked reduction in lead is attributed in large part to the prohibition of lead additives in gasoline. EPA data; redrawn from Nebel and Wright, *Environmental science: The Way the World Works.*

formaldehyde. Specific limits are placed on the emission of sulfur and benzene. The act specifies precise minimum standards for gasoline for both summer (the high ozone, or baseline period) and winter use. These specific criteria, which clearly illustrate the details of the

Fuel Property	Standard
API Gravity	57.4
Sulfur, ppm	339
Benzene, %	1.53
RVP, psi	8.7
Octane, R+M/2	87.3
IBP, F	91
10% F	128
50% F	218
90% F	330
End Point, F	415
Aromatics, %	32.0
Olefins, %	9.2
Saturates, %	58.8

TABLE 6.2 Specific properties of gasoline for summertime use set by Congress; 42 USC 7545(10)(B)(i). Generally, Congress does not enact such detail, but leaves standards to a regulatory agency. Congress directed the EPA to formulate additional standards, but these mandated minimums reflect the deep congressional concern over air pollution caused by gasoline consumption.

act and attention given to the problem by Congress, are summarized from the act in Table 6.2.

Part B of this subchapter addresses questions and problems associated with emissions from aircraft engines. It authorizes the administrator to formulate standards, but any action must be in conjunction with the secretary of transportation, and safety cannot be compromised. To date, this short part has had comparatively little effect, except in terms of authorization to study the problems.

Clean Fuel Technology

Part C, which considers the complex issue of alternative fuels, relates clearly to the fuel regulations in Part A. The emphasis on alternative fuels reflected by this part, coupled with available grain from which to produce alcohol, led to the initial efforts to introduce gasohol, a gasoline/alcohol mixture with clean-burning characteristics, to the American public in the 1970s. In addition to these factors, uncertain foreign oil supplies contributed to the emphasis on the development of gasohol. Although the product has not taken over the fuel market, real potential for continued use remains.

The emphasis on clean fuels has directed significant technical attention toward the chemical makeup of gasoline. Efforts have included the development of highly oxygenated fuels whose combustion yields less carbon monoxide than standard gasoline. Although technically feasible, some of these efforts have been criticized because the anticipated reduction in pollutants could be achieved more efficiently by regulating a relatively small number of vehicles that, for a variety of "mechanical" reasons, produce excessive emissions. The mechanical reasons are many and varied. Old worn vehicles are a major problem because of excessive oil consumption and related smog production. Carburetion and ignition problems fall into the same general category. Poor maintenance of pollution control devices also contributes to the problems. In addition, evidence suggests that these "super fuels" may damage parts of the fuel systems of older cars, causing leaks and potential fire hazards. Although the act looks to the use of technology, clearly it illustrates that even the most advanced technology does not always yield practical solutions. Thus policy and regulations should not be based exclusively on emerging technology.

Potential Fuels

Other clean-fuel efforts that have received government attention and support include natural-gas-powered vehicles, and even the development of electric cars. Although not a part of the Clean Air Act, support for the development of new, efficient, dependable mass-transport systems in major metropolitan areas from coast to coast must be considered a significant effort to reduce vehicle traffic, thereby reducing air pollution.

The EPA has continued to emphasize the conversion from conventional motor vehicle fuels, gasoline and diesel, to "clean fuels." Clean fuels display two complicated, but environmentally friendly attributes: They emit fewer hydrocarbons, and the emitted hydrocarbons are less toxic and react more slowly to produce smog. Vehicles using clean fuels could reduce smog emissions by up to 90 percent, and reformulated fuels could reduce smog by as much as 25 percent. The generally recognized advantages and disadvantages of six common clean fuels are summarized in Table 6.3.

Space Technology and Clean Fuel

Chrysler Corporation reported the application of elements of space-age technology to overcome the disadvantages of electric cars noted in Table 6.3. Chrysler proposes the use of fuel cells, devices used extensively in the space industry, to produce hydrogen required to generate electricity. The process would use gasoline as a source of hydrogen but, unlike direct combustion, fuel cell technology is virtually emission free and can increase mileage by up to 50 percent. Vehicle range would increase from the current 100 to 150-mile limit to 400 or more miles. Costs currently prohibit practical applications, but the potential is obvious. Part of the rationale for continuing to work with gasoline stems from economic considerations: the existing distribution system nationwide and businesses associated with it.

Noise Abatement

Noise abatement is the shortest subchapter included in the act, and was part of the original 1955 air quality legislation. Although noise is different from the pollutants considered by the vast majority of the act, Congress recognized it as a problem related to air pollution with

Fuel	Advantages	Disadvantages
ELECTRICITY	• Potential for zero vehicle emissions • Power plant emissions easier to control • Can recharge at night when power demand is low	• Current technology is limited • Higher vehicle cost; lower vehicle range, performance • Less convenient refueling
ETHANOL	• Excellent automotive fuel • Very low emissions of ozone-forming hydrocarbons and toxics • Made from renewable sources • Can be domestically produced	• High fuel cost • Somewhat lower vehicle range
METHANOL	• Excellent automotive fuel • Very low emissions of ozone-forming hydrocarbons and toxics • Can be made from a variety of feedstocks, including renewables	• Fuel would initially be imported • Somewhat lower vehicle range
NATURAL GAS	• Very low emissions of ozone-forming hydrocarbons, toxics, and carbon monoxide • Can be made from a variety of feedstocks, including renewables • Excellent fuel, especially for fleet vehicles	• Higher vehicle cost • Lower vehicle range • Less convenient refueling
PROPANE	• Cheaper than gasoline today • Most widely available clean fuel today • Somewhat lower emissions of ozone-forming hydrocarbons and toxics • Excellent fuel, especially for fleet vehicles	• Cost will rise with demand • Limited supply • No energy security or trade balance benefits
REFORMULATED GASOLINE	• Can be used in all cars without changing vehicles or fuel distribution system. • Somewhat lower emissions of ozone-forming hydrocarbons and toxics.	• Somewhat higher fuel cost

TABLE 6.3 Summary of clean fuels considered to reduce air pollution, with advantages and disadvantages for each.

From *Clean Fuels: An Overview*, EPA-F-92-008.

Fact Sheet OMS-6. U.S. Environmental Protection Agency. January 1993.

at least some common causes, particularly crowding or urbanization. This subchapter calls for abatement of noise at federal facilities; it otherwise authorizes no noise regulations, but calls for study of the problems associated with noise as a pollutant.

ACID RAIN

Although acid rain (or, more generally, acid deposition) is the result of the emission of specific compounds subject to the previously discussed regulation by provisions of the CAA, Congress viewed the problem as serious enough to deserve specific, special consideration. This controversial topic is addressed in Subchapter IV-A of the act. Apparently, the inclusion of two subchapters both designated IV (Noise, just noted, and Acid Rain) reflects a simple numbering error without legislative significance. The subchapter devoted to acid rain is designated Subchapter IV-A and bears no relation to Subchapter IV.

In 42 USC 7651, Congress justified the provisions of this subchapter in its expression of facts and its purpose in enacting the legislation. Congress found that acid compounds represent a general threat to ecosystems, resources, and public health. It also found that burning fossil fuels constituted a major source of acid depositions, and that the pollutants had become an international issue because winds carried them great distances across international borders. The purpose of the legislation, simply stated, is to reduce damage by reducing certain emissions—sulfur and nitrogen oxides—with the target initially to reduce the annual emission level of sulfur dioxide by 10 million tons from the 1980 level and the emission of nitrogen oxides by about 2 million tons.

Respected scientists differ on the impact of acid rain. Few deny that specific air pollutants, notably sulfur dioxide, contribute to acid rain. The issue assumes international proportions in that Canada and, to a lesser extent, Scandinavian countries insist that acid rain resulting from sulfur emissions in the United States is the leading cause of lost fish production in lakes and streams. Although evidence that acid rain comes from American sources is quite conclusive, arguments continue that they cause the reduced productivity. Evidence opposing blame includes the measurable impact of acid rain changing the pH of rivers, lakes, and streams, and suggests natural phenomena that could be responsible for the existing conditions.

Presidents Carter and Bush both made acid rain reduction priority items, and the CAA continues to reflect this priority. The act also recognizes practical economic considerations that are reflected in a variety of provisions and in one very unique feature.

The CAA identified coal-burning electrical generating facilities as prime sources of sulfur emission, and Subchapter IV-A includes very specific emission limitations for individual generating units. The act grants individual emission allowances to specific electrical generating units. The allowance program includes a highly unique feature: Under specified conditions, individual unit owners or operators may sell their allowances to others if the owner does not require the allowance. A unit that is operating below the allowed emission level may sell its authority to emit sulfur to a unit that cannot operate at its designated emission level. Effectively, this says the government allows the sale of the right of individuals to pollute the air. The situation is not quite that extreme, although many strongly disapprove of the auction program for any purpose. Specific regulations to avoid overall reduction of air quality restrict the areas in which allowances can be bought and sold. In spite of the protective restrictions on the use of purchased allowances, environmentalist groups have sought to purchase allowances to prevent industries from discharging additional pollutants represented by the allowances.

PERMITS AND THE PERMITTING PROCESS

Subchapter V, Permits, provides a basis for the enforcement of the major provisions affecting stationary sources as well as acid rain regulations. The act requires permits for the operation of major sources of pollution (sources subject to regulation under the provisions of 42 USC 7411 and 7412, New Stationary Units and Hazardous Pollutants, respectively) as well as for "affected sources" defined in Subchapter IV-A (a unit subject to emission reduction requirements). The basic rule is simple: It is unlawful to violate a permit requirement. Of course, for sources that require permits, it is also unlawful to operate the source without a permit. A major provision of the permit requirement states that every permit issued must have an enforceable emission limitation and standards. The additional requirement of site inspections of sources that are issued permits adds force to the enforcement policy.

Although the CAA places greatest emphasis on major sources of pollution, it does not ignore small businesses. The act calls for states to develop programs parallel to the programs for major sources that are appropriate for small businesses. In terms of required permit fees, the act recognizes the potential economic burden on regulations on small businesses and authorizes either the state or the administrator to make appropriate adjustments.

OZONE AND STRATOSPHERIC OZONE PROTECTION

The final subchapter of Chapter 85 addresses the controversial issue of protection of atmospheric ozone. Part of the controversy stems from the fact that the act identifies ozone in ambient air as a serious pollutant and seeks to reduce emissions, yet it also contains extensive provisions to protect ozone in the atmosphere. Providing a distinction between the two sources would reduce the conflict. Stratospheric ozone is not part of the troposphere, the part of the atmosphere near the surface of the earth that humans breathe.

In the stratosphere, rather than acting as a pollutant, ozone plays a critical role in filtering (holding) high energy (short wave) solar radiation. If this radiation were to reach the earth's surface, massive climatic changes associated with increasing temperatures could occur. The temperature changes would be attributed to a greenhouse effect. The increased, high energy solar radiation is reflected by the earth's surface as lower energy, longer wavelength radiation. This radiation cannot escape through the earth's atmospheric envelope, in part because of the existing air pollution, and in part because of natural forces. As a result, the energy is retained in the atmosphere, which it warms continuously. At a minimum, this warming could affect all forms of life. Among other major potential effects, a temperature increase could cause significant melting of polar ice caps and result in massive flooding.

Evidence has suggested that certain compounds may in fact tend to destroy the protective layer of stratospheric ozone. Chlorofluorocarbons (CFCs), a special family of hydrocarbons (organic compounds), constitute a major threat to the ozone layer. These compounds are used in nearly all types of refrigeration units—refrigerators, air conditioners, and similar heat-transfer equipment. As the equipment ages or is damaged, the compounds escape into the environment to become air pollutants. CFCs also are commonly used in the manufacture of plastics and in the computer industry for cleaning sophisticated electronic parts. Although no longer used in the United States, CFCs are a common aerosol propellant elsewhere. Scientific arguments continue as to the potential harm CFCs represent. Many claim evidence is inadequate to justify the regulations imposed on the manufacture and use of CFCs. Others firmly believe the danger is real, and that the magnitude of the potential justifies regulation, in spite of technical uncertainties. Congress has acted with great certainty.

Subchapter VI of Chapter 85 effectively prohibits the use and manufacture of certain types of CFCs. The baseline year for regulation is established as 1986, and the act recognizes two major classes of CFCs to be regulated, with five separate groups in Class I. The act, 42 USC 7671c, provides a phase-out schedule for the various compounds. All Class I compounds shall be phased out by January 1, 1999, except for methyl chloroform, whose production shall be limited to 20 percent of the production in the baseline year. Class II compounds shall be phased out by 2015, based on restrictions of their movement in interstate commerce.

These regulations have had a relatively significant impact on the private citizen. Refrigerants (certain types of freon) used in many auto air conditioners are outlawed. As a result, the cost of air conditioner repairs has increased dramatically.

NEW CLEAN AIR STANDARDS

By law, every five years the EPA must review and revise the air quality standards set under the CAA to take into consideration the most recent information regarding the health effects of various air pollutants. Current reviews focus on more restrictive standards for ozone and particulate matter. Proposed ozone regulations would reduce ozone accumulations by 33 percent, new rules would reduce the standard for particulate matter from 10 to 2.5 micrometers, and the average annual concentration would be reduced to 15 micrograms per cubic meter of air sampled.

Proponents of the new regulations point to increasing evidence of respiratory problems associated with exposure to both ozone and small particulate matter. Opponents claim that the costs of compliance far exceed any measurable benefits and that benefits are questionable, regardless of costs. Congress has consequently been subject to intense lobbying from both sides. The EPA insists that available technology, or soon-to-be-available technology, will cover up to 70 percent of the areas the proposed new regulations would classify as nonattainment.

Opponents further contend that the efforts are dealing with trivia. They point to establishing emission standards for home lawn mowers and similar equipment by 2001 and for heavier but similar equipment by 2005. Equipment currently in use would be exempt from such regulations.

Clearly, compliance with more stringent air quality standards includes significant economic considerations. Costs will ultimately be passed on to consumers, and the total cost, which may be difficult, if not impossible, to estimate, must be balanced with the benefits to be derived including health care considerations and intangibles such as improved individual health.

CONCLUSIONS

Congress initially expressed its concern over air quality in the mid-1950s. Early legislation lacked the strength and the focus to adequately address the deterioration of air quality nationwide. The Clean Air Act, passed in 1970, marked a major change in the congressional policy or philosophy related to air quality regulation. Today, the 1970 act, as significantly amended in 1976 and in 1990, provides the basis for a massive and comprehensive federal role in air quality regulation. Numerous factors contributed to the more rigorous 1970 congressional action. For example, the lack of progress by states to effect air quality improvement and the continued deterioration of air quality dissatisfied Congress. Congress apparently acted partly in the belief that the individual states potentially suffered too much pressure from industry to minimize air quality and pollution control regulations. The 1970 act created a strong federal-state partnership with federal standards to improve air quality to be administered by individual states. This partnership has resulted in more vigorous air quality regulation and in measured improvement of the air quality, although unmet target dates and concessions in the interpretation of certain automotive criteria remain sources of criticism.

The focal point of the Clean Air Act is the National Ambient Air Quality (NAAQ) program and the accompanying State Implementation Plan effort. The NAAQ effort addresses six pollutants identified on medical grounds to be serious threats to human health, the so-called "criteria" pollutants. Lead replaced hydrocarbons on the initial list; reduction of lead in ambient air as a result of the prohibition of fuel additives containing lead represents a major success story for the Act.

The 1990 Clean Air Act amendments, which recognize 189 hazardous pollutants, provide the legislative basis for extensive air quality regulation and represent a major step toward continued air quality improvement. In spite of continuing challenges, less-than-targeted progress, and authorized delays in meeting pollution control standards, massive data support the conclusion that the Clean Air Act has resulted in measurable improvement in air quality in the United States. The adoption and continued implementation of the standard of "maximum achievable technology" for major sources of pollution will further reduce air pollution.

QUESTIONS AND CONCEPTS FOR DISCUSSION AND RESEARCH

1. Discuss the historic issues of clean air, including causes and early regulations.
2. What were the initial federal acts addressing air quality issues, and what were their major strengths and weaknesses?
3. Why is the Clean Air Act of 1970 viewed as relatively strong legislation compared with earlier legislation focused on air quality?

4. Comment on the significance of the following provisions or aspects of the CAA of 1970: national ambient air quality standards; SIPs; attainment and nonattainment regions; air pollution credits and permits; the basis of designation of a region as attainment or nonattainment.

5. What are the two major sources of air pollution addressed by the act? Is this distinction reasonable?

6. What are the major weaknesses of the act?

REFERENCES AND SELECTED READING

Kubasek, Nancy K., and Gary S. Silverman. 1994. *Environmental Law.* Englewood Cliffs, NJ: Prentice Hall.

Nebel, Bernard J., and Richard T. Wright. 1993. *Environmental Science: The Way the World Works.* Englewood Cliffs, NJ: Prentice Hall.

U.S. Environmental Protection Agency. August 1989. *Environmental Backgrounder: Acid Rain.* Office of Public Affairs (A-107). Washington, DC.

————. December 1989. *Glossary of Environmental Terms and Acronym List.* EPA 19K-1002. Washington, DC.

————. October 1992. *What You Can Do to Reduce Air Pollution.* EPA 450-K-92-002. Washington, DC.

————. April 1993. *Plain English Guide to the Clean Air Act.* EPA 400-K-93-001. Washington, DC.

————. December 1995. *National Air Quality and Trends Report, 1994.* EPA 454/R-95-014. Washington, DC.

7

Clean Water and Water Quality Considerations

INTRODUCTION

Importance of Water Resources

Water constitutes up to 90 percent of all living matter in plants and animals. No form of life can survive without some dependable supply of this simple, yet critically complex combination of hydrogen and oxygen. Water also constitutes a basic component of many of the world's varied ecosystems, and ecologists and other scientists worldwide recognize it as a key component in many habitats.

Water has also played a central role in the evolution of human society and commerce. The histories of many civilizations are written in and along the banks of major rivers and lakes as well as in transoceanic exploration. Society evolved around rivers, exploration followed river courses, and today rivers remain major highways for commerce. Running water continues to serve as a major source of power for an energy-demanding nation, from the earliest days of the water wheel and mill to today's massive hydrogeneration systems.

Settlements sprouted along the banks of the world's rivers, and the earliest settlers recognized the value of a dependable supply of safe water for a variety of purposes: personal needs and habitat for valued wildlife and plants initially, followed rapidly by transportation. Too frequently, rivers and streams became convenient systems for waste disposal. Unfortunately, the quality of many sources of water has been seriously lowered by a variety of sources of pollution.

Today, the availability of water significantly affects the value of land as well as commercial development. In the semi-arid regions of the western United States, water for irrigation determines the value of farm land, and available, clean water is a prerequisite for industrial development. Even though water covers nearly three-quarters of the earth's surface area, in many parts of the world, and in most of the United States, supplies are in danger and water has come under increasingly rigorous regulation by individual states and the federal government.

The Status of the Nation's Water Supplies and Water Use

Deterioration of water quality is not a new problem, although recognition of the magnitude of the problem is fairly recent. In 1992, in response to a federal legislative mandate, the states reported the extent of water pollution and sources of pollution to Congress. In terms of water resources, the states estimated the nation has:

1. over 3.5 million miles of rivers and streams

2. approximately 40 million acres of lakes, ponds, and reservoirs

3. more than 56,000 miles of ocean shoreline, including Alaska

4. nearly 5,400 miles of Great Lakes shoreline

5. over 277 million acres of wetlands, more than half of which are in Alaska

The report includes only samples, ranging from 99 percent of the Great Lakes shoreline to 18 percent of the rivers and streams, 6 percent of the ocean coastal waters, and 46 percent of lakes, ponds, and reservoirs. Although incomplete, this report provides a sound appraisal of the quality of the nation's water resources.

The report characterizes water quality as "fully supporting" (quality adequate to support a designated use, no serious pollution problem), "threatened" (supporting, but in some danger from pollution), "partially supporting" (some loss attributable to pollution), "not supporting," and "not attainable" (loss from pollution such that the water source cannot be improved to support a designated use). For rivers and streams, 62 percent qualified as supporting or only threatened and 56 percent of the lakes were similarly classified, except that only 3 percent of the Great Lakes reached these desired levels; obviously, the Great Lakes suffer serious pollution problems. Sixty-eight percent of the estuaries sampled, 87 percent of the ocean waters, and 51 percent of the wetlands achieved either the fully supporting or threatened status.

The individual states reported many types and sources of pollutants. Categories of pollutants included sediment, nutrients (such as nitrates from fertilizers and sewage that overstimulate growth of aquatic plants, which ultimately results in oxygen deficiencies). Water pollutants also include silt from agriculture, forestry and developments, pathogens (bacteria, fungi, and viruses) from sewage, medical waste, and livestock. Coliform bacteria suggest the presence of untreated sewage in the water.

Many sources account for accumulations of organic matter as a pollutant: Sewage, leaves and garden clippings, and runoff from livestock feedlots are common sources. Organisms that decay organic matter require oxygen and create a high biological oxygen demand (BOD). Thus BOD is a measure of organic pollutants; a high BOD reflects relatively high concentrations of raw organic material in the water and is undesirable because of potential harm to fish and other forms of aquatic life that must compete for the available oxygen.

Industries contribute heavy metals (such as lead and mercury) and a wide array of organic chemicals, many of which come from petroleum compounds. Leaching from landfills represents a continuing threat to water quality, making landfills subject to strict regulations (see chapter 8). Residues from agricultural chemicals, both pesticides and fertilizers—many of which are also used in urban settings such as golf courses—represent a significant nonpoint source of pollution.

INTRODUCTION TO WATER LAW

Water resources are subject to four broad areas of regulation involving both state and federal laws and regulations. Laws that establish criteria for water quality and preservation of water resources generally are based on federal law and rules authorized by two major federal laws: the Clean Water Act and the Safe Drinking Water Act. In addition, laws regulating waste disposal focus on protecting water quality.

Generally, state laws regulate health issues related to water safety and quality, although the Safe Drinking Water Act addresses some of these issues. By convention, state water laws that address purely health-related water issues are not considered "environmental regulations."

Water Use and Water Rights

The regulation of the use of water and allocation of water resources from lakes, rivers, streams, and even wells remain generally controlled by state law. However, federal law becomes operative when federal water projects are involved and when water sources, such as many major rivers, serve more than one state.

Water laws and regulations can be divided into two major categories: laws affecting the rights to "own" or use water for any purpose (other than navigation, which is beyond the scope of this discussion), and laws and regulations that address establishing or maintaining specific levels of water quality or purity, including the regulation of water pollution.

WATER RIGHTS: OWNERSHIP CONSIDERATIONS

Generally, issues of water ownership involve water use more than water quality. Conflicts take the form of disputes over water rights, and such disputes have played a significant part in the development of the more arid portions of the western United States. With the exception of use limitations established by the federal government for water delivered by federal water projects, such as the Central Valley Project in California, and interstate disputes over the rights to river water, such as the Colorado River and disputes between California and other states through which it runs, ownership disputes are a matter of state law.

Ownership interests in water traditionally are limited to supplies of freshwater, and the immediate source of the water can play a central role in the nature of the water rights. State regulations recognize two basic sources of water: surface water, which is water in naturally flowing rivers and streams and commonly includes lakes; and groundwater, which is water found in underground strata that is tapped by wells and extracted by pumps. It may include some types of springs, before spring flow becomes a measured surface source.

In the case of surface water, a water right grants the right to use the water, but it does not grant ownership of the water itself. Regulation of the rights to surface water fall under one of two doctrines: the *riparian doctrine,* which has its roots in common law and links ownership of property adjacent to a body of water to the use of that water; and rights claimed by *appropriation,* which allow individuals to claim water and to divert it for use apart from its channel or source. The appropriation right frequently is associated with a state requirement for a permit to divert the water. These two basic doctrines include other important provisions and reflect additional differences.

Riparian Rights

The doctrine of riparian rights to surface water trace to English common law. The basic right states that owners of land adjacent to a body of water have the right to use that water so long as the water is returned undiminished in quality and quantity to the channel from which it was diverted, before the channel leaves the user's property. States in the more humid eastern parts of the country follow this doctrine. The riparian doctrine seems reasonable for water rights associated with the use of water for power, but uses that actually "consume" water, such as irrigation, where the water obviously cannot be returned to the channel from which it was diverted, clearly violate the basic provisions of the doctrine. These violations appear to create no conflicts, so long as adequate water is available. However, when such diversions adversely affect others who claim similar rights along the same body of water, conflicts arise and litigation follows.

In terms of ownership, the riparian right is transferred with the land: The owner of the land owns the right to use the water, and when the land is sold, the riparian right is sold with it. In addition, the owner's right is limited to use on the riparian land, meaning that riparian water generally cannot be diverted to locations removed from the body of water, even when the land to which it is transferred is owned by the same individual.

Increased consumptive use of water has seriously eroded the continued acceptance of the riparian doctrine, even in states that traditionally have enjoyed plentiful supplies of water. Traditional riparian states have addressed these problems by statutory modification of the doctrine, or by similar judicial interpretation of the riparian doctrine. Many states have formulated water plans that establish priorities for water use, the riparian doctrine notwithstanding. In the face of drought emergency conditions, such plans allow the state government to suspend riparian water rights.

Appropriation Rights

In the drier areas of the United States, water rights have been established by appropriation. In the simplest sense, appropriation means use: An individual diverts water from a river or stream (appropriates it) and claims the right to use a specified amount of water. This right is traditionally established on the basis of "first in time gets first in right"; that is, the first person to divert and use water beneficially has the first right to it. The requirement to divert and use is critical because it effectively limits claims for all of the water in a given stream. So long as the flow of a stream has not been entirely appropriated, individuals may claim water rights. However, in many states, to avoid conflicts, enforceable claims require a state permit in addition to the diversion and use criteria. Of course, problems arise in dry periods when stream flow is inadequate to satisfy all appropriations. In such instances, the "first in time" doctrine becomes critical: The earliest claimants have first right to all the water they initially claimed, before later claimants receive any flow. In most states, this right can be sold or rented independently of title to any land.

In many instances, water appropriations on a given stream exceed the normal flow of the stream. As a result, later appropriations are of little value. Part of the "overappropriation" comes from multiple appropriations of water to be used for the same purpose. In recent years, states have reviewed the validity of such multiple claims in an attempt to identify valid claims and to reduce cases of apparent overappropriation of rivers and streams. The state of Montana, for example, has been a leader in efforts to reject needless multiple claims while protecting the rights of claimants under the traditional precepts of "first in time is first in right." By legislation, every person claiming a water right was required to refile the claim. If an individual made more than one claim to irrigate the same parcel of land, generally the state denied the multiple claims, but allowed the earliest priority claim. In addition, Montana has established a special Water Court to hear and settle disputes involving water rights.

Groundwater

Although they did not own surface water, traditionally landowners owned the water, or at least the right to the water, beneath their land. (This is the same general principle associated with the ownership of minerals, although the rights to minerals have far more frequently been separated from the sale of the land.) In recent years, the exercise of this ownership right has come under increasing regulation. Increased demands for groundwater resulting from urban growth and massive expansion of and dependency on irrigation for agricultural purposes, coupled with the development of high volume, high powered pumping systems, have created serious threats to supplies of groundwater and to conflicts among users.

Aquifers

The major sources of groundwater exist in *aquifers,* subterranean paths of slow water movement that may extend hundreds or even thousands of miles, although some are relatively local in extent. Water may be extracted from an aquifer great distances from the site where surface waters enter (recharge) the aquifer, and within relatively small distances several users may seek to pump water from the same aquifer.

Aquifers are far more complex than an underground river of freely flowing water or a subterranean lake; their geology reveals complex, frequently ancient structures that are sturdy, yet fragile. The internal structure of aquifers subjected to excessive withdrawals of water may deteriorate, so that even if adequate water at the recharge sites is available, the aquifers can no longer support the same flow as before the withdrawals. Normal paths of water flow may be blocked and the resources damaged, if not lost. Even if an aquifer is not damaged in terms of its capacity to transport water, its value can be permanently reduced.

In the coastal areas of South Carolina near the border with Georgia, for example, rapid urban growth over the past decade has accelerated the demands for water, most of which is supplied from groundwater resources. Demands have exceeded recharge rates, and the water level in wells has dropped dramatically. In fact, the level in some wells has dropped below sea level. As a result, salt water has encroached on the freshwater supply entering the well; the normal flow of the aquifer is inadequate to flush the salt water from these wells. Effectively, the overuse of wells represents a critical first step in contamination of the aquifer and its loss as a major source of fresh water.

Regulating Groundwater Use

Because the water in question did not exist as a lake under an individual's property, claims of ownership rights to the use of groundwater have been more difficult to sustain. In dry years, water levels drop, and shallow wells may suffer. Proof that the operation of a new, deeper well with a large pumping system directly caused a problem with a smaller well is difficult to establish, but courts in some states have recognized the right to water in a common "cone of depression" such that an individual cannot increase groundwater withdrawals to the detriment of others' historic use of that supply of groundwater.

Unlike regulation of surface water, the regulation of the use of groundwater supplies is relatively new. This in part reflects the fact that until fairly recently, supplies of groundwater have generally matched the demand. Now, as new technology allows far greater exploitation of this resource, demands exceed supply, and the need for regulation becomes apparent. In addition to regulations to foster the fair distribution of this valued resource, from an environmental perspective, regulations are needed to protect the resource itself.

In addition to protecting water rights to groundwater based on basic precepts of prior use and on historic withdrawals, some states have legislated water plans that address the regulation of both surface water and groundwater resources. For example, the state of Washington requires permits for the development and operation for all but domestic water wells (wells that provide water for household purposes), and South Carolina has established a statutory basis to protect groundwater resources by monitoring uses and avoiding excessive withdrawals. Many other states are following the pattern of introducing groundwater regulations and water rights in addition to traditional rights associated with surface waters. Such regulation certainly is part of environmental law because it regulates a critical natural resource.

WATER QUALITY

Virtually all human activities depend on an adequate supply of reasonably pure water. In a very real sense, the purity of available water reflects the quality of the local environment. Water is sensitive to many sources of environmental abuse. Human activities account for the deterioration of water quality, and human efforts have demonstrated that deterioration not only can be slowed, but can be stopped and indeed be reversed.

Table 7.1 summarizes a variety of sources of water pollution and associated types of pollutants identified by the EPA.

Category	Example
Industrial	Pulp and paper mills, chemical manufacturers, steel plants, textile manufacturers, food processing plants
Municipal	Publicly owned sewage treatment plants that may receive indirect discharge from industrial facilities or businesses
Combined Sewers	Single facilities that treat both storm water and sanitary sewage, which may become overloaded during storms and discharge untreated waters into surface waters
Storm sewers/urban runoff	Runoff from impervious surfaces (including streets, buildings, lawns, and other paved areas) that enters a sewer, pipe, or ditch before discharge into surface waters
Agricultural	Crop production, pasture, rangeland, feedlots, other animal holding areas
Silvicultural	Forest management, tree harvesting, logging, road construction
Construction	Land development, road construction
Resource extraction	Mining, petroleum drilling, runoff from mine tailing sites
Land Disposal	Leachate or discharge from septic tanks, landfills, and hazardous waste sites
Hydrologic modification	Channelization, dredging, dam construction, stream bank modification

TABLE 7.1 Categories of sources of pollution and examples of related industries or activities used in the EPA water quality report. These categories reflect the major sources of water pollution reported by the states as required by the Clean Water Act. From *The Quality of Our Nation's Waters: 1992.* EPA 84-S-94-002. U.S. Environmental Protection Agency. March 1994.

Waste Disposal

Throughout recorded history, efforts were made to protect domestic water supplies. In the westward expansion across the United States, for example, settlers recognized and valued sources of "sweet water." Unfortunately, in spite of concerns for supplies of domestic water, water sources have traditionally been viewed and used as convenient avenues for waste disposal. Even in the United States, until fairly recent decades, society has accepted dumping garbage and human sewage into rivers and bays. Water courses have long been accepted as sites for the disposal of manufacturing waste and by-products. As a result, the waters of many of the nation's rivers, lakes, and bays are polluted to the point that they pose significant health hazards, to say nothing of the loss of wildlife habitat, destroyed fisheries, and the nuisance associated with odor and debris accumulations. The historic use of waterways for transportation has exposed them to added burdens of pollution from both vessels and passengers. Recreational uses of major waterways continues to increase the potential burden of pollution.

Runoff

Waterways seem to be natural sites for the accumulation of wastes not originally deposited in them. Many of the nation's rivers and lakes have been polluted by farm chemicals carried long distances in runoff waters and accumulated from diverse sources. Agricultural chemicals and animal waste are two major sources of nonpoint source pollution, the control of which is of growing national concern. Some livestock facilities, depending on the number and class of livestock handled, are classified and regulated as point sources of pollution and are subject to rigorous standards under federal and state laws.

Runoff from the nation's landfill facilities reaches rivers and lakes as pollutants carried by surface sources and as leachates in contaminated groundwater supplies. Aging underground fuel storage tanks of various types represent a source of growing concern in terms of pollution of groundwater and surface water supplies.

Urban development represents an increasingly serious potential source of water pollution: Runoff from streets, highways, and parking lots carries a variety of toxic substances, many of which are by-products of gasoline and road surfacing materials. Even snow removal presents risks of water pollution from both the runoff of the snow and disposal of snow in rivers and lakes, when roads have been treated with salt or other deicing compounds.

THE FOCAL POINT OF FEDERAL WATER QUALITY REGULATIONS

Considering the importance of water quality, the fact that water pollutants cross state lines, the importance of water in both manufacturing processes and products, hence in interstate commerce, and the obvious impacts of water quality on human health and welfare, extensive government regulation of water quality should come as no surprise. The Clean Water Act represents the initial focus of federal regulation of water quality and the greatest body of federal water quality regulations. This act is found in Title 33 of the *United States Code,* Navigable Waters. On its face, the act focuses on the impact of water pollution on the nation's waterways, rivers, harbors, and bays but does not address health issues related to water pollution, although clearly health and water pollution cannot be separated.

Provisions of the Safe Drinking Water Act address issues related to the protection of drinking water supplies and pollution control, regardless of the source of the water. This obviously health-related act is found in Title 42 of the *United States Code,* The Public Health and Welfare.

Title 33 includes two other acts that reflect congressional concern over the unregulated, continuing pollution of waterways, the Ocean Dumping Act and the Oil Pollution Act of 1990. The provisions of both of these acts focus more on general damages than on health-related issues, although compliance with their provisions should have positive health effects.

THE CLEAN WATER ACT

The Federal Water Pollution Control Act (FWPCA), commonly known as the Clean Water Act, traces to the Federal Water Pollution Control Act of 1948, as amended. The act is found in Chapter 26 (Water Pollution Prevention) of Title 33 (Navigable Waters) of the *United States Code*. Early legislation provided a broad definition of navigable waters, and court decisions have further expanded the definition well beyond waters that directly support shipping or related activities.

Clearly, the FWPCA encompasses significant health-related issues, in addition to general environmental issues and concerns. Like the Clean Air Act, the FWPCA is an immense and complex package of legislation from which equally complex sets of rules and regulations have evolved. The act comprises ninety-six sections and subsections numbered 33 USC 1251 through 1387, covering 161 pages of text. Chapter 26 is divided into six subchapters that provide a broad overview of the scope of the act. Congress specified that the administrator of the EPA will administer the act, which includes specific rule-making authorization.

Provisions of the Act

Subchapter I, Research

The title of Subchapter I, Research and Related Programs, fails to reveal critical subject matter comprising 33 USC 1251 (a) and (b), the first sections of the subchapter, in which Congress clearly expresses the intent of the legislation: "to restore and maintain the chemical, physical, and biological integrity of the Nation's waters." In this one statement, Congress recognized national water quality problems by calling for the restoration of the integrity of the nation's waters.

Goals.   With this broad purpose established, the same section presents seven goals or policy statements that set the basic tone of the act:

1. Eliminate the discharge of pollutants into the nation's waters by 1985. Obviously, this ambitious goal has not been met; as is typical for many initial regulatory efforts, initial steps overestimated what could be accomplished. (At times such over ambitious efforts lead to ridicule of the intent and inhibit progress.) Nonetheless, the basic intent is clear—polluting of the nation's waters must stop.

2. Where attainable, develop an interim water quality goal to protect fish, shellfish, and wildlife and provide for recreation by July 1983.

3. Prohibit the discharge of toxic pollutants in toxic amounts. In this statement, the act recognizes two critical facts—that pollutants differ in their toxicity (the harm they may cause), and that regulations should address the discharge of toxic amounts, not all discharges. Of course, controversy continues over what constitutes a harmful amount when possible accumulation in the environment is considered. This issue becomes part of the ongoing considerations in risk assessment and risk management.

4. Provide financial assistance for waste treatment facilities. In this statement, the federal government recognizes that the cost of abating pollution of the nation's waters is greater than state budgets can tolerate. In the act, Congress authorized appropriations; this authorization is not in itself an appropriation. The effectiveness of this "commitment to the states" is directly linked with the willingness of Congress to appropriate funds on a continuing basis. In addition, the limit on appropriations for assistance to the states "to construct publicly owned waste treatment works" plainly identifies what Congress views as

one of the most serious water pollution problems: direct discharge of sewage into the waters of the United States, or indirect discharge in the form of inadequately treated discharge from sewage treatment plants.

5. Support area-wide planning for waste treatment management.

6. Set the policy that major research and demonstration efforts are needed to develop technology suitable for the control of pollutants in all bodies of water. This policy clearly implies that federal funds should be appropriated for such research.

7. Place increasing emphasis on nonpoint sources of pollution.

These seven statements reflect the massive intended scope of activity of the federal government, the recognition that sewage represents a major problem, and an initial commitment that the federal government must bear a significant share of the cost to address these problems.

The first section includes another very significant statement of policy: Congress declared that the responsibility to "prevent, reduce, and eliminate" water pollution rests with the states; 33 USC 1251(b). In addition, Congress mandated that the states manage programs authorized under the Clean Water Act.

Subchapter I also describes a comprehensive plan that addresses pollution control of both surface (navigable) and groundwater sources of water. The specific inclusion of groundwater further illustrates congressional concern over the extent of water pollution. The inclusion of pollution control in Title 33, Navigable Waters, reflects two points: the emphasis of the act on surface (navigable) waters and the fact that the subject matter of the individual titles of the code can be very diverse. In addition to addressing both surface water and groundwater, in this section, Congress considers another significant issue, regulation of nonpoint sources of pollution.

Congress has emphasized controlling or eliminating water pollution arising from identified (i.e., point) sources. The facts, unfortunately, are clear: Significant amounts of water pollutants arise from nonpoint sources, and to achieve the stated goals of the chapter, problems associated with these sources require attention. The act does not define "nonpoint source," but it does define "point source": "any discernable, confined and discrete conveyance, including, but not limited to any pipe, ditch, channel, tunnel, conduit, well, discrete fissures, container, rolling stock, concentrated animal feeding operation, or vessel or other floating craft from which pollutants are or may be discharged." The final goal/policy statement calls for emphasis on nonpoint sources of water pollution.

The remainder of Subchapter I reflects the intent of Congress to develop essential information to fight water pollution. This subchapter calls on the administrator of the EPA to develop cooperative pollution control efforts involving all levels of government—federal, state, and local—and to render technical assistance to public and private pollution control agencies. The subsection authorizes grants to states for virtually all activities related to water pollution control, from research and demonstrations to surveys and studies concerning the causes, effects, extent, and, ultimately, the elimination of pollution.

Types of Federally Supported Activities. In the act, Congress narrows the initial research on health effects by placing "special emphasis" on the effects of bioaccumulation of pollutants on the commercial and sporting value of aquatic species. This provision initially was not part of the FWPCA, but was introduced as part of the 1987 Water Quality Act. Now it is found in Subchapter I of the act at 33 USC 1254(a).

Treatment of municipal sewage remains a central, but not exclusive, target of the provisions of this subchapter. Other specific targets for attention include water quality of the Great Lakes, and lakes in general, with attention to the nutrient accumulation and vegetative growth in polluted lakes, waste disposal equipment for ships, study of the disposal of waste oil, and comprehensive studies of the effects of water pollution of ecologically fragile regions, such as estuary zones.

Support for Undergraduate Students.   In Subchapter I of the act, Congress recognizes both the need for and deficiency of technically trained specialists to address the multitudes of technical problems associated with the goal of eliminating water pollution. Congress authorized appropriations to facilitate the development of essential human resources and technical expertise to implement the mandated efforts to eliminate water pollution, including research and graduate fellowships and support for undergraduate scholarships. This level of authorized support for a specific purpose, water pollution elimination, is unique and further reflects the congressional position of the critical need for action.

Subchapter V, Administration

Subchapter V (sections 1361 through 1377) includes the administrative details for the implementation of the provisions of the act as well as specific definitions that are critical to the provisions of the act. (As was true with the Clean Air Act, reviewing the subchapters of the Clean Water Act out of numeric sequence facilitates a general analysis and understanding of this complex body of legislation.)

The administrative regulation of the act includes key definitions that set limits and the scope of the legislation that frequently reflect the legislative intent of Congress. In addition to the definition of "point source" just introduced, Subchapter V defines nineteen terms and concepts; 33 USC 1362 (1 through 20). All are important in the administration of the act, but the following ten are critical to understanding its scope and its regulatory provisions:

1. "Pollutant" is all encompassing. It includes dredged spoils, incinerator residue, sewage, garbage, sludge, munitions, chemical waste, biological materials, radioactive materials, heat, discarded equipment, and industrial, municipal, and agricultural materials discharged into water.

2. "Navigable water" means the waters of the United States, including territorial seas. This definition has been interpreted by federal courts and will be expanded in the discussion that follows concerning wetlands, which come under federal regulation as part of the Clean Water Act.

3. "Territorial sea" broadly means the sea extending three miles from shore at low tide.

4. "Contiguous zone" relates to seas and includes any area established by the United States under Article 24 of the Convention of the Territorial Sea and Contiguous Zone.

5. "Ocean" is any portion of the sea beyond the contiguous zone.

6. "Effluent limitation" is any restriction established by a state or the administrator on the quantities, rate, or concentrations of chemical, physical, biological, and other constituents that are discharged from point sources into navigable waters, waters of the contiguous zone, or the ocean. (Note that the limitation considers point sources, and that

landfills, pursuant to section 507 of Public Law 100.4, now are recognized as point sources, but many agricultural and urban sources still escape regulation as nonpoint sources.)

7. "Discharge of a pollutant" means what it says—the addition of any pollutant from a point source into the navigable waters of the United States.

8. "Toxic pollutants" include disease-causing agents that directly or by incorporation in the food chain cause death, behavioral abnormalities, cancer, genetic mutations, or other harm to individuals or their offspring. Obviously, this definition provides a wide latitude in identifying any substance as "toxic" for the purpose of control under the provisions of this act.

9. "Pollution" includes any man-made or induced change in the chemical, physical, biological, or radiological integrity of water.

10. "Medical waste" refers to all medical instruments (sharps) and infected or potentially infected human waste or remains, including blood and surgical waste (which includes dressings and bedding).

The definition of "discharge of pollutants" initially limits the FWPCA to point sources of pollution. This definition does not preclude regulation of nonpoint sources, but it does reflect at least the initial congressional concern. Increasingly, nonpoint sources appear as major contributors to water pollution, and they will receive additional attention through amendments to this legislation.

Two additional administrative provisions of the act reflect the intent of Congress to encourage the interest of individuals in protecting the quality of the nation's water. First, the act grants a private right of action, which means that an individual can sue to have the provisions of the act enforced; this right is also granted under provisions of the Clean Air Act. Second, the act includes provision to protect whistle-blowers from retaliation by employers.

Subchapter II, Waste Water Treatment

Subchapter II focuses on one of the major aspects of the act, waste water treatment, or sewage treatment plants. Congress expresses its purposes: "to require and assist the development and implementation of waste treatment management plans." Congress recognized sewage as a major source of water pollution and that federal assistance is needed to resolve the problems. Provisions of this subchapter clearly express congressional policy regarding waste treatment.

The legislation requires waste treatment management plans to apply the best practicable waste treatment technology before waste is discharged into any water source, stream, river, or lake. The provisions of this portion of the act encourage waste treatment programs that produce revenue through recycling and other efforts. Waste treatment plans must include reclaiming and recycling of water, confined disposal of pollutants to avoid additional environmental pollution, and consideration of advanced waste management techniques.

In addressing the problems of sewage treatment, Congress recognized the creation of another potential problem, the disposal of sludge, the residue of waste water treatment. Congress called for the disposal of this material in an environmentally safe manner, which includes disposal in landfill facilities and spreading on agricultural lands. Although the sludge may contain valuable plant nutrients, it also represents a serious potential source of pollution, because the concentrations of pollutants, such as heavy metals in the waste water, are increased in this by-product of waste water treatment.

Subchapter II authorizes federal assistance for the development of waste treatment facilities and establishes the distribution of funds appropriated, although the act itself cannot appropriate funds. Appropriations in the form of entitlement to the states are based on population. The basic policy logically reflects the fact that states with larger populations generate more sewage and have greater need for assistance.

In the first period authorized for funding, fiscal years 1982 through 1985, New York and California received the greatest authorizations (11.3097 and 7.2901 percent respectively), and rural, sparsely populated states such as Montana, North Dakota, South Dakota, and Wyoming and the smaller states such as Delaware and Vermont (excluding the territories of the United States) received the lowest authorizations, 0.4965 percent each. The water quality standards to be satisfied, of course, are the same for all states, regardless of funding.

Subchapter III, Standards and Enforcement

In terms of environmental regulations, Subchapter III, 33 USC 1311 through 1330, Standards and Enforcement, is the core of the act. The initial provisions of this subchapter set the tone of the act, with specified exceptions: "the discharge of any pollutant by any person shall be illegal." For other than publicly owned point sources of pollution, Congress established the standards that must be satisfied as "the application of the best practicable control technology currently available". For discharges into publicly owned treatment facilities, Congress set more rigorous requirements for meeting pretreatment effluent limitation standards. The tone of this critical subchapter reflects the most serious intent of Congress to stop water pollution. Even with this strongly stated intent, the act includes provisions for existing versus new treatment facilities, meaning that standards for existing water treatment facilities are less rigorous than those for new facilities developed in compliance with the act. For new sources, the act requires consideration of the costs of achieving such effluent reductions and the nonwater environmental and energy impacts of such new standards. Clearly, the act recognizes that issues other than water pollution reduction must be addressed.

In considering water pollution in general, Congress established broad categories of pollutants found in essentially all water sources. These are characterized as *conventional pollutants,* which are defined as pollutants that are well understood by scientists. Congress listed four conventional pollutants that generally indicate water quality, and authorized additions to the following list as required: biological oxygen demand (BOD—a measure of organic matter in water), suspended solids, fecal coliform (colon bacterium), and pH. Congress specifically excluded thermal discharge as a conventional pollutant. The list of conventional pollutants now is current in 40 CFR 401.16 and adds oil and grease to the original congressional list.

Standards of Performance.   Two sections represent the heart of the subchapter, 33 USC 1316, National Standards of Performance, and Toxic and Pretreatment Effluent Treatment Standards, 33 USC 1317. In expressing the National Standards of Performance, Congress took a politically courageous step and identified specific industrial point sources of pollution targeted for regulation. The target industries (grouped and identified as categories in the legislation) are listed in Table 7.1 (see page 148). The law directs the administrator to add to the list from time to time when necessary; these additions are included in the CFRs. In defining "standards of performance," Congress specified its ultimate goal, indicating that, where practicable, the standard should permit "no discharge of pollutants."

This list, which Congress identified as a minimal list, reveals several key points. First, Congress recognized an extraordinarily wide array of point sources. The targeted industries directly or indirectly involve essentially every phase or type of manufacturing and product produced in the United States today. Second, regulations focus on point sources, which exclude the majority of pollution arising from agriculturally related sources, but include feed lots as identified point sources. Although the application of pesticides is not addressed, the provisions of the act recognize hazards associated with their manufacture. Third, the scope of the industries targeted in Table 7.1 clearly establishes that some activities in every state fall under the provisions of this act.

Nonpoint Source Pollution

The nature of nonpoint source pollution (NPS) and its causes are fairly simple to describe. Agriculture is a major contributor to NPS through the use of excessive amounts of fertilizers, particularly nitrogen, that leach through the soil to contaminate groundwater or that move with runoff to pollute surface waters. Nitrogen is a prime cause of the eutrophication, excessive algae growth that harms other forms of aquatic life by competing for oxygen in the water. Pollution from fertilizers also trace to urban uses such as golf courses, but like agriculture, a specific point cannot be identified for control purposes. Like fertilizers, pesticides and pesticide residues from excessive agricultural and urban uses move with water.

Livestock represent a serious source of NPS. Feedlots are recognized as point sources and are subject to effective regulations, "on farm" production is not regulated, and grazing stock pollute rivers, lakes, and streams.

Urban conditions also contribute to NPS. Runoff from roads and parking lots, for example, carries petroleum products and toxic by-products through drainage systems into water sources either directly or through sewage treatment plants that are not designed to manage such pollutants.

Poorly defined or undefined sources make the management of NPS challenging. Consequently, individual responsibility in the use of agricultural chemicals is an essential first step. Technology exists that can predict with great accuracy the type and amount of fertilizers a crop will require; following those recommendations will reduce overuse and the related runoff problems. In addition, it is economically wise for producers to avoid waste. Proper use of pesticides is required by law and will minimize them as a source of pollution. Stricter enforcement of rules may be required, and extra care in cleaning equipment and the disposal of containers must be actively encouraged. Currently, no suggestion has been made to limit fertilizer supplies to producers to avoid pollution problems. Currently, control of livestock to protect water supplies is up to the individual producer. Even if specific regulations are formulated, compliance must effectively be voluntary because of the enormous areas to be considered. Compliance could include fencing to exclude stock from water supplies.

Controlling urban runoff is equally complex. In many communities, storm sewers, which carry toxic pollutants, drain directly into streams, lakes, and rivers. Runoff from such storm water systems may pass through treatment plants. All too frequently, however, the treatment facility is not designed to monitor the problem, let alone correct it by appropriate treatment. As a result, steps that minimize the generation of these pollutants seem to hold the most immediate hope for preventing further damage. Runoff control for new developments will be part of the solution, and frequently is included in local or state development regulations.

Special Considerations.   The complex issues of a product that represents multiple environmental threats deserve special note. Potential pollutants must be viewed from several points: Their manufacture, use, and disposal each may pose a unique problem. In some instances, the issue is far more manufacture than use, whereas in others, use represents the greatest environmental threat. In addition, disposal nearly always poses some environmental threat. Wide discrepancies exist in the regulation of the three phases, and regulations are spread among diverse bodies of legislation. For example, the FWPCA recognizes dangers from the manufacture of pesticides, but the use of pesticides is regulated by the Federal Insecticide, Fungicide, and Rodenticide Act, FIFRA. Issues related to pesticide residues in food are addressed by the Federal Food, Drug, and Cosmetic Act.

Structure of the Standards

The list of industries suggests the types of pollutants to be regulated, from asbestos to organic chemicals and biological residues or heavy metals. Actual performance standards to comply with discharge limitations are published in exhaustive detail in the CFRs. The extent of these regulations is staggering. Effluent Guidelines and Standards are found in 40 CFR 425 *et seq.,* identified in the CFR as Chapter I, Subchapter N. Subchapter O regulates sewage sludge, Subchapter P is reserved for future use, and Subchapter Q considers energy policy.

Subchapter N spans over 500 pages of regulations in 40 CFR. Its 326 separate parts regulate point sources ranging from leather tanning to nonferrous metals forming and metal powders. Table 7.2 summarizes the specific industries for which the EPA has formulated standards. Note that, depending on the point source, the standard may include criteria such as "best available technology" or "best practicable technology" as well as distinctions between existing and new sources. See, for example, the varied standards reflecting these differences for the coal mining point source; 40 CFR 434.

The second major point of this subchapter, 33 USC 1317, focuses on toxic and pretreatment effluent standards. Thirty-six compounds or groups of compounds identified as toxic pollutants are listed in 40 CFR 401.15; this list incorporates a shorter list found in 40 CFR 129.4. Classification considers toxicity of the pollutant, its persistence in the environment, its degradability, and its effects on organisms in the water. According to the law, toxic pollutants shall be subject to effluent limitations based on the best available technology economically achievable for the applicable category or class of point pollutant. The thirty-six compounds are listed in Table 7.3.

Pretreatment Regulations.   Pretreatment of waste water is a major portion of the regulatory process. Industries must pretreat effluent before it is discharged into public waste

1. Pulp and paper mills
2. Paperboard, builders paper, and board mills
3. Meat product and rendering processing
4. Dairy product processing
5. Grain mills
6. Canned and preserved fruit and vegetable processing
7. Canned and preserved seafood processing
8. Sugar processing
9. Textile processing
10. Cement manufacturing
11. Feedlots
12. Electroplating
13. Organic chemical manufacturing
14. Inorganic chemical manufacturing
15. Plastic and synthetic material manufacturing
16. Soap and detergent manufacturing
17. Fertilizer manufacturing
18. Petroleum refining
19. Iron and steel manufacturing
20. Nonferrous metal manufacturing
21. Phosphate manufacturing
22. Steam electric power plants
23. Ferroalloy manufacturing
24. Leather tanning and finishing
25. Glass and asbestos manufacturing
26. Rubber processing
27. Timber product processing

TABLE 7.2 General categories of industries identified as potential sources of water pollution that Congress found should be subject to regulation. Summarized from 33 USC 1316(b).

treatment facilities, which places a major portion of the cleanup responsibility at the source of the pollution. Pretreatment criteria and standards vary among industries, but they all center on the same target: minimizing harmful discharges at their source. Consider two vastly different industries—petroleum refining and the canned and preserved fruit industry.

Petroleum Refining.   The petroleum refining industry is the source of a wide variety of pollutants, which is reflected in the fact that pretreatment regulations for the petroleum refining industry involve standards to satisfy ten specific criteria:

1. BOD5—the five-day biological oxygen demand, which is a measure of the amount of organic material in the waste water.

2. TSS—total suspended, nonfilterable solids. These are minute solids that resist separation by conventional physical means.

3. COD—similar to BOD5, but a measure of chemical pollutants that create a demand for oxygen in the water.

4. Oil and grease.

Compound	Compound
1. Acenaphthene	19. Chloroform
2. Acrolein	20. 2-chlorophenols
3. Acrylonitrile	21. Chromium and compounds
4. Aldrin/Dieldrin	22. Copper and compounds
5. Antimonium and compounds	23. Cyanides
6. Arsenic and compounds	24. DDT and metabolites
7. Asbestos	25. Dichlorobenzenes
8. Benzene	26. Dichlorobenzidine
9. Benzidine	27. Dichloroethylenes
10. Beryllium and compounds	28. 2, 4-dichlorophenol
11. Cadmium and compounds	29. Dichloropropane and Dichloropropene
12. Carbon tetrachloride	30. 2, 4-dimethylphenol
13. Chlordane	31. Dinitrotoluene
14. Chlorinated benzenes	32. Diphenylhydrazine
15. Chlorinated ethanes	33. Endosulfan and metabolites
16. Chloroalky ethers	34. Endrin and metabolites
17. Chlorinated naphthalene	35. Ethylbenzene
18. Chlorinated phenols	36. Fluoranthene

TABLE 7.3 Compounds identified by EPA as toxic pollutants and subject to regulation as such under the CWA. Summarized from 40 CFR 401.15.

5. Phenolic compounds—an entire family of volatile, highly toxic organic compounds.

6. Ammonia, measured as nitrogen.

7. Sulfides.

8. Total chromium, a heavy metal.

9. Hexavalent chromium—a chemically active form of chromium.

10. pH—a measure of relative acidity or alkalinity; the hydrogen ion concentration on a logarithmic scale. A pH of 7.0 is neutral, and a pH of 5.0 is ten times more acidic than a pH of 6.0. Values above 7.0 reflect basic conditions of alkalinity. For the petroleum refining industry, the allowable pH of effluent ranges from 6.0 to 9.0.

Obviously, the petroleum industry represents significant threats to water quality and requires extensive regulations. Compliance efforts involve an equally broad spectrum of specialty disciplines including engineering, physics, and chemistry. Currently, scientists applying the most innovative biotechnology methods are working to develop microorganisms that will degrade or neutralize many of the toxic products associated with the petroleum refining industry.

Canned Fruit Industry. By contrast, the canned and preserved fruit industry faces only three of the criteria the petroleum industry must satisfy: BOD5, TSS, and pH. The BOD5 concern reflects the enormous quantities of raw plant material this industry generates. TSS and pH are concerns associated with essentially all industries that require water in their processing activities.

Although the goal is constant, obviously, not all criteria apply to all industries, and achievable standards vary with the industry. The CFR specifies the specific standards for each criterion for each regulated industry. A discussion of the complex technology for each industrial area, criterion, and pollutant is beyond the scope of this text; the individual technical fields should provide that type of specific technical information.

Subchapter IV, Permits and Wetland Regulations

The construction or operation of any facility that might result in the discharge of pollutants into the waters of the United States requires a permit or license. Subchapter IV sets licensing standards and criteria. Under authority of 334 USC 1341(a), the administrator may issue permits for the discharge of pollutants so long as the provisions of the law are satisfied. This subchapter includes Section 404 of the Clean Water Act (33 USC 1344), which specifically considers the discharge of dredge or fill material into the navigable waters of the United States. This section provides the statutory basis for one of the more controversial elements of the act, the regulation of draining or filling wetlands.

Wetlands and Permits.   The act vests regulatory authority in the Secretary of the Army, through the Army Corps of Engineers, to issue permits to discharge dredge or fill materials into the navigable waters of the United States: wetlands are included in the definition of navigable waters. The EPA retains veto power over permits. The history of wetland regulation explains the role of the Corps in the permitting process.

At the close of the last century, Congress amended the Rivers and Harbors Act and empowered the Corps to include in its authority with respect to river and harbor development and maintenance the authority to issue permits for the discharge of dredge and fill materials into the navigable waters of the United States. This is the authority exercised in wetlands regulations.

An Initial Issue.   The definition of "navigable waters" presented one of the first issues associated with this authority. Court decisions defined these waters in a very broad sense, with little direct link to actual commercial navigation. Bodies of water with a remote path to the navigable waters of the United States also fall under the authority of this section. The definition or identification of wetlands presented a similar controversy.

The Delineation Issue.   By agreement among affected agencies, the criteria include specific soils factors associated with hydromorphic soils, vegetation that is typical of "swamplike" areas, periodic flooding or water table criteria, and the hydrology of the area. Although the criteria are to apply nationwide, controversies still arise from regional differences in both soils and plant communities. In addition, several agencies have been involved with decision making regarding wetland delineations.

In 1994, the government clarified many of these issues through presidential directives and interagency agreements. Currently, wetland delineation criteria are based on the 1985 *Corps Delineation Manual.* The Corps retains permitting responsibility and general responsibility for all wetlands except agricultural lands, which, except for permitting, fall under the authority of the Soil Conservation Service.

These regulatory changes were made in response to widespread criticisms that no agency had final authority and that too frequently landowners received different answers from different agencies. At least for agricultural purposes, the situation has been simplified. Part of the special treatment for agriculture stems from the fact that agricultural lands fell under the Farm Act "Swamp Buster" provisions, which denied farmers farm bill benefits for damaging wetlands, thereby requiring agricultural producers always to work on wetland questions with at least two agencies, the Corps of Engineers and the Soil Conservation Service.

Exemptions.   The provisions of 33 USC 1344 have led to a series of rules in the CFR. These include nationwide exemptions to the permitting process for "normal farming and silvicultural activities" and a series of national (preexisting) permits for special, limited purposes ranging from navigational aids and bridge work to water-measuring devices. The permits have specific conditions that must be satisfied before activity can be undertaken.

The provisions of this section apply only for identified wetlands. Both the Corps and SCS have adopted the policy articulated by President George Bush prior to his election in 1990—no net loss of wetlands. If a permit is granted to disturb a wetland, the development must compensate for lost wetlands by creating additional wetlands. Plans involving wetlands must show how damage will be mitigated and minimized. Developers are encouraged to mitigate bank wetlands: develop and preserve wetlands in one area before seeking to disturb them in any other area. The CFR addresses mitigation criteria.

Federal Legislation

Provisions of the CWA just discussed, including extensive administrative rules, provide the substantive federal law regulating wetlands. Congress has stated general policy regarding the preservation of wetlands in Title 16, Conservation. Chapters 59 and 59a of Title 16, 16 USC 3901 *et seq.,* express both reasons to preserve wetlands and general policy. In its finding of facts, Congress recognized eight points regarding the value of and threats to the nation's wetland resources:

1. Wetlands play an integrated role in maintaining the quality of life through material contributions to national economy, flood control, and forest, wildlife, and plant resources, thus benefiting human health and welfare.
2. Wetlands provide critical habitat for wildlife, fish, and migratory fowl, including endangered species.
3. Migratory bird treaties with Canada, Mexico, Japan, and (the former) USSR require continued protection of America's wetlands.
4. Wetlands produce significant commercial benefits, up to $10 billion annually.
5. Wetlands enhance water quality.
6. Wetlands provide flood and erosion control.
7. Wetlands constitute only a small portion of the lands of the United States.

8. Some federal government agencies have harmed wetlands.

With these findings, Congress declared it is the policy of the United States to cooperate in the preservation of wetlands.

Subchapter VI, Funding Authorization

The final subchapter, Subchapter VI (33 USC 1381 through 1387), is the shortest of the FWPCA. It provides authorization for, and directs the administrator to make, capitalization grants to each state to establish a water pollution control revolving fund to assist in the construction of treatment works, to implement plans for nonpoint pollution control, and to protect natural resources under the National Estuary Program. This brief section considers the administration of the financial aid program with little additional substantive regulation of water quality, although it does reflect congressional awareness of a federal responsibility to assist states in meeting federally imposed rules and regulations.

SAFE DRINKING WATER

Although the Water Pollution Control Act considers health issues, in the Safe Drinking Water Act (SDWA), 42 USC 300a through 300j-25, Congress addressed the health-related issues of drinking water safety and public health in specific detail. This short act evolved from the Public Health Act of 1944, and now is found as Subchapter XII, Chapter 6A, Title 42, The Public Health and Welfare, of the *United States Code*. The act is relatively short—thirty-four pages of text—but it covers a complex area critical to public health and is divided into six parts, lettered A through F. The subject matter of the parts provides an overview of the provisions and scope of the act:

Part A, Definitions

Part B, Public water systems

Part C, Protecting underground sources of drinking water

Part D, Emergency powers

Part E, General provisions

Part F, Additional requirements

Specific definitions delineate the scope and intent of Congress with respect to the act. Key definitions include (1) "primary drinking water regulation," which means regulations applying to public water systems concerning specific contaminants that affect public health; (2) "public water systems," which are systems that provide piped water for the public; and (3) "maximum contaminant level," defined as the maximum allowable level of a contaminant delivered to a user of a public water system. As in other acts, the administrator is defined as the administrator of the EPA.

Part E treats the general administration of the act. The first section, 42 USC 300j, establishes the importance Congress places on ensuring the safety of public water supplies. It effectively guarantees that chemicals needed for treating water will be made available to public water systems. In addition, the administrator is authorized to initiate research programs related to human health effects of contaminated water. This part also authorizes the administrator to make specific grants to states, authorizes appropriations for such grants, and requires development of water quality guidelines for a specific group of contaminants—including microbiological, viral, radiological, organic, and inorganic contaminants—and for any grant for demonstration projects involving water recycling, reclamation, and reuse. The act grants citizens a private right of action to have the provisions of the act enforced.

In terms of regulations, Part B, Public Water Systems, contains the heart of the act. Congress places primary responsibility for enforcement of drinking water standards on the states. The act refers to national or interim standards and directs the administrator to revise them as appropriate. The current standards are found in 40 CFR 141 *et seq.* The subdivision of Part 141 reflects the detailed complexity of the standards. This part comprises eight subparts, the most significant of which are B, Maximum Contaminant Levels; F, Maximum Contaminant Level Goals; G, Revised Goals and Effective Dates; and H, Filtration and Disinfection Standards. The initial contaminants included organic and inorganic compounds, turbidity, and several types and sources of radioactive materials. The goals include standards for organic and inorganic compounds and microbiological contaminants. These regulations also set the standards for the control of lead and copper in drinking water.

Part F addresses lead specifically with a narrow focus on lead in coolers; it defines "coolers" as any mechanical device that is part of a drinking water system and that cools water for consumption. "Lead free" essentially refers to all plumbing associated with coolers, including pipes, and sets a maximum lead concentration allowable in the system. The major focus of this section is the elimination of lead from cooler systems in schools because of the greater potential harm associated with exposure of young children to lead, but the act extends protection from lead to everyone by prohibiting the use of lead pipes, solder, or flux in public water systems as well as in residential and nonresidential facilities connected to public water systems.

In Part B, Congress specifically requires the administrator to hold public hearings prior to promulgation of drinking water standards. Recall that the Federal Administrative Procedure Act requires notice and comment, but not public hearings unless required by Congress. Clearly Congress recognizes the intense public interest in the provisions of the act and the continued resentment to the imposition of federal rules on the states. The required hearings modify problems and, of course, provide meaningful input to the rule markers.

Part C addresses the protection of groundwater supplies and, like the delegation of responsibility in Part B, places this responsibility on the states. This part also regulates specific activities that might otherwise adversely affect underground water supplies, such as underground injections and similar hydrological activities. It also provides specifically for wellhead protection and requires each state to develop a plan for protecting areas around wellheads from contaminants.

The last part to be considered, Part D, Emergency Powers, allows the administrator to take action to protect any public water system or groundwater source threatened with a contaminant when state authorities fail to take appropriate action. In recent decades, in response to severe drought conditions coupled with increasing demands for water, states have also adopted emergency authority legislation to supplement the actions under the emergency provisions of the Safe Drinking Water Act. The heart of many state plans is water-rationing authority vested in the governor of the state.

CONCLUSIONS

Clearly, pollution threatens many of the nation's water resources. Congress has recognized this continuing problem and has taken strong steps to address both the reduction of pollution and the prevention of continued pollution from point sources. Nonpoint sources represent the biggest, but currently inadequately regulated, source of water pollution. Agriculture continues to be targeted as a serious nonpoint source polluter, but many urban activities also contribute as nonpoint source polluters.

QUESTIONS AND CONCEPTS FOR DISCUSSION AND RESEARCH

1. Discuss the concepts and fundamental differences between riparian and "appropriation" water rights. Note how rights to groundwater are similar to or different from these two basic rights to surface water.

2. Characterize the scope and congressional intent of the Clean Water Act.

3. What critical terms with specific definitions apply to the Clean Water Act?

4. What are the major policy aspects of the Clean Water Act?

5. Congress took a unique step in identifying industrial sources of water pollution in the CWA. Describe several of these industries and the pollutants they produce.

6. What is the history and statutory basis for federal regulation of wetlands? What are the national permits? What are the origin and significance of the no net loss policy?

7. What basic issues does the Safe Drinking Water Act address? What are the major pollutants of concern? What is the major policy emphasis of the act?

REFERENCES AND SELECTED READING

Kubasek, Nancy K., and Gary S. Silverman. 1994. *Environmental Law.* Englewood Cliffs, NJ: Prentice Hall.

Nebel, Bernard J., and Richard T. Wright. 1993. *Environmental Science: The Way the World Works.* Englewood Cliffs, NJ: Prentice Hall.

U.S. Environmental Protection Agency. February 1988. *America's Wetlands, Our Vital Link Between Land and Water.* EPA-87-016. Washington, DC.

————. December 1989. *Glossary of Environmental Terms and Acronym List.* EPA 19K-1002. Washington, DC.

————. April 1990. *Citizen's Guide to Groundwater Protection.* EPA 841-S-94-002. Washington, DC.

————. 1992. *The Quality of Our Nation's Waters.* EPA 841-S-94-002. Washington, DC.

————. May 1994. *Is Your Drinking Water Safe?* EPA 810-F-94-002. Washington, DC.

PART FOUR

Waste Management

8

Waste and Waste Disposal

INTRODUCTION

The accumulation of waste from industrial, commercial, and residential sources has become one of the nation's leading environmental concerns. The magnitude of the problem of waste disposal generates the grim image that America may be "drowning" in its garbage! Although overstated in these terms, the problem of waste disposal has reached a critical level.

Growth of the Problem

Waste disposal is not a new problem. It accelerated after World War II for a variety of reasons: New products—plastics and man-made fibers—became readily available, the economy flourished, consumer demands for goods skyrocketed, and the nation's population grew dramatically with the post-War baby boom. Despite intensified efforts to reduce waste, the Environmental Protection Agency predicts continued increases in municipal solid waste as well as in hazardous and toxic wastes and nuclear wastes.

Table 8.1 reflects the pattern of increase in the generation of municipal solid waste (common household garbage) and suggests several important issues. First, paper and paper products represent the major component of waste currently going to landfill facilities. However, paper can be recycled, which can reduce this source of waste dramatically. Second, plastics represent a serious source of waste, but these data do not adequately reflect two important considerations: (1) increasingly successful recent efforts to recycle plastics, and (2) major efforts to render many plastics more "biodegradable" so that they do not persist in landfills seemingly indefinitely. The greatest progress in recycling seems to have been

Material	Year		
	1970	**1986**	**2000**
paper and paperboard	32.5	50.1	66.0
glass	12.5	11.8	12.0
metals	13.5	12.6	14.4
plastics	3.0	10.3	15.6
rubber, leather, textiles, wood	9.0	12.5	13.2
food waste	12.8	12.5	12.3
other nonfood product waste	0.1	0.1	0.1
yard waste	23.2	28.3	32.0
miscellaneous inorganics	1.9	2.6	3.2

TABLE 8.1 Material discarded as municipal solid waste for the period 1970–2000, expressed in millions of tons. From *The Waste System.* U.S. Environmental Protection Agency. November 1988.

realized with aluminum cans, and as more states enact bottle deposit laws, greater progress in recycling glass should be anticipated as well. Regardless of all positive efforts, waste accumulation remains a most serious problem in the United States.

The Impact of Humans

Unfortunately, human activity unavoidably generates certain amounts of waste. In the past, two factors minimized the serious nature of waste disposal recognized today: In the United States, adequate open land abounded, and waste conveniently was dumped "out of sight, out of mind." In addition, prior to World War II, the nature and quantity of much of the waste dumped in open pits and spilled or dumped into rivers and lakes did not represent the serious problems that waste of today poses in terms of toxicity and degradability.

The Price of Convenience

The American consumer enjoys a fantastic array of all types of products, from necessities such as food to conveniences and luxury items. In addition to their abundance and diversity, several features characterize consumer products today. Two have enormous impact on waste accumulation.

A single word characterizes many products and explains part of the negative environmental impact of the products—convenience, in the form of packaging, including the type of packaging materials used, and the continuously growing number of throwaway, disposable, or one-time-use items virtually all Americans enjoy daily.

Packaging

Many food products provide familiar examples of packaging:

- the styrofoam fast-food containers that all too frequently litter roadsides;
- precooked, packaged meals;
- individually packaged, single servings of meats, dairy products, and diet foods, and even individually wrapped pieces of fruit.

Food products are not the only offenders. Health care and personal hygiene products commonly are packaged for safety and convenience of single-dosage units. The list goes on to include everything from toys to recreational and sporting equipment and household and home repair products.

The type of material used for packaging represents a potential environmental problem. Table 8.1 indicates paper products as a major source of waste; much of this waste is in the form of excessive packaging materials, and paper does not degrade rapidly in a dump environment. Increasingly, plastics are used as packing materials and wrappers; consider the number of items sealed in plastic mounted on a paper base or back. These represent more materials for the landfill that resist natural degradation.

Excessive packaging poses a serious waste problem, but neither the packaging industry nor wholesale or retail distributors should bear the entire blame. Much of the packaging is in response to consumer demands. Packaging plays a significant role in marketing, and modern packaging technology increases convenience and adds to product quality and safety. The issue is not the elimination of packaging, but rather reduction of excessive, waste-generating packaging that seems to serve only the purpose of consumer convenience combined with efforts to make packaging materials either easier to recycle or more susceptible to natural degradation.

Disposables

Convenience impacts waste accumulation through increasing consumer use of "throwaway" or single-use items that modern technology and materials have made readily available: plastic tableware, plastic-treated takeout containers, and "no deposit-no return" bottles, plus the vast array of "replace, do not repair" appliances—everything from battery-operated pencil sharpeners and letter openers to hair dryers, throwaway razors, and multitudes of toys and "gadgets" for the home and office. The increase in the use of battery-operated appliances and toys has generated two problems: disposal of the appliance or toy and disposal of the battery that represents a source of heavy-metal pollution.

The story could continue endlessly, but consider a final example, the disposable diaper. Manufacturers recognize that these popular products represent a significant source of waste. The necessary plastic liners limit their biodegradability and add to their persistence in landfills. However, this convenience could be environmentally friendly: paper/disposable diapers eliminate the environmental cost of washing diapers—heating water and frequent detergent discharge to sewage systems.

Manufacturing

Manufacturing in general represents a major source of waste, including toxic and hazardous waste products whose safe disposal requires special technical considerations. In response to increasing awareness of the problems and strict pollution control regulations, potential harm from hazardous waste has been reduced, but the problem remains significant in terms of generation of wastes. EPA data reveal several major industrial types that generate large quantities of hazardous waste: These include the chemical industries, with all types of compounds from corrosive agents, acids, and organic chemical compounds to pesticides; the fabricated metal industry, with heavy-metal residues in waste water sludge and electrical equipment, with solvents and degreasing compounds and polychlorinated biphenols (PCBs); and petroleum refineries. Numerous other industries, including leather tanning, the wood and wood pulp industries, and textile industries, generate various types of hazardous waste.

Waste Generated to Protect the Environment

Ironically, the technology available to reduce air and water pollution can lead to the production of solid wastes and hazardous wastes; sludge from water treatment facilities presents an excellent example. Treatment technology allows a variety of hazardous and toxic substances to be removed from waste water before that water is allowed to enter a stream, a lake, or the ocean. Unfortunately, the treatment process yields sludge in which the hazardous materials accumulate, and may be more concentrated than in the polluted water. The sludge then becomes a waste product that commonly finds its way to landfills and represents a truly hazardous material. The same types of problems exist with respect to incinerators and disposal of residue from the incineration of various types of wastes.

In many instances, the hazardous waste is a by-product of the manufacturing process, not a matter of choice to the manufacturer. As a result, waste control efforts assume several forms: improve technology to reduce the waste produced, recycle products to reduce waste produced, and formulate new products whose manufacture does not generate hazardous waste materials. Because elimination of such wastes seems to be effectively impossible, major emphasis is also placed on the ultimate safe disposal of the waste material. Governmental regulations address this complex topic from several vantage points: waste reduction at the source; new manufacturing processes and products; and strict regulation of disposal sites. Federal regulations distinguish municipal solid waste and hazardous waste and recognize two major problem areas—currently active waste disposal sites and closed waste disposal sites—that continue to pose serious environmental threats.

WASTE DISPOSAL

By the end of the second decade following World War II, Americans realized that the generation and disposal of solid waste had become a problem of national proportion. This recognition included increasing awareness that the old methods of using open dumps and discharging all kinds of waste into lakes, rivers, and the oceans constituted a truly serious health threat. During this same era, general public interest over the environment was touching virtually every facet of life as the nation entered a period of active concern over the degradation of the environment.

Early Legislative History

Congress first addressed the solid waste issue in 1965, passing the Solid Waste Disposal Act. In 1970, recognizing the potential value of materials commonly disposed of as municipal solid waste, Congress amended the Solid Waste Disposal Act and gave birth to the Resource Recovery Act. The amendments placed the federal government squarely in the waste management scene. In 1976, the act was amended to give rise to the Resource Conservation and Recovery Act, RCRA, 42 USC 6901 *et seq.* (Solid Waste Disposal). The 1976 legislation effectively brought waste disposal under federal regulation. This act addresses issues related to currently operating landfill (dump) sites. Subsequent to RCRA, Congress enacted the Superfund, which addresses issues related to closed or inactive dump sites.

The Resource Conservation and Recovery Act

Congress clearly expressed its intent in RCRA in terms of the primary goals of the legislation:

1. To protect human health and the environment,
2. To conserve energy and natural resources,
3. To reduce waste generated, including hazardous waste, and
4. To ensure environmentally safe waste management.

In the provisions of RCRA, Congress distinguished between "municipal solid waste" and "hazardous waste," a distinction that at times may appear to lack logic, but one that is reflected throughout the act.

Implementing RCRA to achieve these very wide-sweeping goals has required the formulation of a plan for an integrated approach to waste management; many of the rules and regulations promulgated under the authority of this act reflect this integration. The efforts involve every phase of waste generation and disposal, from reduction at the source and energy conservation in manufacture to recycling and reuse, including composting organic materials and even the capture and use of gas (methane) produced as a result of natural decaying processes, the use of waste as a source of fuel, and the use of heat from incinerators as a source of energy.

For both hazardous waste and municipal solid waste, the provisions of RCRA reflect the most serious concern for protecting water sources. The emphasis on waste reduction and recycling reflects this in part, but the very specific requirements for landfill design for disposal of either category of waste leave no doubt about the serious nature of the problem or congressional intent to address that issue.

Structure of RCRA

The Resource Conservation and Recovery Act is codified as Chapter 82 of Title 42, The Public Health, and is cited as 42 USC 690-1 *et seq.* This act is divided into ten subchapters, designated I through X. In terms of actual waste management and disposal, three subchapters are of critical importance: Subchapter III—Hazardous Waste Management; Subchapter IV—State and Regional Solid Waste Management Plans; and Subchapter X—Underground Storage Tanks. Subchapter X is discussed in chapter 9 and the other two in the following pages, which also include other provisions of the act.

In some instances, reference is made to the subtitles of the actual act as written by Congress rather than to the comparable subchapter of the *Code.* Thus, Subchapter III, 42

USC 6921–6932, may be referred to as "Subtitle C" of the act, and facilities required by this legislation as "a Subtitle C landfill." The same confusion may be found for Subchapter IV, 42 USC 6941–6949, and Subtitle D, or Subtitle D facilities. Regardless of the designation, the law is exactly the same.

The act is lengthy and complex in that it distinguishes various types of wastes and specifies regulations for the various categories. The first major distinction is household and municipal solid waste separated from hazardous waste, although household and municipal solid waste may, at times, include substances that are considered hazardous. Thus, definitions that specify what types of waste fall under which legislative provisions become critical. Because a major danger arising from disposal of all forms of waste involves the potential of water pollution, of either surface water or groundwater, the act incorporates definitions and standards that have their origins in the Clean Water Act and/or the Safe Drinking Water Act and are even tied to provisions of the Clean Air Act.

As codified, the act consists of ten subchapters that provide an overview of the act:

1. General provisions
2. Office of Solid Waste, authority of the administrator
3. Hazardous Waste Management (Subtitle C of the act)
4. State or regional solid waste plans (Subtitle D of the act)
5. Directing the secretary of commerce's role in resource recovery
6. Federal responsibilities
7. Miscellaneous provisions
8. Research and development/information
9. Regulation of underground storage tanks (Subtitle I of the act)
10. Demonstration, medical waste tracking

General Provisions

In the general provisions, Subchapter I, 42 USC 6901 *et seq.*, Congress expresses broad concern over four related topics: solid waste, environment and health, materials, and energy.

With respect to the first topic, Congress addresses the accumulation of solid waste and specifically notes the problems associated with packaging and discarded materials. In addition, Congress looks to a high standard of living that has resulted in the demolition of older buildings, new construction, and new roads that have yielded "a tide of waste," and to the fact that urbanization has concentrated waste and waste disposal problems. Finally, Congress asserted that the management of these problems should remain a state, regional, or local function, but their magnitude makes them national concerns.

Land Utilization as a Special Issue

Congress expressed growing concern that waste disposal used increasing areas of valuable land and noted that land disposal of waste presented a serious health hazard when not carefully planned and managed. Congress further recognized that other environmental legislation—notably, the Clean Air Act and Water Pollution Control Act—contributes to the problem by leading to the production of sludge that requires disposal, frequently in land-fills. Linked with this is the clear realization that open dumping endangers both surface wa-ter and groundwater supplies. Focusing on hazardous waste, Congress stated that mismanagement of such materials leads to serious health problems, and that problem pre-vention is superior to remediation. Congress also noted the high cost of correcting or clean-ing up problems from the initial mishandling of hazardous waste materials. Finally, in expressing a major policy position, Congress declared that landfills are not dependable and should be the last choice for waste disposal. This position alone sounded the cry for a com-prehensive, integrated approach to waste management.

The Case for Recycling and Reuse

In addition to concerns over the fate of waste materials as health and environmental hazards, Congress observed that much waste material annually included millions of tons of material that could be recovered and reused or otherwise recycled. Not only is such re-covery environmentally sound but, as Congress noted, it will reduce the nation's depen-dency on foreign oil and generally conserve energy. With regard to this "recycling emphasis," Congress noted that the technology to separate materials to implement these steps is available.

Finally, concerning energy, Congress noted two key points in the act. First, much waste is suitable for use as fuel, and second, the nation must strive to develop alternative forms of fuel. The Congress asserted that the technology also exists to develop such alter-native forms of energy that might use solid wastes.

Congressional Objectives and Policies

Given the preceding goals, Congress formulated specific objectives and policies to meet them. Objectives of the act encompass three major points:

1. Protect health and the environment,
2. Provide technical and financial assistance to improve waste management, and
3. Prohibit open dumping.

The prohibition of dumping does not end land disposal of waste, but it requires application of technology to the design and operation of landfill facilities in an environmentally safe manner, coupled with all efforts to minimize waste destined for landfills.

The act clearly expresses the nation's policy regarding waste management: WHERE FEASIBLE, REDUCE (OR ELIMINATE) THE GENERATION OF HAZARDOUS WASTE AS RAPIDLY AS POSSIBLE. This policy of elimination of waste extends to municipal solid waste as well. The act calls in effect for a coordinated effort to reduce waste at the source, recycle waste, including composting as much waste as possible, re-cover energy from waste, and, finally, dispose of the minimum amount of waste in landfill facilities.

Subchapter I includes key definitions on which much of the substance of the act de-pends; see 42 USC 6903 for the list of definitions. The act defines "hazardous waste" as a solid waste, or combination of solid waste, which because of its quantity, concentration, or physical, chemical, or infectious characteristics may—

(A) cause, or significantly contribute to an increase in mortality or an increase in serious, irreversible illness, or

(B) pose a substantial present or potential hazard to human health or the environment when improperly treated, stored, transported, or disposed of or otherwise managed.

Hazardous waste displays one or more of the following hazardous characteristics: ignitability, corrosivity, reactivity, or toxicity. Based on these criteria, 40 CFR 261 provides a detailed list of specific hazardous waste materials; currently over 400 wastes are listed.

Congress excluded "household garbage" and "municipal solid waste" from its definition of hazardous waste. These extensive sources of waste are treated as municipal solid waste according to the act. Such waste comes from single- and multiple-family dwellings, hotels and motels, and from manufacturing processes that do not produce hazardous waste.

Subchapters II, V, VI, VII, VIII, IX, and X

No subchapter should be viewed as unimportant, but these seven are not central to the basic discussion of the management of solid and hazardous waste. They can conveniently be discussed briefly in a single group.

Subchapter II considers administration of the act through the Office of Solid Waste and provides guidelines for the authority of the Administrator regarding waste management programs. Subchapter V confirms the congressional intent to stress recycling. This subchapter directs the secretary of commerce to formulate plans to ensure the use and commercial success of recycled materials as far as possible. Subchapter VI focuses on federal responsibilities regarding the provisions of the act. These include both compliance with the provisions of the act and the use of recycled materials.

Subchapter VII includes several provisions of public interest. It provides "whistleblower" protection from retaliation by an employer for people who report violations of provisions of the act. Subchapter VII also grants individual citizens the judicial, private right of action to bring suit to have provisions of the act enforced through court orders and to have violators penalized, and it calls for public participation in formulating waste management plans. This public participation becomes increasingly significant in decisions regarding locating and operating new landfill facilities.

Subchapter VIII deals with research and development activities and federal support of research efforts. Subchapter IX considers the specific and serious problems associated with leaking underground storage tanks. Finally, Subchapter X details a demonstration program for tracking medical wastes.

HAZARDOUS WASTE MANAGEMENT

Hazardous waste, as defined by the act, is primarily the product of the nation's industries. Leading producers include the petroleum refining industry and chemical industries. Table 8.2 summarizes general groups of industries and the types of hazardous wastes produced by each. This table also suggests that many of the products commonly used either contain hazardous products, or their manufacture results in the production of hazardous wastes.

Waste Generators	Waste Type
Chemical Manufacturers	Strong Acids and Bases Spent Solvents Reactive Wastes
Vehicle Maintenance Shops	Heavy Metal Paint Wastes Ignitable Wastes Used Lead Acid Batteries Spent Solvents
Printing Industry	Heavy Metal Solutions Waste Inks Spent Solvents Spent Electroplating Wastes Ink Sludges Containing Heavy Metals
Leather Products Manufacturing	Waste Toluene and Benzene
Paper Industry	Paint Wastes Containing Heavy Metals Ignitable Solvents Strong Acids and Bases
Construction Industry	Ignitable Paint Wastes Spent Solvents Strong Acids and Bases
Cleaning Agents and Cosmetics Manufacturing	Heavy Metal Dusts Ignitable Wastes Flammable Solvents Strong Acids and Bases
Furniture and Wood Manufacturing and Refinishing	Ignitable Wastes Spent Solvents
Metal Manufacturing	Paint Wastes Containing Heavy Metals Strong Acids and Bases Cyanide Wastes Sludges Containing Heavy Metals

TABLE 8.2 General types or categories of industries with examples of waste generated by each. From *Solving the Hazardous Waste Problem: EPA's RCRA Program*. EPA/530-SW-86-037. U.S. Environmental Protection Agency. November 1986.

Four general methods are employed to dispose of hazardous waste. The most common, accounting for approximately 60 percent of the waste, is the use of steel- or concrete-lined deep shafts or wells into which liquids are injected under pressure. Up to 35 percent of the waste is stored in surface ponds, lagoons, or pits; leakage and leachate from such facilities is a growing environmental concern. About 5 percent is disposed of in landfills developed with special liners to minimize leakage, and only 1 percent is discharged into open pits or dumps.

Subchapter III, Hazardous Waste Management

By definition, municipal solid waste is not considered hazardous waste, and therefore disposal is not subject to the stringent regulations of Subtitle C of the RCRA, which constitutes Subchapter III of the act, Hazardous Waste Management. The length and detail of Subchapter III reflect the complexity of issues related to the management of hazardous waste and the serious congressional attention devoted to this growing problem.

The first section of subchapter III, 42 USC 6921, suggests the complexity of the entire subchapter in terms of the five subsections that it comprises. The first subsection, 6921(a), specifies criteria for identifying or listing hazardous wastes. The act directs the administrator of the Environmental Protection Agency to establish criteria for identifying hazardous wastes and to cooperate with other agencies to ensure that such listings include carcinogens, mutagens, and tetratogens at levels hazardous to human health. This subsection also specifies initial criteria to be applied for the identification of hazardous wastes. The act directs the administrator to take into consideration "toxicity, persistence, and degradability in nature, potential for accumulation in tissue, and other related factors such as flammability, corrosiveness, and other hazardous characteristics." These factors suggest, but do not repeat, the factors described in the expanded description of hazardous waste that includes "toxicity" and "reactivity" and that now applies to listings found in the CFRs. In addition, this first subsection directs the administrator to conduct a survey so that sites used for the disposal of hazardous wastes can be identified and located in the future.

Large- and Small-Scale Generators of Waste

In terms of regulations, the act distinguishes between large- and small-scale generators of hazardous wastes. Small-scale generators are defined as producing more than 100 kg (220 pounds), but less than 1,000 kg (2,200 pounds) of hazardous wastes per month. The initial focus of regulations centered virtually exclusively on large-scale generators of hazardous wastes, but the act also establishes time frames to develop rules applicable to small-scale generators. Although the act distinguishes generators of hazardous waste based on size, no distinctions are made in terms of wastes to be regulated. A variety of businesses fall under the small-scale generator provisions of the act. For example, commercial dry cleaning operations produce residues from hazardous solvents, and furniture manufacturers produce both combustible by-products and use wood finishing products that leave hazardous by-products. Table 8.3 summarizes a variety of small-scale generator industries and the hazardous wastes they may produce. Note that businesses that produce less than 100 kg (220 pounds) per month are conditionally exempt from regulation under this act.

Finally, this extensive initial section of Subchapter III clarifies the exclusion of municipal solid waste as hazardous waste. To be excluded, such waste must come from single- and multiple-family dwellings, motels and hotels, and from industries that do not discharge listed substances.

Subchapter III has given rise to a multitude of rules found in 40 CFR 260–290, all of which reflect the scope and intent of the act. A single section, 42 USC 6922, applies to the generators of hazardous waste and provides authorization for several major elements of regulations related to record keeping and labeling waste materials. A key point is the requirement that after September 1, 1985, the generator of the hazardous waste is required

Type of Business Typical	How Generated	Types of Wastes
Drycleaning and Laundry Plants	Commercial drycleaning processes	Still residues from solvent distillation, spent filter cartridges, cooked powder residue
Furniture/Wood Manufacturing and Refinishing	Wood cleaning and wax removal, refinishing/stripping, staining, painting, finishing, brush cleaning and spray brush cleaning	Ignitable wastes, toxic wastes, solvent wastes, paint wastes
Construction	Paint preparation and painting, carpentry and floor work, other specialty contracting activities, heavy construction, wrecking and demolition, vehicle and equipment maintenance for construction activities	Ignitable wastes, toxic wastes, solvent wastes, paint wastes, used oil, acids/bases
Laboratories	Diagnostic and other laboratory testing	Spent solvents, unused reagents, reaction products, testing samples, contaminated materials
Vehicle Maintenance	Degreasing, rust removal, paint preparation, spray booth, spray guns, brush cleaning, paint removal, tank cleanout, installing lead-acid batteries	Acids/bases, solvents, ignitable wastes, toxic wastes, paint wastes, batteries
Printing and Allied Industries	Plate preparation, stencil preparation for screen printing, photoprocessing, printing, cleanup	Acids/bases, heavy metal wastes, solvents, toxic wastes, ink
Equipment Repair	Degreasing, equipment cleaning, rust removal, paint preparation, painting, paint removal, spray booth, spray guns, and brush cleaning.	Acids/bases, toxic wastes, ignitable wastes, paint wastes, solvents
Pesticide End-Users/Application Services	Pesticide application and cleanup	Used/unused pesticides, solvent wastes, ignitable wastes, contaminated soil (from spills), contaminated rinsewater, empty containers
Educational and Vocational Shops	Automobile engine and body repair, metalworking, graphic arts-plate preparation, woodworking	Ignitable wastes, solvent wastes, acids/bases, paint wastes

TABLE 8.3 Examples of small businesses with the hazardous wastes they produce and the processes that generate such waste. From *Understanding the Hazardous Waste Rules: A Handbook for Small Business—1996 Update.* EPA 530-K-95-001. U.S. Environmental Protection Agency. June 1996.

to certify efforts to minimize the production of the waste and, as far as practicable, to ensure safety.

Transportation of Waste

A separate section, 42 USC 6923, regulates transportation, including the requirement of a strict manifest system to track the waste from the site of generation to storage and ultimate disposal. Transportation of hazardous waste must comply with the provisions of the Hazardous Waste Transportation Act (49 USC 1801). The Emergency Preparedness and the Community Right to Know Act also regulates aspects of the transportation of hazardous materials.

Treatment, Storage, and Disposal Facilities (TSDFs)

Facilities used for the storage, treatment, or ultimate disposal of hazardous waste constitute a major area of regulation under the provisions of Subchapter III of RCRA. The statutory provisions and rules authorized by statute reflect two related concerns: the dangers from direct contact with the hazardous waste, and the dangers that result from the substances leaking or escaping from treatment, storage, or disposal facilities and contaminating sources of groundwater and surface water. The act contains twenty-five specific provisions related to the regulation of facilities. 42 USC 6924(a)–(g). Each subsection covers one provision.

The first subsection establishes requirements for public hearings prior to establishing standards for record keeping, monitoring manifest requirements, and the location, design, and structure of facilities. Design specifications for all types of facilities and processes are found in 40 CFR 260 *et seq.* The second provision considers a somewhat unique situation, the use of salt domes for storage of hazardous wastes. The storage of uncontainerized materials is prohibited. The third provision addresses the specific rules for disposal of liquids: All liquids now must be in a container, and this subsection calls for steps to minimize liquids containing hazardous substances. The act also requires the inclusion of an absorbent, even with appropriately containerized liquids.

The next subsection prohibits land disposal of specific wastes, except as approved for disposal by injection in deep, lined wells unless the director of the EPA determines that the disposal creates no hazard to human health and to the environment. The director must consider factors such as long-term uncertainties associated with land disposal and the basic goal of handling hazardous waste in an appropriate manner. Specific prohibitions include the following:

1. Anything liquid, including sludge, with free cyanides with a concentration of more than 1,000 mg/l;
2. Liquids, including sludge, with arsenic, cadmium, lead, mercury, nickel, selenium, or thallium in amounts ranging from 500 mg/l to 100 mg/l, depending on the specific metal;
3. Liquids with a pH of 2.0 or less—very strong acids;
4. Liquid hazardous waste with PCBs (polychlorinatedbiphenyls) with concentrations equal to or exceeding 50 ppm.
5. Hazardous waste with halogenated organic compounds containing more than 1,000 mg/kg.

When necessary, the administrator may apply stricter standards. In the eighth subsection, Congress has directed the administrator to review and supplement this list.

The fifth subsection prohibits the disposal of solvents and dioxins, and the sixth establishes special provisions for the disposal of these compounds. The ninth listed subsection provides for variances from the prohibitions for land disposal of hazardous wastes, and the tenth requires the administrator to publish notice of methods determined to be safe for land disposal. The eleventh subsection prohibits the continued storage of hazardous waste that cannot be disposed of. The twelfth subsection defines land disposal as it relates to specific hazardous wastes to include, but not be limited to, "any placement of such hazardous waste in a landfill, surface impoundment, waste pile, injection well, land treatment facility, salt dome formation, salt bed formation, or underground mine or cave." The next subchapter prohibits the use for dust suppression of used oil or other materials that are contaminated with dioxin or any other hazardous waste, which is a common practice in some rural areas to reduce dust on unpaved roads.

The thirteenth subsection directs the administrator to establish standards for the treatment of hazardous waste materials that will allow the safe disposal of those materials. These standards should "substantially diminish the toxicity of the waste or substantially reduce the likelihood of migration of hazardous constituents from the waste so that short-term and long-term threats to human health and the environment are minimized."

Treatment, storage, or disposal facilities for hazardous wastes are operated under permits granted by the EPA. Treatment standards that allow the safe disposal of the waste are set by rules found in 40 CFR 260. A variety of techniques have been proposed to treat hazardous waste to reduce its inherent toxicity. Eight commonly implemented methods follow:

1. Biological treatment—microorganisms are used to degrade or decompose hazardous, generally organic materials into less toxic or nontoxic components. Recently, extensive research efforts have focused on developing "new" organisms to facilitate decomposition, but the application of modern technology to develop such compounds is not without certain environmental hazards.

2. Carbon adsorption techniques used to remove certain organic compounds from liquids;

3. Dechlorination, involving a variety of chemical processes to remove chlorine compounds from waste such as certain groups of pesticides;

4. Incineration, which vaporizes certain compounds and reduces the volume of material, but which may lead to parallel problems of air pollution;

5. Neutralization—various chemical techniques to control or adjust the pH of waste to acceptable levels;

6. Oxidation detoxification—the use of strong oxidizing (chemical) agents—which is effective on some cyanide compounds, phenols, and organic sulfur compounds;

7. Precipitation techniques used to solidify and remove toxic substances from liquids; this technique may allow recovered materials to be recycled;

8. General stabilization or solidification by removing waste water, which also reduces movement (flow) of the toxin in the environment.

The next subsection requires monitoring air at TSDFs. This requirement clearly illustrates the relationship among regulations—waste management and air pollution—and among the diverse forces that cause deterioration of the environment. A landfill facility can be a source of air pollution.

The fifteenth subsection parallels the thirteenth subsection in that it specifies standards for various types of TSDFs. This subsection provides initial standards for landfills that will receive hazardous waste (Subtitle C landfills), and for incinerators that will receive such waste. For landfills, the basic emphasis is devoted to protecting water quality by assuring containment of the hazardous materials and the leachate they produce. For incinerators, the emphasis is on protecting air quality and ensuring destruction of toxic materials. This subsection specifies the "minimum technological requirements" for TSDFs. Additional requirements are detailed in the CFRs. The RCRA calls for liners, sophisticated leachate collection systems, and monitoring systems to protect water resources.

With respect to landfills, these minimum requirements clearly reveal congressional concern about water pollution coming from landfill sites. The requirements specify "the installation of two or more liners" plus a leachate collection system above and between such liners, as well as groundwater monitoring equipment. Only under very limited circumstances does the act authorize the administrator to waive the liner requirements; such conditions usually involve a landfill that receives only a single, specific type of waste (a monofill) that poses only minimal threats to water supplies.

The sixteenth subsection continues the focus on groundwater protection by requiring specific groundwater monitoring activities at TSDFs. The seventeenth subsection provides the regulatory authority for a unique situation, the use of hazardous waste to produce fuel or as a source of fuel itself. This is in keeping with the overall thrust of the act, resource conservation and recovery; in this case, the focus is on recovery of energy in an environmentally safe manner. The eighteenth subsection requires specific labeling of fuels that contain hazardous wastes and specifies record-keeping requirements. The nineteenth subsection establishes financial responsibilities for operators of TSDFs to operate sites safely and in accordance with the law. This also requires insurance, proof of self-insurance, or similar evidence of financial responsibility.

The next two subsections concern requirements to remedy releases of hazardous materials from sources that were established prior to the act and requirements for TSDFs operators to take corrective actions beyond the boundaries of the facilities. The twenty-third subsection deals with regulations for underground storage tanks; see chapter 9. The final two subchapters consider special circumstances surrounding mining and other special wastes and the sensitive issue of disposal of munitions.

The details specified by Congress throughout the RCRA clearly reflect concern about hazardous waste and its safe management. In addition to the unusually extensive statutory treatment, rules established by statutory mandate further restrict the handling and total management of hazardous waste and provide pinpoint focus on specific issues or problems.

Enforcement

Enforcement of the various hazardous waste regulations starts with the permitting process for operators of TSDFs. The vast majority of the detailed permit requirements are found in the CFR. The focus remains strongly on containment of the waste and leachate, as well as on limiting long-term storage of hazardous wastes without plans to treat the material or otherwise render it less toxic.

The act recognizes state hazardous management plans so long as the provisions and management standards are at least as rigorous as those promulgated by the federal government. States retain the ultimate responsibility for waste management.

Congress expressed its serious intent in the enforcement provisions found at 42 USC 6928. The act authorizes the administrator to issue an order that requires immediate compliance or that assesses a civil penalty for any past or current violations, or both; penalties may not exceed $25,000 per day of noncompliance. However, penalties increase dramatically for acts deemed to be criminal. Certain intentional violations call for criminal penalties of up to $50,000 per day and prison sentences of up to five years. Intentional violations that could cause death or serious injury call for even more severe criminal penalties, up to $250,000 and fifteen years imprisonment for individuals, and penalties of up to $1,000,000 for organizations that knowingly violate the act.

Other significant provisions of this subchapter include the requirement for state inventories of hazardous waste sites, restrictions on the use of used oil, and regulation of the export of hazardous waste. People seeking to export hazardous waste must provide proof that the government of the receiving country has consented to accept such waste. This provision prevents the exercise of private economic pressure to flood less developed countries with hazardous waste.

Municipal Solid Waste

Although municipal solid waste (MSW) is perhaps less of a threat than hazardous waste to human health and the environment, the average person is more familiar with the increasing problems associated with the accumulation of MSW. The average private citizen can do more to reduce the generation of MSW and more to "repair" environmental degradation resulting from MSW than is practicable for hazardous waste.

Two figures clearly reflect the major problems related to MSW: Annually, the United States produces nearly 200 million tons of MSW, and estimates suggest this will increase to over 220 million tons by the year 2000. This is about four pounds of garbage per person per day, every day. The sheer mass of this material creates major problems for disposal. Space for landfills is no longer available, and landfills are known to be the least desirable disposal strategy because, even for MSW, leachate represents a serious and increasing threat to water supplies.

The management of MSW focuses on the federally mandated development of solid waste management plans, which is the heart of Subchapter IV, Subtitle D of the act. Compared to regulation of hazardous wastes, this subchapter is relatively short and simple. Both the subchapter and rules authorized by it recognize the increasing problem of the accumulation of litter. In addition, the provisions of this subchapter emphatically reflect the broad scope of the entire act, calling for a four-pronged attack to reduce MSW:

1. reduce sources of waste, or source reduction;

2. reuse or recycle material, which may include composting organic materials;

3. recover energy from waste, which may include using waste as a source of fuel and recovering gas from decomposition of waste; and

4. minimize the amount of materials ultimately disposed of in landfill facilities.

The statement of goals directs the federal government to assist in developing and encouraging environmentally sound waste disposal methods, including the maximum utilization of resources from solid waste and energy conservation both currently and in the future.

Energy recovery and conservation receive special attention. Congress plainly recognizes that waste material represents an untapped source of energy and that using waste for energy production, in addition to conserving domestic energy supplies, will reduce the load on overflowing landfill facilities. Moreover, Congress asserts that the technology to reduce waste and recover energy is available and that such recovery is technically and commercially feasible. In assuming the position of feasibility, Congress effectively eliminated two major excuses for failing to recover energy from waste! The next three sections provide much of the substance of this subchapter: 42 USC 6942 (Federal Guidelines for Plans), 6943 (Requirements for Approval of Plans), and 6944 (Criteria for Sanitary Landfills).

Regional and State Waste Management Plans

Federal guidelines stress the importance of developing regional solid waste management plans. The formulating of such regional plans should consider the size and locations of areas to be included within a region, the volume of solid waste that should be considered for inclusion within an area, and the availability of an organization to coordinate such regional waste management plans with other plans within the state and with the state's waste management plan. The basic guideline for the state plan is to achieve the goals expressed in Subtitle D of the act, as expressed in 42 USC 6941: environmentally safe disposal of solid waste coupled with energy recovery.

Congress directs the states to include a variety of factors in formulating their waste management plans. These include regional differences in climate, hydrology, and other circumstances that might affect how waste is managed. Regardless of the differences, the management must assure reasonable protection of groundwater and surface water from leachate and surface runoff and adequate protection of ambient air quality. In these respects, mandates for the management of solid waste closely parallel those for hazardous waste.

While recognizing common problems, Congress also acknowledged that local conditions must be considered in addressing them. Such local conditions range from methods of collection and storage of solid waste to population density, methods of waste transportation, geographic and geologic conditions that might affect landfill sites, and the nature of industries that contribute to the stream of the solid waste.

In addition, Congress recognized the very practical factors of economic, political, and management considerations as well as the availability of resource recovery facilities. In combination, this suggests that Congress intended strict regulation of solid waste, but clearly recognized that practical nonenvironmental concerns could moderate the ultimate scope of management.

Congress specified minimum requirements for approval of state solid waste management plans. States may impose, and some states have imposed, stricter requirements. The minimum requirements established by Congress include the following:

1. State, regional, and local authorities who will be responsible for implementation of the state plan, for distribution of federal funds, and for coordinating activities must be identified.

2. State plans must prohibit the establishment of new open dumps and must include requirements that all solid waste (but not hazardous waste) will be used for resource recovery and will be disposed of in a sanitary landfill. This requirement reflects a major policy established by Congress in the RCRA. (Note that a sanitary landfill is not the same as an open dump, but rather is a facility that satisfies specific requirements to protect the environment, with continued emphasis on groundwater protection.)

3. The plan must include provisions for closing or upgrading existing open dumps and for any regulatory power necessary for its implementation.

4. Additional requirements mandate that states must be free to enter long-term agreements regarding supplying waste for processing. Finally, the plan must provide for resource recovery or the safe disposal of materials for which contracts are made.

Like similar provisions in the Clean Air Act, the Clean Water Act, and the Safe Drinking Water Act, the requirements for an approved state plan implement the policy that the federal government establishes standards, but states bear the responsibilities of satisfying such standards.

Landfill Design Criteria

The prohibition of disposing of solid waste in open dumps does not preclude placing such waste in landfills. Key provisions require the administrator to formulate criteria for sanitary landfills and mandate that solid waste must be disposed of only in landfills that meet the criteria. The rules promulgated under this authority require consideration of six major factors.

1. *Location* includes four major elements: (i) Airport safety based on the concern that landfills attract birds that might interfere with aircraft operations; (ii) proximity to floodplains because of the dangers of waste being washed out with floodwaters and the contamination of water sources; (iii) protection of wetlands as a major natural resource (which is discussed in chapter 7); (iv) fault areas and seismic zones to prevent the spread of waste from landfills as a result of earthquakes, and unstable areas for reasons similar to the earthquake concerns—the spread of landfill waste as a result of earth slides.

2. *Operation* comprises seven major elements. (i) Sanitary landfills under this subchapter are not designed for the safe disposal of hazardous waste; thus the first operation concern focuses on procedures and regulations to ensure that hazardous wastes do not enter these facilities. (ii) Sanitary landfills must be operated so as to protect the environment adjacent to them. This means control of litter, odor, and pests—rats, flies, mosquitoes. The major emphasis is the requirement of daily covering of materials deposited into sanitary landfills. Generally covering is with a layer of appropriate soil, although synthetic covers for daily use have been suggested. A major problem arises in wet periods when waste cannot be covered adequately. (iii) Decomposition of the waste yields potentially explosive gases. Thus, control of these by-products, or their utilization as a source of energy, is a significant consideration. (iv) Waste sites are obviously dangerous. Access must be restricted for safety and to minimize illegal dumping. (v) Storm water flowing over the surface of a landfill facility poses a very real threat to surface water supplies. Sites must be designed with adequate flood-control devices—ditches, levees, and collection ponds—to minimize potential pollution. (vi) By definition, municipal solid waste includes liquids, semiliquids,

and gases in containers. All such waste much be in containers; this includes wastes discharged directly from transportation vehicles or in drums with a capacity of 55 gallons or more. (vii) Landfills represent potential sources of air pollution and they must be operated so that the provisions of air quality regulations are not violated.

3. *Design* stands as the most unique element of an acceptable solid waste landfill. The major emphasis in design is groundwater protection, which requires consideration of a variety of factors. (i) The modern landfill is built on a base of specified materials, the last layer of which is a liner designed to contain leachate; see Figure 8.1. The design must include a system to trap, collect, and store leachate and control gas. (ii) Modern landfills are not the traditional pit; rather, waste is piled on or near the land surface, and the landfill becomes a mountain of waste; see Figure 8.2. As individual sections of a landfill are completed (filled), in addition to the daily covering with soil, the individual segments are capped with an artificial "blanket," which then is covered by several feet of soil that can be planted with grass or similar vegetative cover. Trees are excluded because their relatively deep roots may rupture the blanket and allow water to enter, thus generating leachate and potential pollution. (iii) The technical criteria for approved landfills certainly provide some protection for water sources, but these new facilities suffer from a variety of criticisms. For example, the life expectancy of the required liner is unknown, but twenty years seems to be a safe minimum. The fate of leachate in the closed landfill after twenty years is unknown, but it represents at best a delayed environmental hazard. (iv) In addition, the liners are subject to damage in filling or covering the facilities. (v) Groundwater monitoring devices are a required part of the plan for new landfills. These devices are to be used during the active use of a landfill and for thirty or more years after the facility is closed. Although the devices may detect leaks in the liners, they do not suggest how to prevent damage from escaping leachate. (vi) Finally, the closed landfill becomes a tomb for the waste deposited in it. The daily cover and closing blanket yield an anaerobic internal environment in the landfill, an environment in which natural decomposition will not occur. Waste can remain for extended periods of time, and it can become an environmental threat when for any reason it is exposed to air.

4. *Groundwater monitoring and corrective action* must be part of the approved plan because the long-term integrity of the liners and blankets is unknown. Damage or the ultimate failure of these devices must be detected and remedied, or the entire effort has only delayed, and perhaps even concentrated, the pollution from municipal solid waste.

5. *Closure and postclosure care* continue the emphasis on early detection of problems, such as liner leakage, and prompt remedial action to forestall environmental disasters. The thirty-year postclosure monitoring period may seem lengthy, but if a landfill facility is used for a period of twenty to forty years, it must be expected to remain a long-term environmental threat because the design tends to minimize natural decomposition.

6. Owners and operators of sanitary landfill facilities will be required to provide adequate *financial assurance* that such facilities will be properly operated, maintained, and monitored after closure.

The RCRA recognizes that the rigorous requirements for sanitary landfills represent a significant expense to local communities and that in certain limited situations, the requirements can be waived. Generally, waiver is for landfills that serve small communities,

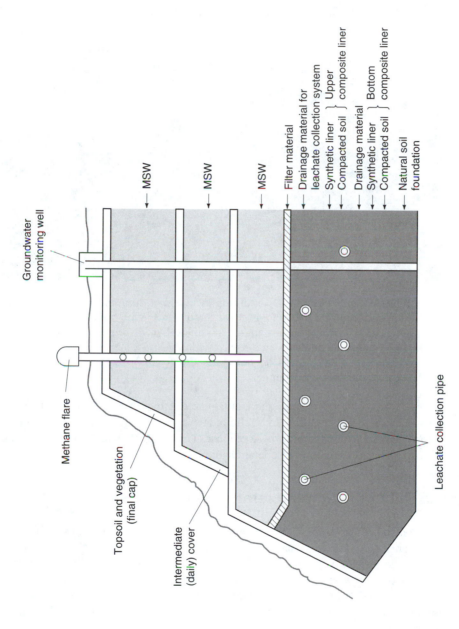

FIGURE 8.1 Diagram of a cross section of a municipal solid waste landfill showing layers of waste and leachate, gas (methane) collection systems, and covers. From Office of Technology Assessment, 1989, after 52FR20226, May 29, 1987.

FIGURE 8.2 Subtitle D landfill is in fact a mountain of garbage, in this case reaching over 160 feet above the ground level, built on a special liner to control leachate and manage runoff. Active disposal areas are covered daily with soil or other material, but litter and odor remain problems in many areas, and liners do not last indefinitely so that ultimately the entombed waste may escape.

fewer than 10,000 individuals, and that handle relatively small amounts of MSW, twenty tons a day or less. In addition, to be eligible for a waiver, such facilities must be located in areas that receive less than twenty-five inches (15.5 cm) of annual rainfall and where there is no evidence of groundwater contamination.

Attempts to Limit Interstate Waste Disposal

Waste disposal has become "big business." In the face of shrinking availability of appropriate sites for waste disposal and increasing demands for disposal, some states have attempted to restrict disposal of waste generated out of state by adding surcharges for the disposal of such waste. In general, however, courts have declared that such charges are unconstitutional. Waste, or waste disposal, is a form of interstate commence that is protected by the Constitution; states cannot act to limit such interstate commerce. Two decisions reflect this policy.

A New Jersey law prohibited bringing into the state any solid or liquid waste that originated outside of the territorial limits of the state. This law affected both private waste site operators and cities that had contracted for out-of-state disposals. Lawsuits sought to allow the import of the waste. Ultimately, the United States Supreme Court decided that the issue was not a waste management or environmental issue, but rather a matter of constitutional law concerning the provisions of the Commerce Clause. The Court thus held the New Jersey law unconstitutional as a violation of the Commerce Clause. *Philadelphia v. New Jersey,* 437 US 617 (1978).

In a 1994 decision, the Supreme Court held that states cannot charge more for the disposal of out-of-state waste than for the disposal of waste generated within the state. The Court held as unconstitutional an Oregon law that allowed a fee of $2.50 per ton for the disposal of "foreign waste" compared with a fee of $0.85 for the disposal of waste generated within the state. The Court noted that the fact that the "foreign waste" was filling the limited waste space in the state did not justify the difference in fees charged. See *Oregon Waste Systems v. Depart. of Env. Quality,* 511 US 93 (1994).

Clearly, states with "space" for waste disposal will not be allowed to profit at the expense of other states. In spite of these decisions, the federal government continues to consider sites in specific states for the disposal of nuclear waste, which frequently are not favored by local citizens and the state government, although such sites may be a source of income. The unique issues of radioactive waste are explored in chapter 9.

NIMBY

The Resource Conservation and Recovery Act mandates the reduction of waste destined for disposal in landfill facilities and provides criteria to protect groundwater and surface water supplies. It does relatively little, however, to minimize the negative impact of waste disposal facilities on adjacent property and landowners. Site criteria strictly limit land that is suitable for waste disposal facilities. As a result, conflicts in use arise with increasing frequency. Public resistance to locating landfills and related facilities in any area further restrict selection of otherwise suitable sites. A simple acronym describes this resistance—NIMBY, Not In My Back Yard.

Numerous factors contribute to the NIMBY syndrome. They all seem to have some validity, but the validity varies. Most relate to two interdependent considerations—the general belief that proximity to a landfill site lowers property values for residential and most commercial purposes, and the related strong belief that landfills constitute a real nuisance resulting from odor and increased insect and rodent populations. Additional concerns include noise, traffic, and litter and dust from the facility.

When landfill facilities expand to include related activities such as recycling and composting (which in fact is a type of recycling), resistance increases. Documented examples exist that these activities add to odor and debris problems, yet the law requires them.

Energy recovery, another mandated aspect of RCRA, creates additional problems. Methane, the gas most commonly generated by waste decomposition, poses a real threat of fire and explosion. At a minimum, in the absence of sophisticated facilities to collect and transport the gas or to use it on-site as a source of energy, the gas is frequently burned, generating a constant, controlled flame or flare that neighbors have found to be a nuisance.

Landowners adjacent to landfill facilities have claimed that the reduced property value resulting from locating landfills near their property constitutes an unconstitutional taking of property. Although developers of private facilities have purchased affected private property, the courts have not found loss to constitute a taking to the extent that owners must be compensated. Some states have proposed laws to compensate property owners, but most states that have considered compensation for landowners have found it too expensive.

No simple answer appears forthcoming. Clearly, part of the solution lies in minimizing waste generation and in maximizing all programs to recycle and reuse waste so that the need for landfills is absolutely minimized.

GROUNDWATER MONITORING

Regardless of the location or the type of waste disposal facility, groundwater protection from waste leachate remains a prime concern. Pursuant to RCRA, the EPA conducts Comprehensive Ground Water Monitoring Evaluations (CME) and Operation and Maintenance Inspections (O & M). Although neither inspection will prevent groundwater pollution, both are designed to provide specific protection against leaks from waste sites.

The CME provides a basis for prevention. It involves site evaluation for monitoring groundwater, including the location of sampling wells to detect leaks and drilling techniques. The O & M follows the CME and determines whether appropriate procedures are being followed to fully utilize the monitoring facilities at the disposal site.

If deficiencies or violations are detected, the facility permit may be suspended or revoked, and operators may be ordered to pay penalties and be liable for damages caused by the violations. In cases of the most serious intentional violations, criminal charges may be brought against the operator of the facility or other responsible individuals.

CONTAMINATION FROM INACTIVE DUMP SITES

Closing the gates to a waste disposal site does not terminate environmental risks there. Tragic events reveal serious environmental problems subsequent to closure that are a direct result of waste disposal. The story of the Love Canal characterizes the problem; this tragic event provided much of the factual impetus for congressional action that led to enactment in 1980 of the Comprehensive Environmental Response, Compensating, and Liability Act (CERCLA), which is commonly called the Superfund Act.

The Love Canal

Until fairly recently, the average citizen did not realize that wastes could significantly affect health. As a result, even highly toxic industrial substances were disposed of merely by dumping them on the ground or in rivers and lakes. This practice led to the creation of uncontrolled or abandoned sites containing hazardous wastes that represent serious threats to human health. The Love Canal represents a tragic example of these practices.

Prior to World War II, a private developer abandoned efforts to build a canal near Niagara Falls, New York. The abandoned canal bed became a convenient disposal site for a variety of industrial waste products, including the burial of over 20,000 tons (thousands of barrels) of toxic wastes such as dioxins. Ultimately the canal was filled and covered with soil. In response to population growth in the area in the post-World War II era, the abandoned site was sold and ultimately became a housing development. Developers were aware of the past use and had apparently been notified of possible escape of toxic substances, if not actually warned of such dangers. This did not stop the development. Over time, as the toxic waste storage containers rusted and corroded away, the wastes escaped and reached the soil surface. Schoolchildren who came in contact with the emerging "goo" experienced a variety of health problems, ranging from simple rashes to chemical burns and serious nervous disorders. Area residents suffered an unusually high rate of miscarriages and birth defects. Ultimately, health officials traced the problem to the "gooey" stuff, which contained, among other products, high concentrations of chlorinated hydrocarbons, chemicals known to cause serious health problems in test animals and strongly suspected of causing serious health problems in humans as well.

The property had been purchased from the city of Niagara Falls, and as the toxic escape problems became more obvious, many people demanded that the city pay to relocate them. Residents filed over $3 billion in health claims against the city. Actual claims were difficult to prove, but eventually the city purchased about 100 homes. The Love Canal disaster received massive media attention. As a result, the federal government sought to determine the extent of potential hazards from abandoned or closed hazardous waste disposal sites.

Following the disclosure of the dangers at Love Canal, two similar situations brought continued media attention and ultimately government action to the problems of abandoned and closed hazardous waste disposal sites. In Kentucky, the Valley of the Drums (located in the northwest part of the state, near Fort Knox and close to the Indiana border) assumed center stage with the discovery of leaking drums of stored hazardous waste materials. Next, the little community of Times Beach, Missouri, appeared in national headlines when stored oil contaminated with highly toxic dioxin contaminated the soil and appeared in the water there. These problems led to federal action in the form of congressional enactment of CERCLA.

Legislative History of the Superfund

President Jimmy Carter signed the Comprehensive Environmental Response, Compensating, and Liability Act into law on December 11, 1980. Congress reauthorized and amended the original act in October 1986 in the Superfund Amendments and Reauthorization Act known also as SARA. In November 1990, Congress further reauthorized CERCLA without additional amendments until 1994, and the taxing authority to generate the Superfund was extended until December 1995.

An Overview of CERCLA

The basic purpose of CERCLA focuses on the cleanup of dangerous closed or abandoned hazardous waste sites. The act calls for establishing a national priority list for sites to be treated. In addition, the act provides for emergency response to spills of hazardous substances and similar accidents. Finally, the act establishes a national trust fund to provide basic funds to clean up hazardous waste sites. Although funds are derived from a variety of sources, the majority come from a tax on chemical manufacturers and the petroleum industry as authorized by the act and its most recent amendments. These funds are used when parties responsible for the storage or disposal of the threatening hazardous waste cannot be found or cannot afford essential cleanup efforts.

CERCLA is codified at 42 USC 9601 *et seq.* The act comprises four subchapters of varying length. The major provisions of the act are found in Subchapter I—Hazardous Substance Release, Liability, Compensation—which encompasses twenty-nine sections, most of which are divided into several subsections.

The first section, 42 USC 9601, provides critical definitions that reveal the scope of the act. Unlike other major legislation, CERCLA does not include a specific statement of congressional intent or findings of fact that explain the purposes of the legislation.

Section 9601 defines thirty-eight terms. All of the definitions are important to the interpretation of the act, but the following explain the scope of the act and elements of the intent of Congress in enacting this legislation:

- "Damage" means damage to natural resources, and the scope of this is apparent from the definition of natural resources that follows.
- "Natural resources" are broadly defined as land, wildlife, biota, air, water, groundwater, drinking water supplies, and other resources belonging to, managed by, held in trust by, appertaining to, or otherwise controlled by the United States.
- Definitions of the terms "drinking water supply" and "groundwater" leave little doubt that a major purpose of the act is protection of water supplies. "Drinking water supply" is any raw or finished source of water that is or that may be used by a public water system, as defined by the Safe Drinking Water Act, or used as drinking water by one or more individuals. "Groundwater" is water in the saturated zone or stratum beneath the surface of land or water.
- "Environment" includes navigable waters, waters of the contiguous zone, and ocean waters over which the United States government exercises management control by international treaty and any other surface water, groundwater, drinking water supply, land surface or subsurface strata, or ambient air within the United States or under the jurisdiction of the United States. This definition reveals a broad-reaching intent of Congress, and again stresses the importance of protecting water supplies.
- The act regulates "facilities," which are broadly defined to include buildings, structures, installations, equipment, pipe or pipelines, wells, pits, ponds or lagoons, impoundments, ditches, landfills, storage containers, motor vehicles, rolling stock, or aircraft in addition to any site or area where a hazardous substance has been deposited, stored, disposed of, placed, or otherwise come to be located. Consumer products in the hands of consumers are excluded, as are vessels.
- The term "hazardous waste" is defined by reference to a variety of other acts, including the Clean Water Act, provisions of the Solid Waste Disposal Act (RCRA), and the Clean Air Act. Any substance that these acts would treat as hazardous will also be considered hazardous by CERCLA.
- Because liability under the act may be attributed to "owners or operators" of "facilities," the definitions of these terms assume great importance. For vessels an owner or operator is any person who owns, operates, or charters vessels. For on- and offshore facilities, the definition is effectively the same. Owners immediately prior to a bankruptcy proceeding are liable too. For transportation, "owner or operator" means the owner or operator of vehicles acting as an independent contractor, but operators

shall not be liable for releases entirely out of their control. The definition of "owner" is further expanded in the section on liability, 42 USC 9607. That section assigns liability to any individual who has owned a solid waste disposal site at any time, not merely to the owner at the time of the waste disposal on the property or to the current owner. However, owners who have no knowledge of the disposal and who could not reasonably be expected to have knowledge may escape liability. This provision may create serious problems in financing land transfers.

- Liability under the act results from the "release" of hazardous materials, which is broadly defined as "spilling, leaking, pumping, pouring, emitting, emptying, discharging, injecting, escaping, leaching, dumping, or disposing into the environment (including the abandonment or discarding of barrels, containers, and other closed receptacles containing any hazardous substance or pollutant or contaminant)." Specific acts related only to workplace exposures are excluded.

The act designates the director of the EPA to enforce the provisions of the act and requires the director to expand the list of hazardous substances. The act establishes specific provisions for notification of unauthorized discharges of hazardous materials and authorizes responses to such releases. The response authority empowers the president to call for cleanup or remediation of damage from spills or unauthorized releases of hazardous materials. The president must act in accordance with the National Contingency Plan.

The National Contingency Plan required by CERCLA to be prepared by the president (i.e., an executive branch plan) focuses on the removal of oil and other hazardous substances. This requirement replaces the plan mandated by the Clean Water Act, 33 USC 1321, and continues to express the emphasis on waste management as it affects water quality. This section also calls for the development of criteria to rank hazardous waste sites by their priority for remediation. The ranking must be based on apparent risks to human health.

Liability Under the Act

As the title of the Comprehensive Environmental Response, Compensating, and Liability Act indicates, one element is assigning liability for damages from the storage or disposal of hazardous waste and for the costs of cleanup of such waste or of remediation. As noted in the definitions, liability extends in general to any person in the chain of ownership from the time of disposal to the present. This broad potential scope of liability has affected many aspects of commerce: Lenders who routinely accept property as security now must consider potential environmental liability in evaluating the financial risks they assume.

If lenders foreclose mortgages on property subject to the provisions of CERCLA, then they have assumed the liability with the ownership. In addition, under the provisions of CERCLA, lenders who play a significant role in the operation of a business they did not own (commonly farming operations) may share environmental liability with the actual landowners. Steps are being taken to reduce this liability. The picture is not entirely clear, but the safe, conservative posture must remain to avoid responsibility by not assuming ownership or participating in management decisions.

The act recognizes certain defenses to liability, but they provide limited protection. For example, if a release of a hazardous substance resulted from an act of God, the owner will generally escape liability. Events characterized as acts of war may be excluded, as are acts of third parties (other than employees or agents of the defendant) with whom the defendant has no contractual relationship, so long as owners or operators of facilities can prove that their actions regarding the release were not the result of a failure to exercise due care and caution. If the third party is an employee, the owner or operator generally will not escape liability.

Liabilities under the act are extensive. The responsible party or parties may be liable for costs of damage to the natural resources, as they are defined in the act, and even for the costs of determining the possible impact on human health and the magnitude of damage caused to the environment; these can include the cost of removing hazardous materials and contaminated material, including soil, plus the potentially enormous costs of properly disposing of the contaminated material. Obviously, liability also includes costs of personal injuries.

Moreover, in addition to costs, the act allows penalties to be assessed for violating the law. These penalties can vary from $25,000 per violation to $25,000 for each day during which a violation continues. CERCLA also includes whistle-blower protection for employees who reveal violations by their employers.

Basic Standards for Cleanup

The act does not specify all details to satisfy cleanup requirements, but it establishes at least a basic standard to be satisfied: (i) permanently and significantly reduce the volume, toxicity, or mobility of the hazardous substance; (ii) avoid the least favored method of remediation, off-site transport of the hazardous material; (iii) protect human health and the environment; and (iv) follow the appropriate standards for safe drinking water. This again reflects the concern with protecting water sources from pollution generated by waste.

The initial list for CERCLA consideration comprised 1,287 sites. By 1983, the list proposed by the states erupted to nearly 39,000 sites. States reporting the most potential superfund sites (50 or more) include California, Florida, Michigan, New Jersey, New York, and Pennsylvania. Experts estimate it will take thirteen to fifteen years to clean up these sites.

Subchapter II established the original fund to be used for site cleanup when responsible parties could not be found. SARA, the 1986 amendments, repealed the provisions of Subchapter II and provided for continuation of the fund and taxing authority through 1995. However, the end of the taxing authority will not mean the end of the other provisions of CERCLA regarding the regulation of the disposal of hazardous waste. The popular feeling suggests that far too many resources have been devoted to legal matters and administration of the program with inadequate efforts devoted to actual cleanup efforts. Many states have implemented individual superfund programs to supplement the federal efforts. Unfortunately, the funds have been seriously depleted, if not exhausted, without major progress in cleanup efforts.

Site Remediation

Experience has proved that the cleanup of many hazardous waste sites is extremely complex, with problems unique to specific sites. The initial belief reflected in CERCLA that current technology would be adequate has proved to be incorrect. Although cleanup emphasis focuses on protecting water resources, after immediate threats to human health and safety are resolved, variations in the site locations, the physical and chemical properties of soil, and proximity to water sources coupled with the vast array of toxic pollutants demand a unique approach for essentially every site. Although some of the lessons learned from the cleanup of one site can certainly be applied to others, each site also presents unique challenges.

In recognition of these complexities, the EPA initiated the Superfund Innovative Technology Evaluation Program (SITE) to develop needed cleanup/remediation technology. The program is a partnership between the public (government, the EPA) and private industry. Efforts have met with increasing success.

Cleanup efforts have required treatment of large quantities of contaminated soil. Merely moving the soil, a massive task in itself in many instances, is inadequate because the pollutants remain a constant threat. Systems to remove volatile and semivolatile materials from the soil at a cost of $200 to 400 per ton have been developed. Many sites require the treatment of thousands of tons of soil. Solvent extract methods have been developed to remove organic compounds, including highly toxic compounds such as PCBs, from soil at a cost of over $100 per ton.

Recent efforts have called for combining methods into "treatment trains" to remedy groups of pollutants. One "train" technique involves employing first an attrition soil washing process to separate contaminated soil from "clean" soil. The contaminated soil is next converted to a fine slurry and various methods are used to remove heavy metals and organic compounds.

Cleanup efforts will increasingly turn to bioremediation, in which genetic engineering techniques "create" forms of microorganisms that will biologically neutralize or otherwise degrade toxic substances such as petroleum products. Such products have been developed and, in fact, have been granted patents by the United States. Of course, issues of risk assessment remain in terms of releasing these human-created forms of life, but they represent a major potential technological breakthrough.

The challenges of site remediation and of waste disposal in general have led to a call for additional legislative action. Developing technology is expensive and a matter of national interest. The call is for a "National Environmental Technology Act." Congress has recognized that environmental technology is more than a "black box" at the end of a pipe.

CONCLUSIONS

In the immediate future, America must dramatically change its attitude about hazardous waste and solid waste problems. Continued emphasis on disposable and convenience products must change. All forms of land disposal of waste must be reduced to an absolute minimum. Not only do landfill facilities threaten the environment even with the best designs, but more important, simply put, space for this use is no longer available.

Waste will be handled in the immediate future by a varied and multifaceted approach with significant statutory requirements. The first step will be the reduction of all waste at its source. The second will be recycling and reuse, including energy recovery. These efforts will include mandatory bottle deposits and similar actions to encourage reuse. Part of the recycling efforts will include the production and use of compost from organic matter. In some regions, where air quality conditions will allow, incineration to reduce waste volume will increase. Finally, the cost of landfill disposal will increase so much that everyone will seek to minimize the production of wastes.

QUESTIONS AND CONCEPTS FOR DISCUSSION AND RESEARCH

1. Discuss the factors Congress has cited as causes for the continuing accumulation of waste in the United States.

2. How have other legislative efforts to protect the environment contributed to waste accumulation?

3. Based on statutory statements of findings, goals, and intent, what issues does the Resource Conservation and Recovery Act address? What does it prohibit?

4. What are the criteria for state waste management plans?

5. Why and how are hazardous waste and municipal solid waste distinguished by the act?

6. In what situation is the concept of large-quantity versus small-quantity generator significant? What is its significance?

7. What are the major similarities and differences between Subtitle C and Subtitle D of RCRA?

8. What groups of industries are targeted for regulation under RCRA and for what purpose?

9. What issues does CERCLA address? What are the major differences between CERCLA and RCRA?

10. What statutory definitions suggest the broad scope of CERCLA?

11. What appear to be the greatest strengths of RCRA? of CERCLA? What are the greatest weaknesses of CERCLA? of RCRA?

REFERENCES AND SELECTED READING

Kubasek, Nancy K., and Gary S. Silverman. 1994. *Environmental Law.* Englewood Cliffs, NJ: Prentice Hall.

Superfund Fact Book, CRS Report for Congress. May 1994. Congressional Research Service, Library of Congress. Washington, DC.

U.S. Environmental Protection Agency. November 1986. *Solving the Hazardous Waste Problem: EPA's RCRA Program.* EPA/530-SW-86-037. Washington, DC.

———. 1988. *The Waste System.* Washington, DC.

———. 1993. *This Is Superfund.* EPA 540-K-93-008. Washington, DC.

———. March 1993. *Safe Disposal for Solid Waste; The Federal Regulations for Landfills.* EPA/530-SW-91-092. Washington, DC.

———. June 1996. *Understanding the Hazardous Waste Rules: A Handbook for Small Business—1996 Update.* EPA 530-K-95-001. Washington, DC.

9

Specific Pollution Control Legislation

This chapter continues the examination of legislation related to pollution and its management. It includes a major addition to the Comprehensive Environmental Response, Compensating and Liability Act in the form of amendments and introduces the regulation of the nuclear energy industry as it relates to human safety and environmental issues, including disposal of radioactive waste. In a return to issues related to water quality, special legislation related to oil spills and the regulation of underground storage tanks by the Clean Water Act are discussed. Although the topics address different subjects, they hold in common continuing legislative concern for human health and environmental degradation.

EMERGENCY PLANNING AND COMMUNITY RIGHT TO KNOW ACT

In 1986, Congress reauthorized the Superfund Act and, through a series of major amendments, added significant new provisions to the act. The reauthorization and amendments are part of SARA, the Superfund Reauthorization and Amendments Act of 1986. In addition to continuing funding authorizations and strengthening the initial focus of CERCLA, SARA added a new focus to the act—the Emergency Planning and Community Right to Know Act (EPCRTKA), Title III of SARA. EPCRTKA is divided into nineteen sections organized in three subchapters: Emergency Planning and Notification, Reporting Requirements, and General Provisions. This legislation is closely tied to the concepts and provision of CERCLA as it initially was legislated, and it expresses this close tie in many provisions. Moreover, this legislation reflects the response of Congress to growing public concern about both human health and environmental safety factors as they relate to dangerous substances developed, used, or stored in local areas.

In the Emergency Planning and Community Right to Know Act, EPCRTKA, Congress recognized the truth of an old adage: An ounce of prevention is worth a pound of cure. The advanced industrial technology of the United States depends on the production and utilization of numerous extremely toxic substances, substances that may be quite harmless in the final product. Commonly, these types of materials are stored in such large quantities that they pose a significant threat to public health and to the environment in the event of an accidental release, including "spills" of all kinds, fires, or similar catastrophes. The EPCRTKA requires communities to plan for possible releases, including releases during transportation, and requires those who manufacture or store such substances to identify what is stored and where it is stored. In this manner, site-specific plans can be formulated for safety and preventive efforts.

Provisions of EPCRTKA

The provisions address three major public safety concerns regarding "dangerous" substances: what is stored, where is it stored, and what happens to it in the event of a leak, spill, or disaster such as a fire at the storage site. Storage includes "inventory," material that will be used in manufacturing or resold, not just storage of waste. Provisions of the act reflect strong links with CERCLA and the Occupational Safety and Health Act (OSHA) because these acts address storage of toxic substances.

Definitions and Concepts Basic to EPCRTKA

Many important definitions are similar in related legislation—CERCLA, RCRA, and OSHA, plus CWA and CAA. Unfortunately, some definitions are not identical, which can be a source of confusion and conflict. Nonetheless, definitions generally make the congressional intent quite clear. The following five definitions are of basic importance to understanding the provisions of EPCRTKA:

1. The scope of the definition of "environment" is quite similar to that formulated in CERCLA. Here environment specifically includes water, air, and land and the interrelationships that exist among and between water, air, land, and all living things.

2. "Extremely Hazardous Substance" is a new concept, identified in 40 CFR 355, Appendix A. Currently, the listing includes over thirty compounds ranging from acetone cyanhydrin to zinc phosphate. The quantities of these extremely hazardous substances to be reported depend on the purpose or use for which they are stored and vary from 1 to 500 pounds. For planning purposes, the amount may range from 10 to 10,000 pounds.

3. The definition of a "facility" closely follows the CERCLA definition: "all buildings, equipment, structures, and other stationary items which are located on a single site or contiguous adjacent sites and which are owned or operated by the same person."

4. "Release" is broadly defined to include "spilling, leaking, pumping, pouring, emitting, emptying, discharging, injecting, escaping, leaching, dumping or disposing into the en-

vironment of any hazardous chemical, extremely hazardous substance or toxic chemicals." This definition includes abandoned barrels or other containers.

5. "Toxic chemicals" are defined by references to a Senate Committee report. The administrator of the EPA may revise the list of toxic chemicals from time to time based on the following statutory criteria: (i) "chemical known to cause or be reasonably anticipated to cause significant adverse acute human health effects at concentrations expected to exist beyond the facility boundaries"; (ii) "chemical known or suspected to be carcinogenic or teratogenic, to affect reproduction, cause neurological disorders, cause heritable mutations, cause other, chronic health problems"; (iii) the harm can be caused by toxicity, toxicity and persistence in the environment, or toxicity and tendency to bioaccumulate in the environment. The list now exceeds 1100 compounds, the release of which requires notification of authorities and the public pursuant to rules found at 40 CFR 372.65.

Initial Steps

Subchapter I, 42 USC 11001 through 11005, provides the first substantive regulatory material. This subchapter specifies initial actions to be completed during the first six to twelve months following passage of the act. These steps include establishment of a variety of planning and emergency response units. The act requires states to establish a state comission, identify planning districts, and make provisions for local committees to deal with emergency preparedness. Typical of environmental legislation, Congress mandates state action to comply with federal law.

The act mandates a three-tiered emergency planning/response structure. The first tier is at the state level. Each state must establish an "umbrella" emergency response commission. The initial duty of the commission was to formulate and establish a procedure through which the public could request information about stored hazardous materials.

The second tier is districts within a state. Within nine months of the passage of the act (October 1986), the act required each state to establish regional districts. The districts facilitate emergency planning and facilitate implementation of the state plan.

Finally, the act requires the establishment of "local" emergency planning committees. These groups represent the front line in planning with respect to stored or released hazardous materials and in providing the public with information to such materials on a local basis. In addition, the act specifies the minimum composition of the local committees: elected state and local officials; law enforcement; civil defense; firefighters; first aid; health care; local environmental groups; hospitals; transportation groups; representatives of the broadcast and print media; community organizations; and facility owners and operators. The composition and scope of membership of the local committees can make them so large as to be ineffective; but seemingly typical of government programs, the act attempts to involve all affected interested groups.

The next section specifies three major elements: substances covered by the act, facilities covered by the act, and notification requirements. The substances are discussed in the definition of extremely hazardous substances and listed in 40 CFR 355 Appendix A. The act required the establishment of interim threshold planning quantity for each substance and requires the administrator of the Environmental Protection Agency to formulate final standards.

The facilities covered represent a key to the broad scope of the act: "a facility is subject to the requirements of this subchapter if a substance on the list referred to in subsection (a) of this section is present at the facility in an amount in excess of the threshold planning quantity established for such substance." This threshold planning amount varies with different substances, and maximum allowable quantities are listed in the CFR. Finally, the act imposes a self-reporting requirement on the owners or operators of facilities at which listed "extremely hazardous substances" may be stored or used. The act requires such reporting whether or not owners or operators are subject to regulation under the act.

Emergency Response Plans

The formulation of emergency response plans by each local emergency planning committee represents a significant element of Subchapter I. The act required that initial plans be formulated within two years following the initial passage of the act, and that plans be reviewed at least annually thereafter.

Minimum content of the emergency response plan includes, but is not limited to, identification of facilities subject to regulation under the act, including identification of routes generally used to transport regulated materials. The concern for transportation reflects awareness of a growing problem: safety in moving hazardous materials by ground, rail, sea, or air, and even by pipelines. Part of the analysis of transportation routes must include identification of other facilities along proposed routes that would constitute potential transportation hazards.

Transportation of Hazardous Substances

A variety of rules affect all aspects of the transportation of hazardous materials. The rules address health and safety concerns and environmental protection, and involve the type of material transported as well as the mode of transportation. For purposes of transportation, hazardous materials are divided into nine distinct groups: (1) explosives, (2) gases, (3) flammable liquids, (4) flammable solids, (5) oxidizing agents, (6) poisonous substances, (7) radioactive materials, (8) corrosive agents, and (9) miscellaneous substances. The rules also specify amounts of these substances that can be transported and limit what substances can safely be shipped together.

Air transport guidelines and rules are given in 49 CFR 175, Transportation of Hazardous Materials (Driving and Parking) in 49 CFR 397, and in 49 CFR 174, Carriage by Rail. In addition, separate provisions are made for routing radioactive materials, including radioactive waste and hazardous nonradioactive materials; see 49 CFR 397, Subparts C and D.

In addition to routing considerations, packaging hazardous materials for transport is subject to extensive regulations that can result in significant penalties if violated. Packaging requirements appear in 49 CFR 173 and encompass ten subparts covering 75 pages including eight appendixes.

Additional Requirements of the Emergency Plan

The plan must include the procedures for owners and operators to notify emergency and medical personnel in the event of a release (including spills) of any regulated substances.

The plan must also designate a community emergency coordinator who will have the responsibility to make necessary determinations to implement the plan and will provide for notification of specified individuals and the public by the facility emergency coordinator and the community emergency coordinator. The plan must also address serious considerations, such as requiring evacuation of an area for health and safety reasons, determining the potential scope of a release and the equipment required to address it, and continued training for all personnel.

Provisions of this act are closely connected with those of other environmental legislation; this is obvious in the requirements for emergency reporting actions resulting from the release of a regulated substance. The act cross-references regulated substances, the release of which requires notification, according to the provisions of CERCLA. However, reporting becomes complicated when it involves substances not subject to CERCLA regulations. For practical purposes, the only release that does not require notification under this act seems to be a release confined exclusively to the facility.

The act recognizes spills of four general groups of chemicals as subject to reporting. 42 USC 11002(a). Chemicals in the four groups may overlap because of the relationship between the Superfund and EPCRTKA. The four general groups are:

- Extremely hazardous substances identified initially for regulation under EPCRTKA;
- Hazardous substances that are listed under the Superfund cleanup regulations;
- Hazardous chemicals that are not on any "preexisting" list, but that OSHA designates as a threat to health; and
- Toxic chemicals initially identified by Congress because of their chronic or long-term toxic effects.

Notice starts with the community emergency coordinator and immediately to the statewide planning commission if the release represents any type of statewide hazard. The minimum content of the notice is specified by statute: the chemical name of the released substance; time and duration of the release; estimated quantity of release; medium into which the release was made (e.g., air, water, land surface); known or anticipated acute health risks; precautions to take, including evacuation; and people to call for additional information.

Required Information

Emergency planning and preparedness are only as good as the information on which the planning and preparation are based. This concept is clearly acknowledged in Subchapter II of EPCRTKA, which addresses varied reporting requirements and the information that establishes the basis for planned responses to unauthorized "releases."

The reporting requirements of Subchapter II provide the foundation for planning and responses to emergencies in order to establish the basic pool of information that describes the type and location of hazardous materials stored in a community. The reporting requirements of the EPCRTKA trace to requirements established by the Occupational Safety and Health Act, OSHA (29 USC 651, *et seq.*; see chapter 11 for a discussion of provisions of this act).

If an owner or operator of any "facility" stores or manufactures any material for which OSHA requires a material safety sheet, EPCRTKA requires the owner or operator to submit either a material safety data sheet or a list of the chemicals to the following groups: local emergency planning committees, the state emergency response commission, and fire departments with "jurisdiction" over the facility. If materials are listed, the list must include (1) a list of hazardous chemicals for which OSHA requires a material safety data sheet grouped as required by health and physical hazards or otherwise as may be required, (2) the chemical name or common name of each such chemical as provided on the material safety data sheet, and (3) any hazardous component of each such chemical as reported on the material safety data sheet. The act authorizes the administrator of the EPA to establish reporting thresholds, so that certain minimal amounts need not be reported.

The act also requires owners or operators of facilities to report actual inventories of designated stored materials. It describes two tiers or levels of information. The first tier is general, aggregated information that is typically available to the public, and that includes estimated ranges in the amounts of hazardous chemicals in each category at a given facility at any time in the preceding year, similar estimates for amounts present on a daily basis, and the general location of the material at the facility. The second tier contains information that may be more confidential for commercial purposes, involving details that are essentially made available on a "need to know" basis. These details include specific names of chemicals as listed on data safety sheets, the basic information on yearly and daily storage as required in tier 1, a brief description of how the material is stored, the location of the stored materials at the facility, and specific requirements if the owner or operator has exercised the right to withhold information from the report for commercial or other reasons.

Finally, Subchapter II requires a formal report of the release of any reported hazardous materials. The requirement to report is limited in that it applies to facilities with ten or more full-time employees and to facilities that are specifically classified under provisions of the system of Standard Industrial Classification Codes. Toxic chemical release reports must be filed if the release involves any of those chemicals previously characterized as hazardous. The same chemicals are also identified as Hazardous Chemicals; see 40 CFR 355, Appendix A for that list. This section also specifies threshold release amounts, below which reporting of releases is not required.

Thresholds vary with the purpose for which the material is stored. For toxic chemicals used at a facility, the threshold is 10,000 pounds per year. For toxic chemicals manufactured or processed, the act established a decreasing standard, starting with 75,000 pounds per year in 1988 and mandated reductions to 50,000 pounds by July 1, 1989, and for reports after July 1, 1990, 25,000 pounds.

Administrative Details

The final subchapter of this act addresses a variety of more administrative details. The act recognizes the rights of manufacturers to protect trade secrets, but also sees potential need to disclose them in emergencies. The act requires owners or operators of facilities to provide information to health care professionals on their written statement explaining why the confidential information is required. Public health concerns may override the provisions of trade secret protection.

Subchapter III also addresses enforcement of the act. It calls for administrative, civil, and, in some circumstances, criminal penalties. Penalties for failing to report releases subject to federal regulation range from fines of $25,000 per day to five years in prison. Increasingly, the law is placing blame on individuals for serious environmental violations. The possibilities of prison are real. In addition, penalties are specified for failure to report inventories of stored materials.

NUCLEAR SAFETY AND NUCLEAR WASTE

The proliferation of nuclear technology provides the best example of the massive impact of science and technology on the environment, although this controversial topic may not represent the greatest potential threat to the environment. In terms of science, the study of radioactivity dates back to the benchmark research of the French scientists Marie and Pierre Curie, who discovered radium in 1898 and who jointly received the Nobel Prize in Physics and Chemistry for their research in 1903. In terms of the problems of nuclear safety and nuclear waste, the detonation of the first atomic bombs in August 1945 hurled the world into the Nuclear Age with massive destruction in Japan and immediate recognition of the apparently limitless potential of this seemingly inexhaustible source of power.

Initial research and development of nuclear power were the domain of the military, although civilian scientists played key roles. Work was done under the cloak of military secrecy, and little effort was devoted to identifying, let alone preventing, the most serious nuclear-energy-related problem confronting the world today—the safe disposal of nuclear waste. This fact is not especially surprising: Fifty years ago, the emphasis was on military use of nuclear power, and the quantities of waste produced were relatively minimal. Certainly the early efforts considered safety for the workers concerning exposure to radiation. However, the world of science lacked experience in dealing with the new giant, and the post-World War II growth of the peaceful use of nuclear power seemingly surpassed the development of technology to manage the problems of waste accumulation that society now faces.

Early Regulation of Nuclear Power

The Atomic Energy Act of 1954, the initial nonmilitary regulation of nuclear power in the United States, is codified at 42 USC 2011 *et seq.* This is Chapter 23 of Title 42, entitled "Development and Control of Atomic Energy." This basic legislation comprised two distinct divisions. Division A consists of nineteen subchapters considered the basic issues of the development of nuclear energy and the regulation of the entire industry. Although military applications and national security received huge priority, the act called for the development of nuclear power for peaceful purposes and recognized great peacetime potential for nuclear energy. Division B established a federal corporation for the development of uranium. In terms of the growth of the regulation of the industry, only Division A is discussed here. The basic provisions of this legislation are reflected in the subchapters, with major emphasis on Subchapter I.

Basic Provisions of the Atomic Energy Act of 1954

Subchapter I states the basic post-World War II nuclear development policy of the United States. Congress recognized that nuclear energy has potential peaceful and military uses.

The policy of the United States would be to achieve maximum benefits from the development of nuclear energy subject to *absolute* defense and security considerations. Congress declared regulation of nuclear power to be in the nation's interest, and at the onset recognized that nuclear waste could be a problem. Congress imposed the responsibility for disposal of "low-level" nuclear waste on the states and suggested that disposal might best be achieved by development of regional facilities. Thus, congressional policy as it relates to nuclear energy appears to foreshadow other environmental legislation: federal regulation with state responsibilities and, in this case, the suggestion of regional cooperation.

Other subchapters establish the general administrative organization for nuclear regulation and call for the establishment of a new regulatory organization, the Atomic Energy Commission, as the lead agency in nuclear development. However, Congress apparently was unwilling to relinquish total regulatory authority to the Atomic Energy Commission because it established a joint Committee on Atomic Energy to watch over the evolution and regulation of the industry.

Additional provisions range from the regulation of special nuclear material and military applications of nuclear technology, to licensing provisions for the use, processing, and transportation of nuclear materials. The act also authorized international cooperation in the emerging area of nuclear technology and related fields.

The Energy Reorganization Act of 1974

The provisions of the Atomic Energy Act of 1954 failed to recognize the problems that emerged with the rapid growth and expansion of the nuclear industry in the United States and with increasing public concern over nuclear safety. In 1974, Congress enacted the Energy Reorganization Act (42 USC 5801 *et seq.*) that effectively revised the entire scheme of federal regulation of the nuclear industry. One major provision of the 1974 act was the establishment of the Nuclear Regulatory Commission (NRC) as the watchdog organization for the development of nuclear energy.

The NRC is an independent civilian organization. The stated purpose of the organization is to ensure adequate protection of public health and safety, the common defense and security, and the environment in the use of nuclear materials in the United States. This body replaced the Atomic Energy Commission of the 1954 legislation and the joint legislative committee. Congress imposed broad regulatory responsibilities on the commission and authorized significant regulatory power. The commission is responsible for the regulation of nuclear power reactors, nonpower research, tests, and training. It also regulates fuel cycles, and medical, academic, and industrial uses of nuclear materials. Finally, NRC regulates the transportation, storage, and disposal of nuclear waste.

Current Focus on Nuclear Waste

The post-World War II growth of civilian use of nuclear energy has led to a major problem with unquestioned health implications: the disposal of nuclear waste. Although public concern continues over the safe use of nuclear energy, with electrical power generation a major target of concern, Congress has currently turned more toward issues related to the safe disposal of the waste products of the nuclear energy industry. The problems are real and undeniable; the dangers from exposure to radiation are scientifically well documented. The nature of radioactive materials used commercially yields waste products whose hazards will persist for hundreds of years. As a result, any solution must be based on truly long-term considerations, not short-term remedies and convenience.

Nuclear waste is classified as either "low-level" or "high-level" waste based on the level of radioactivity. Disposal requirements differ for each category of waste. The nation produces a staggering amount of nuclear waste. In 1993, for example, over eight hundred thousand tons of low-level nuclear waste required disposal; this was down 45 percent from the previous year. The reduction represents in part industrial efforts to reduce waste generation and to compact the products to conserve disposal space. In addition, some waste was disposed of by incineration. High-level waste obviously represents a greater danger, but is produced in lesser amounts. In 1993, some 28,000 metric tons of high-level waste was stored at commercial reactors. The amount is expected to increase to 48,000 metric tons by the end of the year 2003. Clearly, this "on-site" storage is a temporary remedy for a long-term problem.

Congress has addressed this continuing problem through a series of acts and amendments. Efforts started with the Nuclear Waste Policy Act of 1984, 42 USC 10101 *et seq.,* Chapter 108 of Title 42. The act sets the basic foundation for the continuing evolution of the management and regulation of the disposal of nuclear waste. It distinguishes high- and low-level nuclear waste based on the differences in radioactivity, although the distinction lacks a technical definition. High-level nuclear waste (HLW) is defined in 10 CFR 60.1 as: (1) irradiated reactor fuel; (2) liquid waste resulting from the operation of first-cycle solvent extraction systems, or equivalent, and the concentrated waste from subsequent extraction cycles, or equivalent, in a facility for reprocessing irradiated reactor fuels; and (3) solids into which such liquid wastes have been converted.

The general subject matter of the five subchapters comprising the act provides an overview of the scope of this basic legislation. Subchapter I addresses the major issues: disposal and storage of high-level radioactive waste, spent nuclear fuel, and low-level radioactive waste. It also provides specific guidelines for waste repositories. These guidelines take the form of provisions for licensing disposal facilities. They include physical suitability of a proposed site, geology, seismology (earthquake and related threats), water (or the potential of pollution from the site), proximity to natural resources, and population density.

This subchapter consists of eight parts:

1. repositories and their location;

2. interim storage programs, which remain a serious concern;

3. monitored, retrievable storage;

4. low-level radioactive waste;

5. redirection of the nuclear waste program (the Yucca Mountain, Nevada) site;

6. and 7. benefits;

8. transportation, clear recognition that moving nuclear waste represents a special hazard to human health and to the environment. Specific regulations for the transport of nuclear waste are given in 49 CFR 397, subpart D.

Subchapter II considers research and development activities. Subchapter III generalizes "other considerations" related to radioactive waste. Subchapter IV recognizes the need for nuclear waste negotiations and a nuclear waste negotiator. Subchapter V, the last subchapter, establishes a nuclear waste review board. The brief history of nuclear waste as a recognized environmental problem has repeatedly led to controversy and conflict in which negotiations play a critical role, but have not at all times prevented litigation.

Low-Level Waste

In 1984, Congress targeted low-level radioactive waste in the Low-Level Radioactive Waste Policy Amendments Act. These amendments to the 1982 act recognized the continuing problems associated with the disposal of nuclear waste and the need for further regulatory action. The 1984 amendments recognized the practical value to states of forming regional compacts and authorized their formation. To date, nine compacts have been formed. In addition, the amendments recognized the rights of members of a compact to exclude waste from nonmembers. In general, courts have frowned on such exclusions based on the Interstate Commerce Clause of the Constitution. Apparently, however, these provisions do not breach the Constitution. In addition, the amendments established a system to encourage states and compact members to be responsible for the waste they generate. The system involves both rewards and penalties, as appropriate.

By law, nuclear waste facilities must be licensed by NRC. Currently, a facility at Barnwell, South Carolina, is licensed to receive low-level waste. A facility at Hanford, Washington, is also licensed, but disposal is limited to members of the Northwest and Intermountain compacts. A site at Clieve, Utah, is limited to the disposal of a limited group of specific types of nuclear waste. In 1993, NRC licensed a disposal site in Ward Valley, California, contingent on the state's acquiring title to it; this is still in litigation. The site at Beatty, Nevada, terminated accepting nuclear waste in January 1993. Sites currently under review include Boyd County, Nebraska, Hudspeth County, Texas, and Wake County, North Carolina.

High-Level Waste

Disposal sites for high-level radioactive waste present an even greater problem. In 1990, in recognition of the need for at least a temporary solution, the NRC amended its rules to allow on-site storage of spent fuel in approved storage containers. Both the Nuclear Waste Storage Act of 1982 and the Nuclear Waste Amendments Act of 1987 address the issue of high-level waste.

Combined, the 1982 act and the 1987 amendments mandate a detailed approach to the disposal of high-level radioactive waste. Responsibilities are divided: The Department of Energy has operational responsibility and the NRC has regulatory responsibility of all phases of disposal from transportation and storage to ultimate, geological disposal of the waste. Disposal decisions must consider health and environmental impacts thousands of years into the future; for disposal, material will be converted to a solid state and be deposited in a licensed, stable, deep geological structure. The 1987 amendments focus on a single site, Yucca Mountain, Nevada; see 42 USC 10,171 (the specific amendment is 101 Stat. 1330). "Geological disposal" is defined by 10 CFR 60.2 as a system intended for disposal in an excavated geological medium.

The following "favorable conditions" are specific criteria for locating disposal sites for high-level radioactive waste:

1. the nature and rate of tectonic (earthquake potential), hydrogeological, geochemical, and geomorphic processes;

2. in the saturated zone, host rock permeability and vertical permeability;

3. geothermal conditions favoring precipitation or sorption of radioactive nucleotides and inhibiting the formation of colloids and similar complexes that favor the mobility of waste material;

4. mineral assemblages;

5. minimum depth of 300 meters (essentially 1,000 feet);

6. low population density;

7. 100-year groundwater protection; and

8. in the unsaturated zone low moisture flux and low water table. 10 CFR 60.122(b).

Conclusions Regarding Nuclear Energy

An energy-hungry society will continue to depend in part on nuclear energy for power. Moreover, nuclear energy will become more a part of everyday life, from medical applications to industrial uses. Improving technology has brought safe use with respect to both human welfare and environmental protection to acceptable levels, and the technology continues to improve. The memories of Chernobyl and Three Mile Island may dim with time, but the potential for disaster will not be ignored. Nonetheless, the major concern lies with the threat represented by the waste products generated by this growing industry.

The government has recognized the long-term nature of the problem and the serious nature of the hazards. The basic nature of the waste cannot be changed with technology available today, or in the foreseeable future. Emphasis will be on minimizing waste and then on storing it only in a form and at sites and in a manner that the best technology deems to be acceptably safe. However, absolute safety cannot be assured. This type of risk, at least, is subject to technically sophisticated analysis that will continue to provide essential factual materials for management decisions. Like any waste disposal issue, political pressure must be anticipated as a factor in locating disposal facilities. To further complicate the matter, the nature of the waste and the growth of the use of nuclear energy worldwide will require significant levels of international cooperation to continue to ensure reasonable, acceptable levels of safety. Radioactive pollution will not respect political boundaries any more than air and other water pollutants respect them.

OIL SPILLS

In spite of the growth of nuclear energy and all other alternative forms of energy, for the foreseeable future, fossil fuel (petroleum products) will continue to be the mainstay of America's energy supply, particularly for transportation purposes. In addition to problems of oil pollution associated with refining and burning fossil fuels, petroleum represents a continuing threat as a pollutant, with a potential major impact on water and related resources.

This particular environmental threat is not the result of consuming or using the product; rather, it arises from transporting the raw product from the site of production to the processing facilities, from oil fields to refineries, and at times from refineries to wholesale distributors or to the ultimate consumer. The threat is damage caused by accidental spills of the material during transport. Such spills take many forms: Leaks from pipelines, trucks, and railroad tank cars are frequently reported "environmental accidents." More extensive pollution occurs from major accidents, such as those involving ocean-going tankers that transport enormous quantities of crude oil and other potential pollutants.

Accidents of all kinds involving the discharge of oil into the environment pose significant threats to wildlife and their habitat, threats of pollution of surface waters and, to a lesser extent, of groundwater sources, and threats of fire or explosion. A variety of laws and related regulations at least recognize safety issues with respect to trucking and pipeline safety. Because of the enormous quantities involved, major spills from ships carrying crude oil from field to refinery, represent a potential major disaster, which became a cataclysmic reality in February 1989.

The Oil Pollution Act of 1990

Shortly after midnight on February 3, 1989, the *Exxon Valdez,* an enormous oil tanker, left port in Prince William Sound, Alaska, loaded with crude oil. Shortly thereafter, the ship ran aground on Bligh Reef, ripping her hull open and ultimately spilling approximately 11 million gallons of crude oil. This environmental havoc extended 600 miles from the spill site, killing wildlife and polluting the coastline. The magnitude of the damages and losses may never be fully documented. This disaster led to extensive litigation involving Exxon Corporation and the captain of the ship.

The legal issues of liability are not essential to this discussion, but the result is critical: Effectively in response to the *Valdez* spill, Congress enacted the Oil Pollution Act of 1990, 33 USC 2701 through 2761. It considers pollution of the navigable waters of the United States. Some treat it as part of the Clean Water Act, but this is not correct: It is independent legislation. This act reflects the emerging federal policy of seeking to fix blame and assess damages to those who harm the environment.

Structure of the Act

Compared with other legislation, the Oil Pollution Act of 1990 is a relatively brief act. It focuses on a single environmental issue—oil spills associated with sea transportation of oil and with offshore drilling for oil and onshore spills that result in pollution of "navigable waters of the United States or the adjoining shorelines." The act comprises four subchapters, and reflects the assignment of liability aspects of CERCLA.

Subchapter I encompasses the major substance of the act under the heading of "oil pollution liability and compensation." The basic policy is "you spill, you pay." In addition, this subchapter contains several key definitions, including "act of God" (33 USC 2701(1), which provides a defense to liability under the act: "an unanticipated grave natural disaster." Of course, the concept of "unanticipated" may lead to challenges based on predictability of severe weather conditions and failure to prepare for them, or even building in areas with known earthquake potential. "Discharge" is broadly defined to include all emissions, whether intentional or unintentional, except natural seepage. "Facilities" extend to structures and equipment, other than vessels, used in the production of oil, including vehicles and pipelines. The fund specified by the act is the Oil Spill Liability Trust Fund established by 26 USC 9509.

Liability and Damage

In terms of substance, 33 USC 2702, "Elements of Liability," reveals the muscle of this legislation. The law is clear: "each responsible party for a vessel or facility from which oil is discharged, or which poses the substantial threat of a discharge of oil, into or upon the navigable waters or adjoining shorelines or the exclusive economic zone is liable for the removal costs and damages . . . that result from such incident"; 33 USC 2702(a). Removal costs and damages are specified in detail, and include all costs incurred by the United States, a state, or an Indian tribe or incurred by a person acting under provisions of the National Contingency Plan. Allowable damages are exhaustive.

The act recognizes six very general types of damages for which people may be held liable. Several are common to other similar legislation, and some are unique to this act:

1. Damage to natural resources: injury, destruction, loss of use of natural resources, including reasonable cost of damage assessment.

2. Real or personal property: injury or economic loss from the destruction of property recoverable by individuals who own or lease property.

3. Subsistence use: damages due to loss of use of natural resources for subsistence use regardless of who owns them; for example, loss of fishing or hunting for subsistence.

4. Revenues: damages equal to net loss of taxes, royalties, profit shares from the injury, destruction, or loss of real or personal property or natural resources, with recovery of such losses limited to the government of the United States, a state, or a political subdivision thereof.

5. Profits and earning capacity: lost profits and income from loss of real or personal property.

6. Public services: damages in the form of increased costs of providing public services.

Like CERCLA, the Oil Pollution Act imposes strict and extensive liability on those responsible for causing harm. In many ways, identifying responsible parties may be simpler for oil spills. In addition, potential awards of damages to individuals are more extensive with oil spills than with CERCLA or other environmental legislation, and more extensive recovery is possible for government bodies.

Within very limited circumstances, the act excludes certain discharges from liability: It exempts discharges allowed by a federal permit, those from a "public vessel" (defined as owned by the government), and those from pipelines regulated by the Trans-Alaska Pipeline Authorization Act, 43 USC 1561 *et seq.* The act also recognizes certain specific defenses to liability for discharges.

Discharges resulting from "an act of God" as defined are not subject to liability. Such acts must be unanticipated and not prevented by the exercise of due caution. Discharges resulting from acts of war are also exempt from liability. Although questions could arise about "civil insurrections" and terrorism, the intent of Congress would seem to favor exemption in these cases too.

Damages

The act specifies allowable damages. The amounts allowed are sizable: for ships (tank vessels), the greater of $1,200 per gross ton, or for vessels over 3,000 tons, $10,000,000. The limit for vessels less than 3,000 tons is set at $2,000,000. Vessels not otherwise included face damages of the greater amount of $600 per gross ton or $500,000. For off-shore facilities, damages are set at $75,000,000 plus all removal costs, and for onshore facilities and deep water ports, the limits are set at $350,000,000.

The act focuses on damages to natural resources, 33 USC 2706. Damages include costs to restore, rehabilitate, or replace property, lost value of property, and the costs of assessment of the damages. These damages are paid to government entities, the United States, states, and Indian tribes. Owners may also be liable for damages to private parties.

Subchapter II considers special provisions for Prince William Sound and establishes the Prince William Sound Science and Technology Institute, which is devoted to research, education, and demonstration projects to develop the best available technology for oil spill recovery in the arctic and subarctic marine environment. The act delegates the administration of the Institute to the Secretary of Commerce. In addition to the development of best technology for oil spill recovery, the Institute is directed to complement federal and state damage assessments of the long-range impact of the *Exxon Valdez* spill.

Finally, this subchapter includes provisions for improving aids to navigation to prevent accidents such as the grounding of the *Exxon Valdez* and strengthens standards for spill response plans that vessels are required to maintain. The basic response requirements are specified in provisions of the Clean Water Act, which requires spill-containment plans for tank vessels. The additions call for locating emergency equipment in communities to facilitate responses in Prince William Sound and the use of various types of escort vessels with oil spill recovery capabilities. The stated intent is "protection of the environment, including fish hatcheries," 33 USC 2735(a)(1).

The final two subchapters comprise specific provisions to establish a research program and other miscellaneous provisions. The miscellaneous provisions include a savings clause involving violations of individual constitutional rights and survival of the act in the event of a challenge, authorizations for appropriations, and provisions to protect fishing and recreation on the Outer Banks of North Carolina.

Conclusions Regarding Oil Spills

The danger of environmental disasters from oil spills cannot be eliminated. Crude oil and refined petroleum products represent serious potential pollutants. To satisfy the nation's continuing appetite for energy, enormous quantities of crude oil will still be transported from production sites worldwide to refining facilities, and refined products will continue to be transported to dealers, and ultimately to consumers. Each step, including the ultimate consumption of fossil fuels, represents a threat to the environment.

Provisions of the Oil Pollution Act provide a basis for remedy more than for prevention. Emphasis must be placed on preparedness, but ultimately the focus must turn to prevention. Steps have been taken in this direction, including redesign of tankers to provide double hulls that will not split and spill as easily as the *Valdez*. Aids to navigation, training, and technology all will contribute to reducing spills, but the ultimate responsibility must rest with those transporting these necessary, but dangerous products to act with care beyond legislative mandates.

UNDERGROUND STORAGE TANKS

Chapter 8 of the Resource Conservation and Recovery Act (RCRA), 42 USC 6991, comprises a single section devoted exclusively to problems associated with pollution caused by leaking underground storage tanks. Although the problem is part of RCRA, the provisions are very specific and are appropriately considered separately. In this portion of RCRA, Congress recognized a serious problem, contamination of groundwater coming from underground storage tanks. The major culprits appeared to be tanks used to store various petroleum products, from gasoline and diesel fuel to heating oil.

For the purposes of this legislation, a storage tank is considered to be an underground tank even if only 10 percent of its volume is buried. In addition, the definition of an underground tank includes associated pipes and valves. The law excludes a fairly small array of tanks: residential underground storage tanks with a capacity of less than 1100 gallons that are used for storing motor fuel for noncommercial purposes, and tanks used for storing residential heating oil for use on the premises. Septic tanks also are specifically excluded, along with tanks regulated under the provisions of the 1968 Pipeline Safety Act, or the 1979 Liquid Pipeline Safety Act.

Existing Tanks

The intent of legislation is to hold owners of tanks responsible for damage (pollution) caused by leaks from the tanks. In some ways, liability parallels CERCLA liability. Anyone owning a tank after November 8, 1984, may be liable for pollution caused by leaks from that tank. To be excluded from such liability, the tank must have been nonoperational as of that date: no material dispensed from it and not filled since November 8, 1984. The law requires tanks remaining in use to be modified to guard against leaks and resulting pollution.

Modifications include a leak detection system and inventory control to monitor input to and output from the tank to detect possible leaks. Owners are required to report leaks and spills (releases), with severe penalties for the failure to report a release. Closure of the tank requires removal and disposal of the tank, which has become a problem with respect to the nature of contaminated tank material. In addition to metal tanks, concrete used in the construction of some older underground facilities poses a series of novel problems, because the concrete saturated with petroleum products may represent a hazardous substance and building debris that require special, frequently costly disposal considerations. Consequently, in many areas, service station sites have been abandoned to avoid the expense of removal and the liability of continued operation of aging tanks.

New Installation

New tanks are subject to specific design requirements to minimize leaks and spills. In addition to spill containment considerations, new tanks must be equipped with liners to guard against breakdowns and subsequent leaking. These provisions have naturally affected the retail market of gasoline. New service stations provide an excellent example of how small retail businesses are faced with the expenses of complying with this type of regulation. Of course, the costs are ultimately passed on to the consumer.

Along with other potential sources of pollution, underground storage tanks have become a target of environmental assessment activities to protect investors in real estate transactions. Disposal of the abandoned tanks is a topic of growing concern. The material is extensive in volume and weight and may pose a significant threat of a new form of pollution when removed from the ground.

CONCLUSIONS

Portions of numerous other acts may affect the environment; but those discussed here are of general interest. Other acts worth note involve a short-term study of track medical waste following serious pollution of East Coast beaches, and numerous acts that address transportation safety. Legislative designation of an act as "environmentally oriented" may reflect congressional intent more clearly, but the critical issue is whether any act provides authority or standards that are designed to protect the environment. For example, the most significant single topic not discussed in this text is soil conservation. Clearly, this is a major environmental problem, and Congress has addressed related issues in a variety of acts. However, the subject is too broad for a single-chapter discussion. Moreover, soil conservation commonly is treated as a separate subject and addressed in depth in a variety of agricultural courses and in ecology courses. At an opposite extreme, many would argue that much of the food safety regulation should be included as part of "environmental regulations." The choice here was to limit this topic to pesticides and residue issues. The key point: Look for the issue, not the classification of the law!

QUESTIONS AND CONCEPTS FOR DISCUSSION AND RESEARCH

1. For what reasons did Congress enact the Emergency Planning Community Right to Know Act? How is this Act related to OSHA, RCRA, SARA, and CERCLA? What are the major provisions of the EPCRTKA?

2. How and why has the policy regarding nuclear energy changed with respect to agency responsibility?

3. What are the major regulatory issues regarding nuclear energy faced by the legislature today?

4. What is the intent of the Oil Pollution Act of 1990? To what other environmental legislation is this act similar in intent?

5. What is the major issue addressed by the regulation of underground storage tanks? How is this issue expressed in the legislation?

REFERENCES AND SELECTED READING

U.S. Environmental Protection Agency. September 1988. *Chemicals in Your Community: A Guide to the Emergency Planning and Community Right to Know Act.* Washington, DC.

————. December 1989. *Glossary of Environmental Terms and Acronym List.* EPA 19K-1002. Washington, DC.

————. *September 1994. Guide to EPA Materials on Underground Storage Tanks.* EPA-510-B-94-007. Washington, DC.

PART FIVE

Pesticide Safety, Food Safety, and Personal Issues

10

Food Safety and Pesticide Regulation

The diet of the average American is envied worldwide for numerous reasons: the quantity and diversity of food generally available to the consumer, the relatively low cost of food, and the high nutritional quality and safety of food. Unfortunately, certain agricultural practices that contribute to America's agricultural bounty also represent potential threats both to the environment and to the safety of the food in which we take such pride. These practices involve pest management and the potential impacts that various pesticides used mainly in crop production have on food quality and safety, and on the environment.

PESTICIDES AND THE PESTICIDE INDUSTRY

Frequently, the term "pesticide" is equated with "insecticide," a major group of pesticides that includes numerous toxic materials used to control insect pests that attack crops in the field, forests, stored crops, livestock, and even structures. Some insects attack humans directly, and many are vectors of plant and animal diseases, including diseases that affect humans. Although not technically correct, materials applied to control spiders, mites, and even nematodes frequently are grouped as "insecticides."

Pesticides include at least three other major groups of materials: (1) herbicides, or weed killers, which, in terms of quantity, are the most widely used pesticides and have the lowest levels of toxicity to humans and apparent threat to the environment; (2) fungicides, used to control a variety of plant diseases; and (3) rodenticides, used to control small animals, such as mice and related pests. Although not used as extensively as other pesticides, rodenticides represent a significant threat to animals, including humans. Many types of wood preservatives are also considered pesticides and are regulated with them. However, the spectrum of materials related to animal health used in livestock is not generally included with pesticides.

The EPA defines a pesticide as a "substance or mixture of substances intended for preventing, destroying, repelling, or mitigating any pest." This definition includes any substance or mixture of substances intended for use as a plant regulator, defoliant, or desiccant and notes that pesticides can accumulate in the food chain and/or contaminate the environment if misused. It reveals clearly that the agency recognizes both the potential danger in using pesticides and the fact that these substances can be used safely. The definition is based on controlling "pests"; thus, the definition of a pest becomes of critical importance. The EPA defines a pest as an insect, rodent, nematode, fungus, weed, or other form of terrestrial or aquatic plant or animal life or virus, bacteria, or microorganism that is injurious to health or the environment. The definition of "injurious" is not given, but it obviously includes economic losses.

In the United States, the manufacture and distribution of pesticides is big business. Annual sales of all categories of pesticides top $6 billion, which represent the manufacture of over a billion pounds of active ingredients. The active ingredient is usually the toxic substance. It constitutes a minor portion of the material sold and ultimately applied in the field. Generally, regulations focus on the active material.

About 30 major companies produce most of the active pesticide ingredients in the United States, with approximately 100 additional companies contributing small amounts. Some 3,000 firms actually formulate the final products by mixing ingredients with inert materials, and then package them. Pesticides are sold through thousands of retail establishments.

Pesticide Use in the United States

In the United States, agriculture accounts for approximately 75 percent of the pesticides used. This extensive use is a portion of the concern focused on agriculture as a nonpoint source polluter: pesticides or pesticide residues washing from fields into lakes, rivers, and streams, and potentially polluting sources of groundwater as well. Seven percent of the pesticides find use in homes and gardens. Proportionately this is a relatively small amount, yet some experts claim that comparatively, homeowners are responsible for a disproportionately high level of pesticide misuse.

Pesticide Pollution

Although rarely documented in terms of causing harm, pesticide residues in or on all types of food products represent a continuing concern. The exposure of workers who handle or apply pesticides and those who work in orchards and fields treated with pesticides constitutes a serious concern. Finally, the overall impact on the environment cannot be ignored. This involves the direct impact of pesticides on nontarget organisms, the longer-term effects of pesticide bioaccumulation, and habitat modification resulting in part from pesticides disrupting the balance of nature, including pollution of surface water and groundwater sources.

Few documented cases of harm from the proper use of pesticides can be cited. Nonetheless, public concern over pesticide use continues, and the pesticide controversy involves complex, technical, and emotion-packed issues. Pesticide proponents justify current practices on the basis of recognized safety of the nation's food supply and on the fact that, in spite of massive efforts to develop effective alternatives, many facets of American agriculture depend on the use of a wide variety of pesticides to maintain crop yields and quality. On the other hand, opponents point to the unknown elements of pesticide use, particularly long-term effects of current exposures to less-than-toxic levels of various pesticides and to the fact that different groups of consumers are exposed to different total amounts of pesticide residues based on their normal diets. They argue that long-term uncertainties related to low-dose exposures demand that until a chemical is known to be safe, it should not be used, or discharged into the environment. Proponents base their position on the record of safety and on assurances that approved uses do not represent a significant threat to human health or the environment. The issue is to a large extent one of risk assessment.

In her widely read 1962 book, *Silent Spring,* Rachel Carson sounded an effective alarm for greater regulation of pesticides. Disagreement continues about the accuracy of some claims of pesticide-induced environmental harm and food safety. Nonetheless, Carson's writing brought massive public attention to the potential dangers from the misuse of modern pesticides, the high levels of toxicity of many modern pesticides, bioaccumulation of pesticides, and the lack of adequate training for those using pesticides. The impact of *Silent Spring* triggered congressional concern that led ultimately to increased federal regulation of pesticides through the provisions of the Federal Insecticide, Fungicide, and Rodenticide Act, FIFRA, passed in October 1972.

THE FEDERAL INSECTICIDE, FUNGICIDE, AND RODENTICIDE ACT

The Federal Insecticide, Fungicide, and Rodenticide Act, 7 USC 136 *et seq.,* consists of a single section and twenty-five subsections. In the initial act, Congress addressed two continuing public concerns: identification and regulation of pesticides based on their toxicity, and education of applicators to help ensure safer use of these toxic substances. Although FIFRA is relatively short, it has yielded extensive rules and regulations. Congress has amended FIFRA twice, in 1988 and through significant amendments in 1996, which included both FIFRA and the Federal Food, Drug, and Cosmetic Act through provisions of the 1996 Food Quality Protection Act.

Definitions and the Scope of the Act

Congress did not include stated goals or findings of facts in FIFRA, yet the act clearly recognizes the dangers from the unnecessary and unregulated frequent overuse of toxic substances by individuals who are not adequately trained to use such materials safely. Although Title 7 is limited to agriculture, Congress designated the EPA to administer FIFRA. The act includes thirty-three specific definitions that suggest the scope of authority and congressional intent. Critical definitions include the following:

- "Pest"—"(1) any insect, rodent, nematode, fungus, weed, or (2) any other form of terrestrial or aquatic life or virus, bacteria, or other microorganism (except viruses, bacteria, or other microorganisms on or in living man or other living animals)." Note that weeds are included as pests, although they are not part of the title of the act; in fact, weed control represents a major use of pesticides. Also note the specific exclusion of pests that affect humans or living animals. Clearly, Congress did not intend for this act to regulate medical materials, including veterinary medicines.

- "Pesticides"—"(1) any substance or mixture of substances intended for preventing, destroying, repelling, or mitigating any pest and (2) any substance or mixture of substances intended for use as a plant regulator, defoliant, or desiccant." Note that this statutory definition of a pesticide is not as broad as the EPA's definition cited in the preceding brief discussion of pesticides and the pesticide industry. In formulating rules, regulatory agencies frequently modify established definitions to enable legislation to better cover their anticipated scope of regulation or to tighten and better define the law. Although multiple definitions may seem confusing and certainly are not desirable, to date they have not been the basis of any significant challenge to the act.
- "Weed"—follows a very traditional agricultural definition: "any plant which grows where not wanted."
- "Unreasonable adverse effects on the environment"—the limits embodied in the definition of this phrase establish the standards for regulating any pesticide that threatens to harm the environment: "any unreasonable risk to man or the environment taking into account the economic, social, and environmental costs and benefits of the use of any pesticide." This does not provide a definition of the concept of "unreasonable," but it clearly indicates the congressional intent that economic factors are to be considered. In addition, adverse effects to the environment include harm to humans, according to the specific wording of the definition.

Other definitions are important, but these four shape much of the very broad focus of FIFRA.

Pesticide Registration

The basic regulatory posture of FIFRA is clearly expressed in a single statement: "no person in any state may distribute or sell to any person any pesticide that is not registered under this subchapter"; 7 USC 136 (a). The purpose of the registration is to identify the type of pesticides used and to define the conditions under which they may be used. The criteria for registration illustrate this intent. According to FIFRA (7 USC 136[c]), applications for registration must provide the following information:

1. The name and address of the applicant.
2. Name of the pesticide.
3. A complete copy of the labeling of the pesticide, a statement of all claims to be made for it, and any directions for use. This information provides the foundation for increased pesticide safety. The label instructions must specify how and when the pesticide can be used, including the pests to be controlled, the crops on which the materials can be applied, and the stage of development of the crop at which applications can be made. Users are required by law to follow label directions precisely; failure to follow directions constitutes unauthorized use of the pesticide and violates the law.
4. Complete chemical formulas of the pesticide.

5. A request that the pesticide be classified for general use, for restricted use, or for both under different circumstances. The designation of general use versus restricted use establishes another major regulatory aspect of FIFRA. Pesticides classified for *general use* cause no unreasonable threat to the environment when used in accordance with the directions, warnings, and cautions specified for the registered use of such a pesticide. By contrast, pesticides designed as *restricted use* represent an unreasonable threat to the environment, even when used in accordance with directions and warnings. Restricted-use pesticides may be applied only by, or under the direct supervision of, a certified applicator. Unfortunately, the law restricts who may apply restricted use pesticides, not who may purchase them. As a result, inadequately trained individuals may secure and apply restricted-use pesticides in violation of the law.

FIFRA also requires the reregistration of pesticides initially registered prior to November 4, 1984, to ensure that effectively all pesticides in use would ultimately be subject to the registration requirements. The act allows the cancellation of the registration of a pesticide and has provisions for the experimental uses of pesticides.

In addition to registration of pesticides, FIFRA requires the registration of pesticide manufacturers. The manufacturer registration requirement is not designed to deny the right to manufacture pesticides; rather, the purpose is to monitor what products are in production to better inform both manufacturers and users of problems or policy changes affecting the manufacture or use of a product. Registered producers must report annually as to the types and amounts of pesticides produced and distributed. The act ensures confidentiality of information provided to protect the commercial interests of manufacturers.

Applicator Certification

In addition to requiring applicator certification for the application of restricted-use pesticides, FIFRA specifies minimum certification standards. The act also authorizes individual states to institute certification programs based on a plan approved by the administrator of the EPA. For approval, a state plan must include at least the following:

- Designation of a state agency responsible for administration of the certification program;
- Assurance of legal authority and technical competency to carry out the plan;
- Assurance that required reports will be made; and
- Assurance that the state certification standards will conform with minimum federal certification standards.

Approved state plans seemingly "preempt" the federal regulations. However, this is not entirely accurate because, for approval, a state plan must satisfy the intent and minimum provisions of FIFRA.

Certification programs must include training in at least eight specific subject areas:

1. Pesticide label and labeling comprehension

2. Pesticide safety considerations

3. Environmental issues, including weather factors and the land characteristics that might affect safe use of the pesticide

4. Pests and target pest considerations

5. Pesticide technology

6. Equipment calibration and operation

7. Pesticide application techniques

8. Laws, rules, and regulations affecting the use of pesticides

Different specific standards for certification pertain to commercial versus private applicators. In addition, programs are to provide information about integrated pest management techniques that may reduce or minimize the use of pesticides.

User Safety

The act does not specifically address the use of safety equipment by pesticide applicators, although if label directions called for the use of equipment, failure to use such equipment would constitute violation of the law. The overall emphasis on safety clearly justifies agency rules for user protection. Such rules are found under "Worker Protection Standards." The purpose of the rule is "to reduce the risk of illness or injury resulting from workers' and handlers' occupational exposure to pesticides used in the production of agricultural plants on farms or in nurseries, greenhouses, and forests and also from the accidental exposure of workers and other persons from such pesticides." Certain users are exempt from the provisions of these worker safety regulations; these include livestock producers and nonfarm (crop and forestry) users; 40 CFR 170 *et seq.*

The rules continue to specify types of equipment—including respirators—clothing, and shoes required for the application of various pesticides. The rules address exposure resulting from workers' entering fields, orchards, greenhouses, or similar facilities following applications of restricted-use pesticides. The rules set minimum times that must elapse before workers may reenter fields.

Power to Stop Sales

FIFRA authorizes the EPA to stop the sale of a pesticide, to have supplies removed from sales shelves, and to confiscate supplies of any pesticide whose manufacture or distribution violates the registration requirements of the act. The agency can also suspend or cancel the registration of a pesticide if it is found to represent an unacceptable risk. If the registration of a pesticide is suspended or canceled, FIFRA authorizes federal indemnification to those who suffer financial losses as a result of possessing supplies that no longer may lawfully be applied to crops.

Summary and Conclusions Concerning Pesticides

FIFRA regulates the manufacturing and use of pesticides in crop production. Registration distinctions between general- and restricted-use pesticides provide the basis for training applicators in the safe handling and use of the most toxic pesticides. Registration standards for all agricultural pesticides require specific information on the pesticide container; this includes details concerning the uses of the pesticide allowed by law and critical safety information. Failure to follow the label instructions violates the law and can lead to civil and criminal penalties.

FIFRA provides a solid legislative foundation for pesticide safety. This act does not address issues of pesticide residues on or in food products, although, in theory, properly used pesticides should leave no excessive residues. Food safety issues related to pesticides are addressed by separate statutory law.

THE FEDERAL FOOD, DRUG, AND COSMETIC ACT

The evolution of human culture and society parallels the growth and evolution of agriculture. Part of this evolution includes the foundations of regulations of the food industry. Some of the earliest laws established systems of weights and measures to assure that buyers and sellers received a fair measure in their commercial transactions. Subsequently, regulations addressed quality, including the addition of "fillers" as well as of potentially toxic materials that enhanced the appearance or "flavor" of some products, such as copper compounds to tea, or alum to beer. Legislation to preserve food safety and quality is relatively recent.

Historical Background

In the United States at the end of the nineteenth century, a variety of problems suggested the need for federal regulation of quality and safety of food and related products. Although several early attempts addressed food quality issues, the Federal Food, Drug, and Cosmetic Act of 1938 (FFDCA), 21 USC 301 *et seq.*, corrected weaknesses in earlier legislation and established the basis of federal food quality regulation today. The act is an enormous body of legislation that has undergone significant amendments, including some provisions of the 1996 Food Quality Protection Act.

Basic Provisions

The basic provisions of the act prohibit the "introduction or delivery for introduction into interstate commerce any food, drug, or cosmetic that is adulterated or misbranded." The act calls on the Commerce Clause of the Constitution for justification. Most other provisions of this act fall well beyond the scope of even the broadest consideration of environmental regulation. Nonetheless, the provisions of FFDCA that regulate pesticide residues in foods clearly are related to environmental policy as it relates to pesticide regulation and merit consideration in any comprehensive discussion of environmental law and policy.

Food Policy

Food regulations appear in Subchapter IV of Chapter 1 of Title 21, Public Health. This subchapter starts at 21 USC 341 with basic definitions of food and regulatory standards. The act grants the secretary of agriculture great latitude in establishing rules and regulations, and authorizes any action by the secretary that promotes honesty and fair dealing in the interest of consumers in terms of identity, quality standards, or "reasonable standards of fill of container." With respect to environmental considerations, the major regulatory authority comes from the concepts of "adulterated food" (21 USC 342) and subsequent authority to regulate pesticide residues in foods (21 USC 346, *et seq.*).

Any food that contains poisonous or deleterious substances that could be harmful to health is characterized as adulterated, and the law prohibits introducing such food to interstate commerce. This general definition has several critical exceptions: naturally occurring substances that do not cause harm, and pesticides. Immediately following this exception, the act prohibits unsafe levels of pesticide residues on raw agricultural products. The act provides a strong basis for determining "unsafe levels of pesticide residues."

Regulation of Pesticide Residues

Initially, the act did not prohibit pesticide residues on raw agricultural products. The act specifies that any product not recognized as safe by appropriate experts will be considered as unsafe on raw agricultural products. From this, the act specifies that tolerance levels for pesticides must be established, and that raw agricultural products with residues that do not exceed these limits shall be considered safe. Based on this statutory authorization, tolerance limits for hundreds of pesticides on a multitude of crops and crop products have been established and ultimately reported in the *Code of Federal Regulations.* Tolerance limits have been changed, and reference to the *Federal Register* is essential to ensure that the most current standards are being followed. The basic law still emphasizes consumer safety: Raw agricultural products contaminated with pesticides are defined as adulterated.

The potential of pesticides for causing cancer remains a major concern in allowing any pesticide residue in or on foods. In the mid-1950s, this concern was expressed in an amendment to the FFDCA; the Delaney Amendment effectively prohibited any residue in food of a pesticide known to cause cancer in test animals or humans. Over time, however, these provisions raised serious regulatory and technical issues. The prohibition was against "any residue"; it did not recognize the minute amounts that might be detected or the rigorous safety standards incorporated into residue allowances set by administrative rules, nor did it consider the dosage that might cause cancer in humans or in test animals. Finally, since its passage, technology has advanced to the extent that residues can be detected at levels of one part per 100 million to one part per billion, whereas in the 1950s, residues might have been detected in amounts of one part per thousand or one part per hundred thousand, with the most rigorous analysis possibly reaching detection of some materials at one part per million. Thus the meaning of "no detectable residue" has changed with time, as smaller amounts are readily detected, without showing that such minute amounts constitute a significant health hazard.

Enforcement of this amendment led to significant controversies. In spite of the wording, the enforcement focused on a reasonable standard of no "harmful" residue. Consumer groups insisted on strict enforcement of the amendment because the residue standards fail to recognize different groups of consumers that might suffer different exposure levels or react differently to the allowed residues. Major emphasis focused on residues on "fresh" fruits and vegetables and the impact of these residues on infants and young children, who not only may consume more of the raw product, but who clearly consume more in proportion to their body weight. Although the amendment issue itself was never resolved, Congress addressed many of the issues in the 1996 Food Quality Protection Act.

The FFDCA also considers pesticide residues in processed food, but the standards are easier to understand: Effectively, if the processed food contains less residue than is allowed on the raw product, the food is allowed in commerce. Certain restrictions apply in terms of processing according to the best technology, and some conflicts have arisen concerning when an agricultural commodity has been processed in terms of establishing when less restrictive residue standards apply.

The FFDCA obviously first considers issues of human health. In terms of environmental focus, considered with FIFRA, the federal government has taken a strong stand to protect human health, to protect the environment, and to continue to allow agricultural producers to use essential pesticides, although regulations impose increasing restrictions on pesticide usage.

THE FOOD QUALITY PROTECTION ACT OF 1996

In recent years, Congress has recognized continued threats to the American food supply and the weakness of existing laws and the rules and regulations derived from those laws. A significant portion of this awareness relates to FFDCA and the issues of zero tolerance of pesticide residues required by the Delaney Amendment. In 1995–1996, Congress addressed a variety of issues and ultimately significantly modified much of the pesticide legislation as it affects food quality and consumer safety.

Congress passed the Food Quality Protection Act of 1996 in August 1996. The act, P.L. 104-170, amends portions of both FIFRA and FFDCA and introduces several new regulatory elements. The full impact of this extensive legislation is not yet apparent. Clearly, it will yield a large body of new rules and regulations as both the USDA and the EPA act to implement its provisions.

Where possible and appropriate in the following discussion, the code sections in which the amendments will appear are indicated. In other parts, reference is made to the act as passed by Congress.

The structure of the act is quite simple. It is divided into five titles: Title I and II amend FIFRA. Title I focuses on pesticide registration, tolerances, and periodic review of registration of pesticides. Title II, Minor Use Pesticides, isolates a specific group of pesticides that were not uniquely considered in the original act. Such pesticides, by definition, are used on crops grown on fewer than 300,000 acres, annually. Such pesticides may also be used on animals. The act specifies the definition as an addition to FIFRA, 7 USC 136.

Title III repeals the Delaney Amendment. This title calls for a detailed survey of food consumption patterns, particularly patterns of infants and children, to determine whether a significant difference to pesticide residue exposure might exist as a result of differences in patterns of consumption, especially with the consumption of fruit. This title is new material, not an amendment to either FIFRA or FFDCA.

Title IV amends FFDCA and builds on the survey requirement of Title III. The major emphasis is on pesticide residue tolerances as they relate to consumption patterns of infants and children. Key definitions not previously established are cross-referenced to FIFRA for consistency. "Processed food" is defined with a specific addition of Subsection "gg" to FFDCA, 21 USC 321, and means any food other than a raw agricultural commodity that has been subject to processing such as canning, cooking, freezing, dehydrating, or milling.

In addition, Title IV provides a new basic standard for the tolerance and exemptions for pesticide chemical residues. This new material specifically amends the pesticide tolerance requirements stated in 21 USC 346(a). The new standards that amend and replace the preceding material provide more precise definitions and standards. The general rule becomes:

> except as provided in paragraph (2) or (3), any pesticide chemical residue in or on a food shall be deemed unsafe for the purposes of section 402(a)(2)(B) (21 USC 231(q), as amended) unless—
>
> > (A) a tolerance for such pesticide chemical residue in or on such food is in effect under this section and the quantity of the residue is within the limits of the tolerance; or
> >
> > (B) an exemption from the requirements for a tolerance is in effect under this section for the pesticide chemical residue.

This statement recognizes that approved residues are allowed and repeals the "no detectable residue" standard.

The act further explains that the term "food" will include both raw agricultural commodities and processed food and considers tolerances applicable to processed foods. Effectively, the act continues the rule that, in the absence of a separate standard, if a residue in a processed food does not exceed the allowable residue tolerance for a commodity from which the product was manufactured, the food is not deemed adulterated.

The act addresses criteria for residue standards. The general rule requires first that a residue is allowed only if it is "safe," and safety must include aggregate exposure to the residue or toxic substance. The initial legislation did not specifically address the issue of aggregate exposure; this inclusion is part of the compromise in repealing the provisions of the Delaney Amendment. Furthermore, tolerances must now consider exposure of infants and children as separate groups. The act requires that risk assessment include data on consumption patterns and address special susceptibilities of infants and children plus account for cumulative exposures or a cumulative effect.

Unlike its predecessor, FFDCA, Title IV of 1996 FQPA sets out detailed criteria for approving pesticide residue tolerances:

1. The validity and completeness of the data on which the request is based
2. The nature of toxic effects demonstrated from studies
3. Relationships to other studies involving human health
4. Available information indicating consumption of food
5. Available information concerning cumulative effects of the pesticide
6. Available information concerning the impact of aggregate exposure
7. The variability among subgroups of potential consumers concerning toxic reactions to the residue
8. Other information the administrator deems helpful

Finally, Title V of the act discusses the collection and use of various fees associated with pesticide reregistration under the provisions of FIFRA. Limits are set for the use and collection of these fees.

CONCLUSIONS

Pesticides represent a threat both to the environment and to humans as a potential adulterant to foods. However, pesticides also contribute to crop yield and quality. The laws that regulate residues also affect the use of pesticides and thus are part of the broad spectrum of environmental regulations.

The provisions of FIFRA and FFDCA, coupled with the 1996 FQPA, provide a solid basis for protecting the environment from pesticide pollution. Emphasis on all steps to minimize pesticide use while continuing the high level of agricultural productivity is essential. Certification of both private and commercial applicators and registration of pesticides and pesticide manufacturers are steps in the right direction to ensure adequate control of these potentially harmful materials. The most perplexing weakness in the legislation appears to be the lack of regulations regarding who can purchase any type of pesticide and the continuing unregulated, nonagricultural uses of pesticides.

QUESTIONS AND CONCEPTS FOR DISCUSSION AND RESEARCH

1. Compare and contrast the purpose and scope of the Federal Insecticide, Fungicide, and Rodenticide Act with the provisions of the Federal Food, Drug, and Cosmetic Act.
2. What are the major environmental provisions of FIFRA?
3. What is the significance of general-use versus restricted-use classifications of pesticides?
4. What factors does FFDCA require to be considered in establishing pesticide residue standards?
5. The Food Quality Protection Act of 1996 repealed the Delaney Amendment; what new provisions of law replaced or substituted for this amendment?
6. For what other major regulatory changes did the FQPA call?

REFERENCES AND SELECTED READING

Carson, Rachel. 1962. *Silent Spring.* Boston: Houghton Mifflin.

U.S. Environmental Protection Agency. *Environmental Backgrounder: Pesticides.* Washington, DC.

————. September 1995. *Citizen's Guide to Pest Control and Pesticide Safety.* EPA 730-K-95-001. Washington, DC.

11

The Workplace Environment, Toxic Substance Control, and Ethics

In addition to legislation that clearly focuses on the environment, numerous other acts or rules authorized by those acts either directly or indirectly affect the environment. To understand the scope of legislative impact on environmental issues, these acts must be introduced and placed in perspective with the acts discussed in the preceding chapters, legislation that protects natural resources, protects our health, and regulates the massive problems associated with waste disposal.

The workplace represents a special environment, but one in which most adults spend the majority of their waking hours. Relatively little federal legislation directly addresses issues unique to the workplace environment in terms of the environment encountered by workers, yet the federal government regulates workplace environmental conditions in the name of worker safety.

The majority of workplace regulations spring from the provisions of the Occupational Safety and Health Act (OSHA). This act addresses two related aspects of the workplace environment. First—the primary emphasis—OSHA focuses on workplace safety and reducing worker accidents and injuries. This focus includes worker protection from physical injuries and accidents ranging from falls on slippery surfaces to injuries from improperly guarded machinery and the need for protective clothing for certain workers. This aspect of OSHA is not generally viewed as environmental legislation. The second major aspect of the act addresses worker illness and injuries not necessarily associated with an individual accident. This concern for the health of the worker involves environmental problems and justifies considering OSHA in part as environmental legislation.

THE OCCUPATIONAL SAFETY AND HEALTH ACT

In considering OSHA, Congress recognized that safety in the workplace is in the nation's interest. Nonetheless, OSHA receives frequent criticism from both labor and management: the latter claims that regulations are too time-consuming and do not significantly improve worker safety, and the former argues that rules are too lax and that too many workplaces are unsafe. Labor calls for stricter workplace safety standards, and management insists it recognizes the need for workplace safety and will act responsibly without legislation.

In 1970, Congress recognized the ongoing conflict of interests between labor and management and enacted OSHA with the express purpose of ensuring workers a safe place to work. The act, 29 USC 651 *et seq.,* is lengthy and complicated. It has been the source of numerous rules, all with a focus on workplace safety.

Congress justified OSHA and provided a clear basis for judicial interpretation of the act in its statement of facts presented in the first section of the OSHA, 29 USC 651(a):

> The Congress finds that personal injuries and illnesses arising out of work situations impose a substantial burden to interstate commerce in terms of lost production, wage loss, medical expenses, and disability compensation payments.

Clearly, OSHA looks first to the economics of workplace safety—productivity and compensation payments. From this vantage point, Congress clearly did not intend that OSHA should focus on environmental protection. Even worker protection seems to arise as a concern associated with lost productivity and increased costs to employers. The subsequently stated purpose of the act seems to be far more concerned with the welfare of the individual.

Congress clearly stated its purpose for OSHA

> through the exercise of its powers to regulate commerce among the several states and with foreign nations and to provide for the general welfare, to assure as far as possible every working man and woman in the Nation safe and healthful working conditions to preserve our human resources. 29 USC 651(b).

Here the emphasis is on workplace safety, which includes the overall environment of the workplace. However, the act does not call for a risk-free work environment; safety is to be assured "as far as possible." OSHA recognizes that some work circumstances are dangerous. The "as far as possible" requirement is vague and has led to disputes as to whether employers have satisfied this requirement.

OSHA, 29 USC 651(b)(1), recognizes shared responsibilities for job safety. In it, Congress called on both employers and employees "to institute new and perfect existing programs for providing safe and healthful working conditions." The act also calls for establishing causal connections between diseases and the work environment.

Setting Safety Standards

In seeking to establish safety standards for the nation's workplaces, Congress recognized the diversity of situations and the value of outside expertise; 29 USC 652(9). OSHA identifies as "national consensus standards" the health and safety standards that have been adopted and promulgated by nationally recognized standards-producing organizations, which have had diverse input into their formulation. In this way, industrial safety standards can be adopted as the official OSHA standard. In addition to major commercial interests, labor unions have had significant input into workplace safety standards based on this section of OSHA.

Relation to EPCRTKA

Part of OSHA involves recognizing workplace hazards. Emphasis is placed on prevention, including monitoring the presence of certain toxic substances that are located at various work sites. OSHA requires employers to maintain material safety data sheets. The information maintained is the same information as that required by the provisions of the Emergency Planning Community Right to Know Act, 42 USC 11001 *et seq.* Here, OSHA clearly interfaces with major environmental legislation. Because OSHA addresses workplace safety involving many of the same toxic pollutants considered by RCRA and other legislation, clearly parts of OSHA must be recognized as environmental law focused on a very diverse but specific type of environment, the workplace.

The Evolution of OSHA

Since the inception of OSHA in 1970, employers have criticized it as being too detailed, with more focus on complying with records and reports than on efforts to address workplace safety. The need for changes has been recognized, and in 1994 Congress amended OSHA to simplify it, to focus more clearly on safety/health issues, and to minimize paperwork and reports. In spite of the initial criticism, OSHA has been effective in improving the environment: Standards set in the textile industry have effectively eliminated brown lung disease, a condition caused by constant exposure to cotton dust. In addition, workers' exposure to lead in battery plants has been greatly reduced; recall that lead is recognized as a serious pollutant and has received specific attention in the CAA as well as the Safe Drinking Water Act. Numerous other environmentally related successes could be cited; however, a downside to OSHA must also be recognized.

Workplace-related chemical exposures cause some 50,000 cases of illness annually. Injuries alone are estimated to cost $110 billion. In addition, about six thousand workplace deaths occur annually. Many of these are safety related, involving the physical safety issue, but illness and exposures to toxic materials obviously are related to the workplace environment. A continuing need exists to improve all aspects of the workplace environment, including emphasis on educating workers to follow safety guidelines and to use available safety equipment, such as eye protection and dust masks.

In the 1994 amendments, the administration recognized the need to reduce paperwork and to focus on activities that increase safety rather than stressing compliance with rules and filing detailed compliance reports and additional accident- or work-related injury reports. The new focus will reduce paperwork and will consider more directly both environmental issues in the workplace and physical safety. Priority areas of environmental concern include conditions contributing to occupational asthma, reproductive problems associated with lead, and exposure to toxic fumes such as asphalt fumes. All of these areas affect health, and all are related to the environment of the workplace. General safety concerns include welding, commercial (deep sea) diving, workplace violence, and motor vehicle accidents.

Through OSHA, Congress has focused attention on the safety of the workplace. Although prevention of many accidents may not appear to be related to environment, protection of workers from workplace environmental pollution in any form is clearly environmental regulation. OSHA includes environmental regulations for the unique but varied environment, the workplace.

INDOOR AIR QUALITY

Few would deny that Congress recognized the importance of protecting air quality. In addition, many states have set air quality standards more rigorous than required by the provisions of the Clean Air Act. Dramatic progress has been realized in reducing some pollutants (e.g., lead) in the ambient air, but all would recognize that serious air pollution problems continue. In addition to "outdoor air," the quality of indoor air has become of increasing concern. Congress, however, has not addressed this issue. Federal legislation seems to ignore any direct regulation of this vital aspect of the human environment: the quality of air indoors, at home, in business places, in public places, and, to a great extent, at work (OSHA does address issues of air quality in the workplace).

Sick Buildings

Poor air quality can be a major problem: It is known to reduce productivity and contribute to employee absenteeism. Air quality is a major element of the "sick building syndrome," a condition workers, employers, and health officials increasingly recognize as real. Workers or residents of a building display "sick building symptoms," which commonly include headaches, irritated eyes, coughs, and, most frequently, increased incidence of colds and upper respiratory tract illnesses.

Many factors contribute to poor indoor air quality and thus to the "sick building syndrome"; these factors include excessively high concentrations of carbon dioxide and carbon monoxide in the air, microorganisms from bacteria to mold, dust and other particulate matter, toxic materials and organic solvents from cleaning compounds and copiers, and cigarette smoke.

Sick buildings share one major feature—poor ventilation. Frequently, as ventilation is improved, health problems are reduced directly. Most new commercial buildings are "sealed"—windows do not open. As a result, air quality depends on the adequacy of the ventilation system and on its proper operation. Renovation of older buildings that does not include appropriate modifications of ventilating systems leads to air quality problems too. This work includes minor additions and partitions that impede air flow.

Except for OSHA requirements, federal law does not specifically address indoor air quality. Rather, state building codes and local regulations set the standards. Of course, OSHA considers worker safety and health, so the scope of federal regulation is effectively limited to the realm of OSHA. Typically for many environmental issues, states have the prerogative to establish plans that, on approval by the appropriate federal agency, set the basis of compliance with federal laws.

In the case of regulating the quality of indoor air, OSHA requires states to have an approved plan associated with building regulations. The plan must involve ventilation design for buildings and must include maintenance as well. It must also designate a party in a building who will be responsible for air quality maintenance. This requirement creates a problem in large buildings with numerous occupants, any one of whom could be responsible for air quality problems. Regardless, the law requires that an individual be identified. Also, the law requires special steps to ensure that occupants are protected from poor air quality that may occur during building renovations. Finally, special, designated smoking areas may be required; such areas must have a negative air pressure so that smoke does not infiltrate the entire ventilation system of the building. In recent years, secondhand smoke has become a significant issue and a national health concern. Secondhand smoke may contribute to the sick building syndrome.

Secondhand Smoke

Secondhand smoke, or passive smoke, has become a major topic of concern related to indoor air quality. Passive smoke represents a serious health threat, according to the EPA. Based on worldwide studies, the EPA estimates that, annually, passive smoke causes three thousand fatal cases of lung cancer in the United States. The EPA classifies smoke as a "group A" carcinogen, the most toxic type. (This group also includes solvents, asbestos, and organic materials such as benzene.) The health risks from passive smoke increase with exposure, but the EPA reported no significant increase in lung cancer among children whose parents smoked.

Public pressure more than likely will force further attention on reducing exposure to passive smoke; further federal action through OSHA may be anticipated. The National Institute for Occupational Health and Safety, an institute created by OSHA, has recommended that workers' exposure to passive smoke be reduced to an absolute minimum. This type of recommendation ultimately will yield regulations from the agency.

In addition to the impact EPA may have on passive smoke through regulations related to indoor air quality, the Office of the United States Surgeon General may play a significant role. The surgeon general could designate nicotine as a drug, and regulate it (or the sale of tobacco products) through the authority of the Federal Food, Drug, and Cosmetic Act. However, regulation of tobacco products historically has been subject to intense lobbying activity, and it is doubtful that in the near future tobacco will be designated as a drug.

TOXIC SUBSTANCE CONTROL

In addition to regulating emissions of various substances through the provisions of general legislation such as the CAA, CWA, and SDWA, Congress has identified several pollutants for "special attention." The Toxic Substance Control Act, 15 USC 2601 *et seq.*, comprises only four subchapters: Subchapter I, Control of Toxic Substances, and Subchapters II, III, and IV that address problems with asbestos, radon, and lead, respectively. Other legislation, CAA and SDWA, also recognizes these three pollutants and seeks to regulate them.

Subchapter I, 15 USC 2601, includes a statement of congressional finding of facts that suggests the reasons for the legislation. The Congress found that "human beings and the environment are being exposed each year to a large number of substances and mixtures." The Congress continued, noting that some of these chemicals and mixtures "may present unreasonable risk of injury to health or the environment," and finally Congress admitted that effective interstate control of these substances requires intrastate control. The finding of the need for both intra- and interstate regulation justifies placing this act under Commerce and Trade, Title 15 of the *United States Code.* The provisions of the act clearly identify it as legislation designed to protect the environment, or humans, from further environmental degradation.

The act seeks to protect individuals from "unreasonable" exposure to pollutants. The act, 15 USC 2601, calls for balancing economic factors with exposure to certain pollutants. In a statement of policy, the act calls for developing essential data, authorizing regulation of specific pollutants, and requires that regulations not impose undue economic hardship on commerce and industry.

Asbestos

Asbestos is a naturally occurring mineral fiber. The term as defined in the act, 15 USC 2642, includes the asbestiform form of several minerals: (1) chrysotite (serpentine), (2) crocodolite (riebeckite), (3) amosite (cummingtonite-grunerite), (4) anthophyllite, (5) tremolite, (6) actinolite. Asbestos has been used as insulation and as a flameproof material. It also is used in roofing materials, floor coverings, and automobile brake shoes and clutch plates. From about 1920 through 1978, asbestos was widely used as insulation in many buildings, including private homes.

Asbestos is not dangerous as it is normally used. The danger arises when materials break down from aging (become friable), and when ultrafine asbestos fibers become airborne. These fibers are less than one-tenth the thickness of a human hair and are essentially impossible to see. Exposure to asbestos fibers can lead to serious lung diseases, including lung cancer. Symptoms usually appear ten to forty years after exposure, as the long-term effects of the irritant develop.

The CAA, 42 USC 7412(b)(1), recognizes asbestos as a pollutant. In the Toxic Substance Control Act, Congress expressed dissatisfaction over the initial EPA rules for asbestos in schools, 15 USC 2641(a), and specifically required school inspections for potential asbestos hazards, 15 USC 2641(b).

In August 1994, the EPA issued its final asbestos rules: Building owners are held responsible for asbestos problems, even when others occupy the premises. The rules recognize four categories of work involving asbestos that cover activities ranging from building maintenance to major renovations involving removal of asbestos insulation, flooring, or roof materials. In addition, owners are required to notify occupants of known or suspected asbestos hazards. Residential structures with fewer than four units are excluded from these regulations, however. In addition, disposal of construction debris that contains asbestos is regulated. Some states have additional regulations as well.

Radon

Radon is a naturally occurring, radioactive, colorless, odorless gas produced by the "decay" of uranium. The CAA considers radon as an air pollutant, 42 USC 7412(b)(1). The Toxic Substance Control Act focuses on radon in buildings where it can accumulate to hazardous levels of concentration.

The act addresses the radon problem in Subchapter III, Indoor Radon Abatement, 15 USC 2661. The United States Surgeon General has declared, "indoor radon gas is a national health problem. Millions of homes have elevated radon levels. Homes should be tested for radon. When levels are elevated, the problem should be corrected." Health experts agree that harm from radon is significantly magnified by smoking. For all radon concentrations studied, smokers suffered more damage than nonsmokers. The joint issue of secondhand smoke and radon was not addressed.

The average radon concentration in ambient air is approximately 0.4 pCi/L (pCi/L is picocuries [a measure of radioactivity] per liter), and the average indoor concentration is approximately 1.3 pCi/L. Repeated or prolonged exposure to radon concentrations of 4.0 pCi/L can be harmful to human health. Studies suggest that radon is a problem in all states, but the magnitude of the problem varies greatly within and among states as a function of the presence of uranium-bearing rocks. Approximately 10 percent of the homes in the United States, some eight million homes, suffer from elevated radon levels. Although the risk can be serious, it is fairly easy to remedy.

Testing for radon is relatively simple and inexpensive. Many home buyers insist on a radon test as a condition to purchasing property. The gas comes from the decay of radioactive rocks and tends to accumulate in basements and similar crawl spaces. Problems with buildup can be remedied with ventilation and sealing compounds to exclude the gas.

Currently, no federal law requires radon testing as any part of real estate sales or financing. Many prospective home buyers insist that a radon test be included in the purchase agreement. The impact of the results of such a test must be viewed on a case-by-case basis, because contracts are effectively private law and different combinations of buyers and sellers could vary with respect to results of a radon test that suggested unreasonable high concentrations of the gas. In the discussion on lead that follows, note that federal rules require sellers to give buyers the opportunity to have homes inspected for lead-based paint.

No standards for radon have been promulgated by OSHA. The Toxic Substance Control Act has established goals for radon reduction: Building air should be as free from radon as the ambient air in the same area; 15 USC 2661. In addition, building codes should be modified to require designs and construction that minimize radon accumulation, and schools should receive special attention and assistance to remedy elevated radon levels.

Lead

Lead has long been recognized as a potentially toxic substance; provisions of the SDWA reflect this knowledge and concern. The CAA reflects the same concern in the prohibition of lead as a fuel additive. Regulations and public awareness, compliance, and cooperation have reduced the level of atmospheric lead and problems associated with this pollutant. Nonetheless, because it has been used for so long in such different ways, lead remains a serious environmental health threat.

At one time, lead was a constituent of many paints. The Department of Housing and Urban Development estimates that lead-based paint was applied to approximately 75 percent of the houses built in the United States prior to 1978. As the paint weathers and wears, lead in the form of dust and minute flakes enters the atmosphere and is inhaled or ingested. Infants and very young children are particularly susceptible to neurological damage from lead poisoning, although adults can also suffer serious harm. This metal also is a significant threat to the health and development of unborn children; thus, lead is commonly viewed as a threat to pregnant women.

Lead-based house paint represents a major area of concern, but it is not the exclusive concern. Children are also exposed to lead-based paint on older toys and may, out of curiosity, ingest numerous items that contain lead.

In addition to the provisions of the SDWA, two other regulatory actions target lead reduction. Neither set of regulations stems from traditional environmental legislation, but both have the effect of reducing lead pollution in the environment and thus must be introduced as part of environmental regulation and policy.

The Consumer Protection Act, 15 USC 2681, calls for the reduction to lead exposure, "to permanently eliminate lead based paint hazard." Subsequent regulations were dramatic, prohibiting the use of lead-based paint; these rules are found in 16 CFR 1303. This single action was a major step in preventing further problems, but it did not consider current problem areas. In 1996, the problem of lead-based paint in residences was addressed by EPA rules. Effective in September 1996 for multiple-family dwellings, and in December 1996 for individual residences, sellers of homes constructed prior to 1978 must notify potential buyers that lead-based paints could have been used in the home and must allow buyers adequate time—ten days, or less by agreement—to have the home inspected; dangerous lead paint may be a reason for the buyer to void a purchase contract. State laws may supplement this provision, in the same way that many states require sellers to notify buyers of hazardous waste disposal or storage sites on property. Finally, the new rules require renovators (contractors or repair workers) to provide clients with a booklet describing possible lead hazards in older homes.

This new rule does not require the seller to remedy the lead paint problem; it merely requires the seller to notify the potential buyer and allows the buyer to include that factor in a decision to purchase the property. The same set of rules also requires landlords to notify renters of potential lead-based paint hazards.

ENVIRONMENTAL ETHICS

An Emerging Discipline

The concept of environmental racism is not widely discussed, but the issue is not new. In 1982, residents of Warren County, North Carolina, protested locating a PCB landfill in their neighborhood; the protesters and the residents of the neighborhood were predominantly African-Americans. Following this protest, the General Accounting Office reported that three out of four hazardous waste sites studied were in predominantly African-American communities. A 1983 study was confined to states in GAO Region 4: Alabama, Florida, Georgia, Kentucky, Mississippi, North Carolina, South Carolina, and Tennessee. Extensive private studies affirmed this pattern nationwide. From 1970 to 1978, three out of four privately owned landfills serving Houston, Texas, were located in predominantly African American neighborhoods. Protests over locating a landfill in King and Queen County, Virginia, revealed a similar pattern. In addition, situations have been documented for both dumps and incinerator facilities in "Cancer Alley" in southern Louisiana and in Alabama's "Black Belt" where waste from superfund cleanup sites is deposited.

A common response to these studies has been that the issue is not ethnic, but economic. Landfills and related facilities are located where land can be purchased relatively inexpensively and where developers and operators will not face stiff opposition to the facilities. Sophisticated statistical techniques have been applied to this issue. No doubt, economics is a serious factor, but when the effects of economics are removed, the major factor remains ethnicity.

In addition to locating landfills and similar facilities, issues of environmental racism have been raised concerning farm workers exposed to pesticides. At least the plurality of farm labor in the United States are of Chicano ancestry. Many farm workers are involved with hand labor in crops that receive extensive applications of pesticides. The argument is that the laborers, because of their ethnicity and economic status, do not receive adequate protection from pesticide residues. Unlike the issue of land use, pesticides are subject to strict regulations, and employers are required to provide workers with adequate safety equipment. Moreover, the law specifies the period following pesticide application during which workers may not enter the fields. Certainly, the law is not always followed, but widespread abuse has not been documented, and some instances of workers' failing to use safety equipment or follow safety regulations account for part of such exposures.

General Considerations

Public awareness of environmental problems, demands for environmental protection, emphasis not only on preserving existing resources, but also on restoring lost resources, and increasing willingness of diverse groups to join in efforts to improve and protect the environment have led to the evolution of a variety of new disciplines, or to new applications of older disciplines. This willingness is strikingly evident, for example, in the remedial and preventive strategies formulated by engineers in efforts to help ensure both clean air and clean water. It is equally evident in the life sciences in efforts to save endangered species and the microbiology of composting, biodegradation of pollutants, and bioremediation. Economic theory and practice have introduced new concepts of valuing natural resources and costs associated with environmental decisions. Even the private individual cannot escape this evolution: Recycling has become a way of life for many who, a mere few years ago, may have viewed recycling as a needless nuisance. In addition, numerous groups contribute to periodic "neighborhood cleanup" efforts.

These same forces have triggered the evolution of environmental law and policy. Congress and state lawmakers look to constitutional principles to apply to solutions of problems that did not exist 100 years ago and that only in the past 25 years have received concentrated attention. Cooperation among diverse interests has become a must, if problems are to be resolved, and both interstate and international efforts will accelerate to protect the environment in which we live and on which we depend.

No field of thought is free of influence from the current focus on the environment. New disciplines emerge, and older fields nurture side shoots or change direction. This fact extends to philosophy, not only in law and policy, but also in the emerging discipline of environmental ethics.

Ethics is an accepted component of traditional philosophy; environmental ethics is emerging as a subfield of the recognized field of applied ethics. The foundation of applied ethics finds its roots in the concepts of the social contract.

Ethical Behavior

Any consideration of environmental ethics must address a variety of broad, fundamental questions. No clear answer leaps forward, but perhaps the benefit is more in seeking the answer than in the answer itself. A logical, but not simple, starting point is to define "ethical behavior." A wide array of laws, rules, and regulations specifies what we may and may not do with respect to many elements of the environment. Many of them regulate "business" more than the individual.

Considering the scope of environmental regulation, a basic question becomes whether ethical responsibility is satisfied simply by obeying the law. At least one answer to this question is *no,* ethical behavior is more than obeying laws. Ethical behavior involves acts enforceable only by one's conscience, not by the letter of the law. This point leads to a related issue: Many professions have codes of conduct or codes of ethical behavior. If complying with laws does not satisfy ethical responsibilities fully, the issue becomes whether conforming to professional codes of conduct guarantees ethical behavior.

In looking at professional codes of conduct, the answer to three critical questions may help determine whether they provide adequate guidelines to ensure ethical behavior or actions: (1) Who wrote the code? (2) What is the purpose of the code? (3) Who enforces the code? In some instances, professional codes are written to protect and enhance the image of the profession, with little concern for external constituencies. In many cases, this is not undesirable: the code may stress superior professional performance, thereby protecting the interests of those served. Codes that are generally "internal" to a profession may not provide adequate guidance, particularly in terms of environmental situations.

If a code requires a specific minimum level of action or performance, and an individual knows or strongly believes that a higher level is required to protect the environment in some way, must that individual act to protect the environment, or are duty and responsibility satisfied by satisfying the provisions of professional codes of conduct? This question immediately raises another closely related issue: whether an individual may (or must) answer to both professional and personal codes of ethics. The problem is not simple.

Consider one example—a situation in which an individual knows that an action taken on behalf of an employer or client will satisfy both the letter of the law and an established code of professional conduct, but the individual knows or believes that a more costly course of action is advised to protect the environment. Suggesting or pursuing the more expensive option is wise environmentally, but it is expensive to either the employer or the client or both. Such circumstances arise daily, and no simple solution exists. As much as anything, awareness of the conflicts and willingness to address them individually, on a case-by-case basis, might be the best of all worlds. Perhaps the opinion of recognized scholars will help direct your thinking.

In a 1790 letter to the Duchess of Auville, Thomas Jefferson described his ethics as follows, "I have but one system of ethics for man and nations—to be grateful, to be faithful to all engagements, and under all circumstances, to be open and generous, promoting in the long run, the interests of both." From this statement, it appears that Jefferson would consider only personal ethics and would seemingly equate them—as they relate to any issue—with honesty and candor. There seems to be no room for conflict of interest, yet conflicts of interest arise daily.

In a slightly different vein, Ralph Waldo Emerson commented in his 1841 *Spiritual World,* "We must hold man amenable to reason for the choice of his daily craft or profession. It is not an excuse any longer that they are the customs of the times. What business has a man with an evil trade?" Certainly, from this point Emerson would not accept professional standards as justification for damage. It also appears that ethical standards, to Emerson, should be evaluated outside of the profession. In Emerson's philosophy, it seems that an avoidable action that degraded the environment would not be acceptable.

Ultimately, humans will determine the quality of the environment in which we live and that we leave for our children and grandchildren. Laws, rules, and regulations will play a key role in protecting the environment, but the concern of each individual will ultimately shape the outcome.

QUESTIONS AND CONCEPTS FOR DISCUSSION AND RESEARCH

1. Considering the impact of OSHA, should it be considered environmental law? Justify your position.

2. What provisions of OSHA suggest a lack of environmental focus? a focus on the environment?

3. Is the issue of "the sick building syndrome" an environmental issue? Is secondhand smoke an environmental issue? Should they be addressed by federal law?

4. On what substances does the Toxic Substance Control Act focus? Are these substances otherwise subject to regulation? Justify the apparent multiple control efforts. Are they unique to these substances?

5. What are the most significant ethical issues related to the environment facing society today? Are there different commercial/industrial issues? Are the issues being addressed adequately? Can they be addressed by statute?

REFERENCES AND SELECTED READING

Axelrad, Bob. 1993. Improving IAQ: EPA's Program. *EPA Journal* 19(4): 14–17.

Browner, Carol M. 1993. Environmental Tobacco Smoke. *EPA Journal* 19(4): 18–19.

Bullard, Robert D. 1992. In Our Backyards. *EPA Journal* 18(5): 11–12.

Leaderer, Brian. 1993. Investigating Sick Buildings. *EPA Journal* 19(4): 25–27.

Mohai, Paul, and Bunyan Bryant. 1992. Race, Poverty, and the Environment. *EPA Journal* 18(5): 6–8.

Perfecto, Ivette, and Baldermar Velasquez. 1992. Farm Workers Among the Least Protected. *EPA Journal* 18(5): 13–14.

Pope, Andrew. 1993. Indoor Allergens. *EPA Journal* 19(4): 13.

Sexton, Ken. 1993. An Inside Look at Air Pollution. *EPA Journal* 19(4): 9–12.

U.S. Environmental Protection Agency. September 1988. *The Inside Story: A Guide to Indoor Air Quality.* EPA/400/1-88/004. Washington, DC.

———. December 1988. *Glossary of Environmental Terms and Acronym List.* EPA 19K-1002. Washington, DC.

———. May 1992. *A Citizen's Guide to Radon.* 2d ed. EPA #402-K92-001. Washington, DC.

———. May 1995. *Protect Your Family from Lead in Your Home.* EPA 747-94-001. Washington, DC.

GLOSSARY

abatement   Eliminating or reducing the degree or intensity of pollution.

acid deposition   A complex atmospheric and chemical phenomenon occurring when emissions of sulfur and nitrogen and other substances are transformed by chemical processes in the atmosphere and deposited in any form of acid precipitation, including dry acid particles.

acid rain   (*See* acid deposition).

active ingredient   In a pesticide, the toxic compound that kills or otherwise controls target pests; regulations focus on the active ingredient.

ADI (allowable daily intake)   Exposure to a pollutant that results in no harm.

administrative law   The body of law created by administrative agencies under the authority of the Administrative Procedure Act and authorized by specific legislation, including rules, regulations, (standards) orders, and agency decisions. Also, the procedures by which such a body of law is created and enforced.

Administrative Procedure Act (The)   Federal law that establishes the rule-making and rule-enforcement procedures for government agencies. States also have similar legislation.

administrative rule(s)   Rules promulgated by administrative (executive) agencies under statutory authority and that have the force and effect of law, including standards and similar regulations.

agricultural pollution   Liquid and solid waste from farming and ranching activities, including runoff and leaching of pesticides and fertilizers.

air pollution   Any substance in air that could, in high enough concentration, harm human health, other animals, vegetation, or other materials.

Note: Many definitions provided in this Glossary have been abbreviated from EPA publications, the most extensively used is: EPA, December 1989. *Glossary of Environmental Terms and Acronym List.* 19K-1002. Definitions from other sources may vary slightly. For legal terms, definitions are from *Black's Law Dictionary,* fifth edition. 1979. West Publishing Co., St. Paul, MN.

air quality control regions   Areas designated by the federal government in which communities share a common air pollution problem.

air quality criteria   The levels of pollutants and lengths of exposure above which adverse health and welfare effects may occur.

alar   A chemical applied to apples to foster the development of red color and natural ripening.

ambient air   Any unconfined portion of the atmosphere. Open air.

appropriative rights   The right to use surface water established by diverting such water from a stream or other source and putting the water to a beneficial use.

aquifer   An underground geological formation containing useable amounts of water that can supply wells or springs.

asbestos   A mineral fiber used in many forms of insulation and fire retardant materials.

atmosphere   The mass of air surrounding the earth, composed mostly of nitrogen and oxygen.

BACT (best available control technology)   Emission limitations based on the maximum degree of emission reduction, which is achievable through the application of best production technology with consideration for energy conservation, other environmental considerations, and economics.

bioaccumulation   Substances that increase in concentration in living organisms.

biochemical oxygen demand (BOD)   A measure of the amount of oxygen consumed in biological processes that break down organic matter in water. The greater the BOD, the greater the level of pollution.

biodegradable   The ability or tendency to break down or decompose under natural conditions.

biodiversity   Describes either inherited differences among individuals of the same species in a population of interbreeding individuals, or the number and type of different species with in a community or ecosystem.

Bureau of Land Management (BLM)   An agency of the US Department of the Interior with the responsibility of managing much of the public grazing lands in the West and throughout the United States.

carbon monoxide (CO)   A colorless, odorless gas that is the product of incomplete combustion of carbon-containing compounds and, if breathed over prolonged periods or in high concentrations, could cause serious health effects or death.

carcinogen   Any substance that can cause or contribute to the production of cancer.

cell   In waste management, the individual units in a landfill into which waste is deposited, compacted, and covered.

CERCLA (Comprehensive Environmental Reporting, Compensating and Liability Act)   Also known as the *Superfund Act,* legislation focused on problems of inactive or abandoned hazardous or toxic waste disposal sites.

chlorinated hydrocarbon   Organic chemical compounds—frequently insecticides—that include chlorine in addition to carbon and hydrogen.

chlorofluorohydrocarbons (CFCs)   A family of inert, nontoxic, easily liquified chemicals that have been used as refrigerants and aerosol propellants. They are reported, in conjunction with chlorine, to damage the ozone layer in the atmosphere.

Clean Air Act (CAA)   Including amendments, federal legislation that sets standards for air quality maintenance and improvement.

Code   The United States Code—the compilation of the statutory laws of the United States.

Code of Federal Regulations (CFR)   Government publication in which agency rules and regulations are published following initial publication in the Federal Register.

Common Law   Law based on tradition and the basic concepts of right and wrong. Comes from English tradition and is a source of law limited by the Constitution to the states. In theory, the federal government has no common law.

conservation easement   A special type of easement recognized by most states in which the easement to protect some aspect of the environment or natural resource is granted to a public agency or public interest organization, without title to the land or other uses being restricted.

consumptive use of water   Use of water that effectively precludes the use by others of the same water. Irrigation is a major consumptive use of water; water used for cooling nuclear generators is a nonconsumptive use.

conventional pollutants   Statutorily listed pollutants that are well understood by scientists.

criteria   Descriptive factors considered by the EPA in setting standards for various pollutants.

criteria pollutants   Six air pollutants designated by the EPA to determine attainment versus nonattainment of air quality for each pollutant in a designated geographic region.

degradation   The process or processes by which a chemical is reduced to a less complex (and frequently a less toxic) form.

designated pollutant   An air pollutant that is neither a criteria pollutant nor a hazardous pollutant as described by the Clean Air Act, but one for which source performance standards exist.

dioxin   Chemical compounds in the dibenzo-p-dioxin family; tests indicate these chemicals, which are found as contaminants in commercial products, are among the most toxic man-made compounds.

Discovery Doctrine   The doctrine, originally from Europe, that asserted that natives occupied but did not own land; as a result, title to the land could be claimed by others.

Earth Day   A day, first celebrated on April 20, 1970, designated to increase public awareness about protecting the environment and conserving natural resources.

easement   The right to use or pass over the property of another.

effluent   Waste water, treated or untreated, that flows out of a treatment plant, sewer, or industrial outfall.

effluent limitation   Restrictions established by a state or by the EPA on quantities, rates, and concentrations allowed in waste water discharges.

Eminent Domain   Right of the government to take or authorize the taking of private property for the public good, but which requires that the owner be fairly compensated.

environment   The sum of all external conditions affecting the life, development, and survival of an organism.

environmental impact statement (EIS)   A document that a government agency may be required to prepare under the mandates of the National Environmental Policy Act that evaluates various alternatives in terms of the adverse effects on the environment resulting from certain types of governmental actions or activities.

EPA (the Environmental Protection Agency)   An independent executive agency established in 1970 to administer the majority of the federal environmental protection programs.

EPCRTKA   Emergency Preparedness/Community Right to Know Act.

ESA   The Engendered Species Act.

fecal coliform bacteria   Microorganisms found in the intestinal tracts of mammals and the presence of which in water supplies provides a basis of estimating water quality and safety for public use.

Federal Register (FR)   Government's daily publication that informs the public of proposed and new rules and regulations and other legal documents of the executive branch of the government.

feed lot   A relatively small area in which animals are confined for controlled feeding and production management. Feed lots are a major source of animal waste, thus of potential pollution.

fee simpler absolute (FAS)   An estate or interest in land granting absolute ownership to an individual, his heirs and assigns, forever, without limitation or conditions. The maximum rights of permanent ownership.

FFDCA   The Federal Food, Drug, and Cosmetic Act.

FIFRA   The Federal Insecticide, Fungicide, and Rodenticide Act.

findings   Congressional findings or findings of fact. In many acts, Congress explains the basis for the legislation in statements that describe the conditions that Congress discovered and on which Congress based its actions.

FLPMA   The Federal Land Policy Management Act.

global warming   A condition some scientists believe to be occurring as a result of deteriorating air quality. It is accompanied by the buildup of gases, such as those that trap solar radiation near the earth's surface and lead to a warming trend that ultimately could have widespread environmental consequences. See *Greenhouse effect*.

greenhouse effect   Potential atmospheric warming caused by the buildup of carbon dioxide and other trace gases in the atmosphere.

groundwater   Supplies of fresh water found beneath the earth's surface, usually in aquifers.

habitat   The place where a population lives; its living and nonliving surroundings.

Hard Rock Mining Act   The only legislation that allows private citizens to patent public land; regulates mining activities on public lands.

hazardous air pollutants   Air pollutants not covered by ambient air quality standards but which, as defined by CAA, may reasonably be expected to harm health or cause death.

hazardous waste   By-products of society that can pose a substantial or potential hazard to human health or the environment.

heavy metals   Metallic elements with high atomic weights such as mercury, chromium, cadmium, arsenic, and lead.

high-level radioactive waste (HLW)   Waste generated in the fuel of a nuclear reactor; found in nuclear reactors and nuclear fuel reprocessing plants.

hydrocarbons   Chemical compounds consisting entirely of carbon and hydrogen.

hydrogen sulfide   Gas produced through the decomposition of organic matter and through petroleum refining processes and combustion.

hydrology   Science dealing with the properties, distribution, and circulation of water.

impact   The effect (frequently expressed as damage) of an action or substance on other substances, activities, or systems.

indoor air   The breathing air inside a habitable structure or conveyance.

injection well   A well into which fluids are injected (or forced) for purposes such as waste disposal.

insecticide   A general term used to describe chemical compound used to kill or control various pests: insects, weeds, pathogens, and even certain mammals and birds. There are some naturally occurring pesticides, but the term most commonly refers to man-made compounds.

judicial precedent   A court decision that establishes the interpretation of the law for a specific set of circumstances.

jurisdiction   A legal concept, the power or authority of a court to hear and decide a case and to enforce its decision. There are two general types of jurisdiction: personal jurisdiction and subject matter jurisdiction.

landfill   Sites for disposal of waste.

land grant colleges   Public colleges established from federal funding of the Morril Act n 1862 or additional legislation in 1890.

LD 50 (lethal dose 50)   Dose of a toxant that will kill 50% of the population of test organisms in a specified period of time. A common measure of comparative toxicity of many chemicals.

leachate   A liquid that results from water collecting contaminants as it trickles through waste, agricultural pesticides, or fertilizers.

liner   A relatively impervious barrier designed to prevent leachate from leaking from a landfill.

litigation   legal action usually involving court proceedings.

lobbying   Formal, organized, and informal efforts to influence political decisions and actions.

Malthus, Thomas   British clergyman/economist that predicted mass starvation on the basis that the rate of population growth exceeded the rate of increasing food production.

Manifest Destiny   The belief or doctrine held in the middle to later part of the 19th century that it was the destiny of the United States to extend over the entire North American continent.

material data safety sheets (MSDS)   Compilations of information required under the Occupational Safety and Health Act to identify stored hazardous materials.

monofills   Landfill facilities that accept only a single, limited type of waste.

multiple use/sustained yield   Use of land for more than one purpose and managing land to maintain a specified continuing level of productivity, frequently measured in the yield of crops, timber, or wildlife.

municipal solid waste   All of the refuse or trash generated by a residential and business community.

mutagen   A chemical that causes or increases the rate of genetic mutations.

national ambient air quality standards (NAAQS)   Air quality standards established by the EPA that apply to outside air throughout the United States.

national emission standards for hazardous air pollutants   Emission standards set by the EPA for air pollution not covered by NAAQS that may cause death or serious illness.

national priority list   EPA's list of the most serious uncontrolled or abandoned hazardous waste sites.

natural resources   With respect to natural ecosystems, resources of value that can be exploited; these may be limited to resources such as water, minerals, timber, and wildlife, or expanded to include less tangible aspects such as beauty or even solitude.

negligence   A civil cause of litigation (tort) which in the simplest sense is an avoidable, careless act that results directly or indirectly in the injury to an individual or to property.

NEPA (National Environmental Policy Act)   The legislation that, among other points, established the requirement for the government to carry out an environmental impact statement (EIS).

NIMBY (not in my backyard)   A commonly cited cause for opposition to the location of landfills and similar undesirable facilities.

non-conventional pollutant   Any pollutant that is not statutorily listed or which is poorly understood by the scientific community.

non-point source pollutant   Pollutants, the sources of which are defuse and do not have a single point of origin or are not introduced into a receiving stream from a specific outlet.

no observable adverse effects (NOAE)   The standard at which no risk exists; the exposure to a suspected harm or danger the magnitude of which results in no observable effect or damage.

NRDC (Natural Resources Defense Council)   A very active environmental lobbying organization.

Nuclear Regulatory Commission (NRC)   The federal agency responsible for the regulation of the use of radioactive (nuclear) materials.

oconogenic   A substance that causes either benign or malignant tumors.

oil spill   Accidental or intentional discharge of oil that reaches bodies of water.

OSHA (Occupational Safety and Health Act)   Legislation initially designed to encourage safety in the workplace. Now includes many environmental factors from noise control to safe storage of hazardous materials; thus, some consider OSHA, in part, as environmental legislation.

ownership (or ownership rights)   Relates to real and personal property and recognized by the legal right to possess, use, enjoy, and convey property; certain environmental regulations may infringe on these individual rights.

oxidant   A substance generally containing oxygen that reacts chemically in air to produce a new substance; the primary ingredient in photochemical smog.

particulates   Fine liquid or solid particles such as dust, smoke, mist, fumes, or smog found in air or emissions.

persistence   Relates to the length of time a compound will remain in the environment after its introduction; resistance to decay.

pH   A measure of acidity or alkalinity of a liquid or a solid; measured as hydrogen ion concentration on a logarithm scale.

picocurie   Measure of radioactivity equalling one million millionth (one trillionth) of a curie.

point source   A stationary location or fixed facility from which pollutants are discharged or emitted.

police power   A source of law reserved by the Constitution to the individual states that allows laws that affect public welfare, health, and morals.

pollutant   Generally, any substance introduced into the environment that adversely affects the usefulness of a resource.

pollution   Generally, the presence of energy or matter whose nature, location, or quantity produces an undesirable environmental effect.

Pollution Prevention Act of 1990   An act that recognize lead, asbestos, and radon as serious potential pollutants and that recognizes the importance of the elimination of sources of pollutants rather than disposal and treatment.

post-closure   The time period following shutdown of a waste management or waste manufacturing facility during which the facility must continue to be monitored as a source of pollution. Has been considered to be up to 30 years.

pretreatment   Processes used to reduce, eliminate, or alter the nature of wastewater pollutants from nondomestic sources before they are discharged into publicly owned treatment works.

public water system   A system that provides piped water to at least 15 service connections or to 25 or more individuals.

quasi-judicial   The function of an agency in enforcing rules and regulations and imposing penalties for violations as allowed by the Administrative Procedure Act.

quasi-legislative   The function of an agency promulgating rules that have the force and effect of statutory law and may be enforced as such.

radiation   Any form of energy propagated as a wave or stream of energetic particles; frequently refers to emissions from atomic nuclei or from x-ray and similar equipment.

radon   A colorless, odorless, naturally occurring radioactive inert gas formed in buildings as a result of the decay of radium in soil or rocks.

raw sewage   Untreated waste water.

RCRA   The Resource Recovery and Conservation Act.

recycling   Minimizing waste by reusing, recovering, or converting or reprocessing into useful forms materials that otherwise would be treated as waste.

regulations   Standards and similar rules promulgated by an agency as authorized by statutory law and acting under the provisions of the Administrative Procedure Act.

remediation   Actual process and activities implemented to correct or dispose of pollutants; practices used to clean abandoned or closed hazardous waste sites.

right of way   The right of an individual or the public to use the property of another. Also, the property used; in a railroad right of way, the area occupied by tracks.

riparian rights   Entitlement of landowner of property adjacent to a body of water to the use of the water, but not the actual ownership of the water itself.

risk assessment   The qualitative and quantitative evaluation performed in an attempt to define the risk posed to human health and/or the environment by the presence, or potential presence, and/or use of a specific pollutant or specific activity such as timbering or mining.

risk management   The process of evaluating alternative regulatory and nonregulatory responses to risk and selecting among them, which also requires consideration of legal, economic, and social factors.

Sagebrush Rebellion   The unsuccessful attempt in the mid-1970s of a coalition of ranchers, miners, loggers, politicians, and other interests to transfer federal public lands in the West to state ownership.

salt dome (salt dome formation)   Geologic term meaning a domelike rock structure formed beneath the earth's surface by the upward movement of a mass of salt. Such structures may reach thousands of feet in height.

sections   (1) Major subdivision of Titles in the US Code; (2) in surveying, an area one mile square, 640 acres.

sick building syndrome   Describes a building, the occupants of which frequently suffer from a variety of symptoms ranging from mild to severe respiratory problems associated with poor air circulation and indoor air pollution.

siltation   The accumulation of soil particles carried by flowing water in rivers, streams, lakes, and at the base of dams. Caused by excessive surface runoff as a result of land development and inappropriate farming and timbering practices.

sludge   A semi-solid residue from any of a number of air or water treatments; sludge can be a hazardous pollutant.

smog   A pollutant associated with oxidants.

smoke   Particles suspended in the air after incomplete combustion (burning) of material.

solid waste   Non-liquid materials ranging from municipal garbage to industrial waste that contains complex, sometimes hazardous substances.

standards   Prescriptive norms that govern actions and establish actual limits on the amount of emissions or pollutants produced or emitted.

stare decisis   Legal doctrine to abide by a rule of law established by a court's decision in a prior, similar case; the rule of legal precedent.

State Implementation Plan (SIP)   EPA-approved state plan for the establishment, regulation, and enforcement of air pollution standards.

stationary source   A fixed, nonmoving producer of air pollution, mainly power plants and other manufacturing facilities using industrial combustion processes.

status quo   The existing state or condition of things at any given time.

statutory law   Laws enacted by Congress or by state legislative bodies.

storm sewers   A system of pipes, separate from sanitary sewers, that carries only runoff water from buildings and land surfaces.

stratosphere   That portion of the atmosphere that is from 10 to 25 miles above the earth's surface.

superfund   The programs operated under the legislative authority of CERCLA or SARA funds to carry out the EPA's solid waste emergency and long term removal and remedial plans for toxic waste sites.

surface water   All water naturally open to the atmosphere.

tailings   Residues of raw materials or wastes separated out during the processing of crops and ore; may also include excess irrigation water that runs off the end of a field.

teratogen   Any substance that causes malformations or serious deviations from normal development of an embryo or fetus.

tetraethyl lead   Lead compound formerly used in premium gasoline as an additive to enhance engine performance. Now illegal to use in the United States.

title   Major subdivision of the US Code; also a subdivision of the legislative act; also ownership as in the title to land or other property, which also includes a formal document as evidence of such ownership.

toxicity   The degree of danger posed by a substance to plant or animal life.

toxic pollutants   Materials contaminating the environment that cause death, diseases, and/or birth defects in organisms that ingest or adsorb them.

treatment storage disposal facility (TSDF)   Facility under permit granted by the EPA for the storage and disposal of hazardous waste.

USDA   United States Department of Agriculture.

waste   Unwanted material left over from processing refuse from places of human habitation.

waste treatment stream   The continuous movement of waste from the generator to treatment and disposal.

waste water   The spent or used water—from individual homes, communities, farms, or industry—that contains dissolved or suspended matter.

water pollution   The presence in water of enough harmful or objectionable material to damage the water quality.

watershed   The land area that drains into a stream or river.

whistle blower   Individual who, without responsibility to act, reports to authorities violations of laws, rules, and regulations—particularly employees who report violations by their employer; some environmental legislation protects whistle blowers from retaliation by their employers.

■ Index